Praise for Betwee

"From the first page of *Between the Two Rivers*, your attention will be captured. Readers won't be able to put the book down. You will hiss at the villains and cheer for the underdogs."

—Carol Hoyer, PhD, for Reader Views

"With this writing, Kouyoumjian joins authors Thea Halo and Peter Balakian, whose finely penned accounts of family members' survival of the Ottoman atrocities are essential reads for the understanding of these genocides."

—Elissa Mugianis, ForeWord Digital Reviews

"Aida Kouyoumjian's rich memories of her mother will be a source of great fascination to anyone interested in the Armenian Genocide."

—Dawn MacKeen, Award-Winning Freelance Journalist

"The book reads like a chapter from *One Thousand and One nights*. An absorbing account that confirms the adage, 'Truth is stranger than fiction' ... The author's visual descriptions touch the senses."

—Mary Terzian, Author of *The Immigrants' Daughter*

"Anyone who has traveled in the Middle East will recognize the authenticity of Aida Kouyoumjian's voice. This story is told with the deep cultural understanding of one born, raised and educated within sight of the minarets of Baghdad. Aida's writing launches the reader into the exotic land of pre-Saddam's Iraq, overflowing with vibrant colors, sights, sounds—and dangers."

—Joyce O'Keefe, Writer and former Foreign Service Officer

"Mannig's spirit, resourcefulness and courage captivate the reader."

—Genie Dickerson, Journalist, Washington, D.C.

"I am impressed with how you have woven personal history with solid research. BRAVO!"

—Helene Moussa, Retired scholar of Coptic art/Author of *Legacy to Modern Egyptian Art*, Toronto, Canada

"I cannot put it away. I knew the story would be incredible. But that is just part of it. The book is also masterfully written, in a very direct and honest manner. It is both touching and thought provoking at the same time. The characters are so alive they seem to have become part of my life. The book is clearly a winner."

—Artak Kalantarian, son of celebrated Armenian author Artashes Kalantarian and Manager, Seattle Armenians Yahoo Group

"I was absolutely fascinated! Your descriptions put such vivid images in my mind, as though I were there next to your mother, hearing and seeing everything. But you left me so hungry for more information ... What a marvelous tribute to a remarkable woman, and yes—a remarkable man!"

—Kelly Givens, Mt. Vernon, Washington

"I feel like I'm there in Mosul in 1918 as a ten-year-old girl, shivering and bloated with hunger ... Family is everything in this book. The fact that Aida Kouyoumjian can retell her mother's story so convincingly is the value of memory ... Her stories teach us how to live and not give up under atrocious circumstances.
"Aida Kouyoumjian moved to America in 1952. The fact that this novel is written in English is a testament to her intellect and very vibrant voice. The book depicts Arabic and Armenian traits and it weaves a carpet for me to get a glimpse of what life was like back then ... Growing up in the '50s, I remember my parents telling me to finish the food on my plate with 'Remember the starving Armenians.' "

—Deborah Cooke, Retired editor/published writer travel

"This is a brutally honest story—nothing seems to be exaggerated or glossed over in this true story—which makes more of an impact on the reader. Kouyoumjian did an amazing job at keeping the authenticity of the subject while writing a novel with great literary value on its own."

—Hasmik Kalantarian, Seattle, Washington

"Aida Kouyoumjian paints in minute details the vivid memories of her mother's daily experiences. We smell, taste, see, hear ... feel, cry and laugh alongside the hero. The powerful depiction of imagery painted in a colorful palette, reminds one of an oriental style painting, we are entertained by exotic places, people, and even humor in the middle of a tragic story."

—Sona Stewart, Retired Art Critic, Issaquah, Washington

"My mind staggers at the disruption of simple human life by the whims and obsessions of others. This is a great book for you to revisit how you see other human beings on the verge of violent and disruptive behavior by those who do not have the right to do so. I just love your book ... It is a labor of love but worth every ounce of your heart and mind you poured into it. You are very gifted as a storyteller."

—Dr. William Rice, Professor of economics at California State University at Fresno.

"Thank you so much for sharing your mother's story with the world. You are a wonderful writer. I feel richer knowing you and your family's story."

—Vicki Heck, Librarian, Mercer Island Library, Washington

"What a great writer you are! Such rich detail, so evocative and emotional, such passion and feeling! Certainly your mother couldn't have told you ALL of this? And although you didn't dwell on the horrors of the Genocide, I was happy to read your book, which still contained so much hope. I can't wait for the sequel—and also wonder when Hollywood will film it?

—Bruce Greeley, Library Systems Analyst, Seattle, WA

"Your Haji-Doo's words: 'If it is written in the heart it will be written by the hand,' certainly became the heart of your ability to write such an important book. Many thanks ... and may God continue to give you that grand voice to write another related book."

—Mary Hall, Mercer Island

"I was instantly pulled into a world of anguish, despair, perseverance, resourcefulness, devotion, hope and pride. It touched me and, in many ways, changed my life forever. I first wanted to thank you for sharing her story, your story and the Armenian story ...."

—Shana Schreiber, student of Dr. Mary Johnson (Columbia College, South Carolina) researching the Armenian Genocide

"It is amazing to think that someone so young had such determination. I loved *Between the Two Rivers* and I want to know more. I highly recommend this book as a good read and great story."

—Catherine, Registered Nurse, Bellevue, Washington

"This book is a valuable and personal account of what many went through at the hands of the Turks at the time. I have sent copies to my daughter, cousin and nieces so that they may also know. Thank you for undertaking this effort."

—Hratch Kouyoumdjian, Architect, San Francisco

"I read your book straight through in a couple of days (a record time for me). I enjoyed it all and had to keep going from page to page. Some girl! Some woman! Some mother! You are a great writer. Keep it up."

—Dr. John Lindberg, retired physician, Mercer Island

"A powerful read—I couldn't put it down. Read it in two and half days and for me that is a 'Wow!' A history lesson for me, too. The book deserves another visit."

—Carole Tye, retired teacher, Mercer Island

"Your unique writing style kept me enthralled throughout the book. I especially liked the last few chapters about how Mannig and Mardiros fell in love and got married."

—Kyle Shanafelt, senior at Mercer Island High School

To Cathy

Thanks for
taking an extra
trip

Between the
Two Rivers

A Story of the Armenian
Genocide

Second Edition

Between the Two Rivers

A Story of the Armenian Genocide

Second Edition

Aida Kouyoumjian

coffeetownpress

Seattle, WA

coffeetownpress

Published by Coffeetown Press
PO Box 70515
Seattle, WA 98127

For more information go to: www.coffeetownpress.com
www.armenianstory.coffeetownpress.com

Cover design by Sabrina Sun

Between the Two Rivers: A Story of the Armenian Genocide
Second Edition

Copyright © 2011 by Aida Kouyoumjian

ISBN: 978-1-60381-111-8 (Trade Paper)
ISBN: 978-1-60381-112-5 (eBook)

Printed in the United States *of* America

ACKNOWLEDGMENTS

I owe my love and dedication for **Between the Two Rivers** to my mother, Mannig Dobajian Kouyoumdjian. She instilled in me the value of memory—not as a human quality but a privileged responsibility to share. I heard her survival stories in the form of lullabies in Felloujah, Abu-Ghraib, Hillah, Mosul and Baghdad—the locales where my father, Mardiros Kouyoum*dj*ian, was assigned to build a dam or engineer the canal-networks for the Irrigation Department of the Iraqi Government. Her melancholic chants ingrained in me how painful it is to lose one's family. Her survival stories taught me not to give up—Mannig, living, and I, telling her story in English. When asked, "How long did it take you to publish her memoirs?"

"A lifetime."

After Mannig immigrated to the United States, she and I spent many hours over a cup of Seattle's delicious coffee talking about her life. We repeated similar scenarios whenever my sister, Maro Kouyoumjian Rogers of South Carolina, visited us. Eventually, my mom handwrote several stories of her memoirs and, just before her death, in 1985, she recorded a short tape.

You will notice I spelled my father's surname with the letter '*d.*' Our family name in Iraq remains under the influence of French spelling, requiring a '*d*' for its accurate pronunciation. On my arrival in America, I wanted to shorten our long and difficult-to-pronounce name. I dropped the letter '*d.*' My mother and my sister followed my example, but my father, who passed on in Baghdad before he could emigrate from Iraq, retained the traditional spelling—as have most members of our kinfolk in the Diaspora.

Personally knowing the principal individuals of *Between the Two Rivers* has been my fortune—their names are factual, such as my *morkor*, Adrine, *deidie* Sebouh Papazian, and diggin Perouz. The Kouyoum**d**jians of Felloujah and Baghdad are also identified by their own names. The remaining characters are real, but their names are fictitious. Any resemblance is purely coincidental. My mother spoke of Dikran, Romella, and the sisters from Van, but their true names had faded from her memory.

Thanks to Zola Ross, the founder of the Pacific Northwest Writers Association, for encouraging me to write Mannig's story and later urged me to enter their annual contest. An award in the non-fiction category inspired me to write of the Armenian Genocide, an issue emotive to living Armenians. Every April 24th, the Republic of Armenia and communities throughout the world commemorate the memory of 1.5–2 millions who were annihilated during World War I. We mourn our loved ones who perished and rejoice with the descendants of survivors whose agonizing stories elucidate and expand our historical knowledge—a continuous renewal of our Armenianness.

My gratitude goes to three award-winners in my critiquing group for their editorial expertise who tracked the progress of my mother's story to its completion. Joyce Lindsey O'Keefe, Genie Dickerson and Mary Kay Windham graciously guided the flow of the progress of *Between the Two Rivers.*

Thanks to Jim Farrell for connecting me with Coffeetown Press, and to Michael Lettini, my neighbor, for his assistance with computer glitches.

I value the tacit support of my sons, Armen, Brian, Roger and their families who never prodded me for a publishing date.

My utmost thankfulness goes to our Lord for protecting my mother from the 'claws of the Ottoman gendarmes' and for all His goodness toward my family.

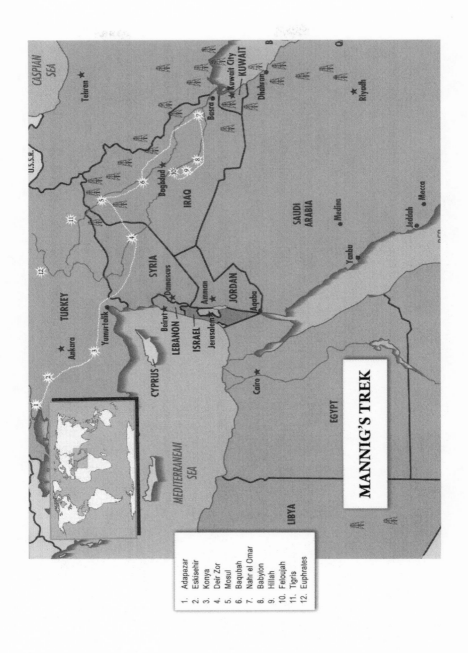

MANNIG'S TREK

1. Adapazar
2. Eskisehir
3. Konya
4. Deir Zor
5. Mosul
6. Baqubah
7. Nahr el Omar
8. Babylon
9. Hillah
10. Feloujah
11. Tigris
12. Euphrates

September 16, 1916—

To the Government of Aleppo:

It was at first communicated to you that the government, by order of the Jemiet, had decided to destroy completely all the Armenians living in Turkey. . . . An end must be put to their existence, however criminal the measures taken may be, and no regard must be paid to either age or sex nor to conscientious scruples.

—TALAAT PASHA, Minister of the Interior

August 22, 1939—I have given orders to my Death Units to exterminate without mercy or pity men, women, and children belonging to the Polish-speaking race. It is only in this manner that we can acquire the vital territory which we need. After all, who remembers today the extermination of the Armenians?

—ADOLF HITLER

Table of Contents

1—Luxury in the Grave

Mannig breathed freely. Ah, but staying alive—a different story. Her fear of whips vanished with the disappearance of the gendarmes—this, after they drove her family from their beautiful home in Adapazar, near Constantinople. Three years later, they abandoned the deportees in the middle of the Mesopotamian Desert and disappeared like a mirage.

Mannig wallowed in freedom now. At the age of ten—more likely younger—she depended on her own wits to fend for herself. She had no skills for survival, but eventually emerged profoundly mature by blocking out horrific memories. She managed to remember only a kaleidoscopic Adapazar from her early childhood—twirling in her yellow dress, air swirling between her legs, melodies on Mama's violin, warmth from the charcoal brazier. *I'm alive! My happy days will survive.* Like the flickering rays of the hurricane lamp in their parlor, bits and pieces of her family's devotion helped her survive her grief. Ignoring pain was her way to resist the suffering brought by the annihilation of her loved ones. *I must not forget.* Who cared if her toe hurt? Foraging for edibles in this famine-stricken city of Mosul absorbed her waking hours.

A chilly November in 1918 summoned a cruel winter in the largest city along the northern shores of the Tigris River. The winds blew in from the rugged Taurus Mountains and swept across the metropolis before cooling the Mesopotamian Desert.

Mannig squinted into a gust of cold wind and shivered. She folded her bare arms and looked at the midday sun. It peeked above the high roofs of the deep alley. Unlike the blistering sun of the desert, this sun barely emitted warmth. *Even their sun is weak.* She slid her hands inside the wide armholes; the tawny burlap sack dangled down her bony shoulders.

1

Ahkh! She yelped at her chilled hands, as her fingertips crawled up and around her hunger-distended belly. *Why is my empty stomach so large?* In Adapazar, her family had laughed when she sucked in her belly to touch her back—even after stuffing herself with *mante*, Mama's specialty of pastry squares stuffed with ground spicy lamb. Her tummy had been flat when she lived with the Bedouin, too. They had sheltered her in their tent for several months after they rescued her from the scorching sun. She had gobbled Arabic bread stuffed with zesty onions and never hungered, but her stomach had been flat then. Now, she hardly found anything to send down to her stomach, yet when she wanted to see her toes, a protruding belly hindered the view.

Mannig's stomach growled—a cue to look for food morsels.

A wad of cloth in a pile of rubbish steered her to forage down the alley. A hop across the open sewer-ditch, and she pulled on the rag. Could it be a coat?

Before salvaging it, she scanned her surroundings for other scavengers preparing to pounce on her. None emerged. Bent in half, she freed a piece of cord from the trash and mud. Disgusted at such a useless find, she almost discarded it, and then she changed her mind— a find is a find, in spite of its stink. She belted the rotten sack and covered her body with it. *Ahkh!* She shuddered. The rotten coarse fibers of the garment scratched against her bare skin; it needled the sores on her chest and back. She pressed her exposed arms close to her ribs and snuggled her hands in her armpits, a stance she often adopted to prevent her budding breasts from peeking from the ragged armholes.

Mannig sauntered into an unfamiliar alley. Chatter, clatter, and smells enticed her deeper into it. A whiff of yeast wafted from the billowing smoke of a chimney. Like the Adapazar bakery? She dashed to the adobe walls and peered through a window-like hole. "*Khattir Allah, Joo'aaneh,*" she sniffed and cried. "For God's sake. I'm hungry."

"*Imshee!*" the woman shooed Mannig away. "Scat! We're all hungry. All of Mosul is starving; millions of us are always hungry."

I don't want bread for all of them; I only want a bite for me.

Not far ahead, a prominent minaret pierced the chilly blue sky, and the *mu'adthin's* melancholic chant reminded the Muslims of their vows. In Adapazar, the opening scores of *Allah-oo-Akbar* had aroused Mannig to sing along the prayer of God is great—if not loudly, at least humming along with the clergy's trills and tremolos. She relished the carefree image of her life four years before.

2

Adapazar belonged to the past.

In Mosul, hunger squashed other sensations.

Across from the bakery, Mannig lingered over the aroma of the seething sesame oil gusting from fritters over an open fire. Her nostrils flared. She smiled at the Kurdish woman poking the embers.

"*Khattir Allah, Joo'aaneh*," she cried, eying the woman.

"*Imshee!*" the woman shooed Mannig off with her arm and crouched closer to her pan. She readjusted her ocher-checkered scarf around her head. "If I give you food today, my own children will waste away tomorrow."

Mannig knew the futility of competing with children who had a mother.

She swerved around just when a jeering "Get out of my way!" shout startled her. She barely dodged a ragged fellow tugging at his donkey. She gazed at the animal. Its back curved low under the weighty water sloshing in goat-skin sacks; the protruding ribs framed its back like the mangy dogs scavenging nearby.

She caught her breath. *Kheghj esh.* Poor donkey! It must be as starved as she.

Her heart thumped in rhythm to the pounding of two coppersmiths. They hammered pretty, shiny bowls a few strikes and then rested to chat with each other.

"We work, and we work," complained the younger one. "But we haven't sold anything since the Ottomans retreated from Mosul."

"Conditions will change as soon as the *Englaizees* arrive," the sage said. "They will promote commerce here, just as they are doing in Basra. Hear my words, young man. They are headed this way even as we speak."

"I wish they would hurry. I want them to drive away the Kurds … and … keep the Turkomen within their separate enclaves." The youth waved his hammer in the air and struck his bowl. "We want Mosul for us, the Arabs. Those ethnic tribes are stealing our businesses, and soon they will wed our women. I hope the *Englaizees* will remember that we, the Arabs, helped them in the Big War. Without us, they wouldn't have crushed the hated Ottomans. When will the English come? "

No food handout here, Mannig told herself. She ambled by while glancing at their brown striped robes, reminiscent of the Bedouin garments.

"They will come soon," the sage said, lifting his hammer.

"Sure they will—after we've starved and gone," the youth said just when Mannig caught his glance. "She's starving too," he pointed the hammer at her. "But I bet she won't for long. She's pretty."

No one had called her pretty in four years. It made her feel nice inside. She flashed a smile, but she stopped short when he shifted his stance and grabbed his crotch. He fondled himself while he ogled her.

Nudged by instinct to shield herself, Mannig tucked her elbows in to hide any bare flesh sneaking through the large armholes of her burlap dress. Spurred by survival energy, she dashed round the bend, out of the bazaar, and into a new alley.

No starvelings here? What luck. Scrawny arms dangling from her shoulders like dried cloth, and skeletal legs like useless sticks, she darted from stone to rubbish. *Ahkh*. Hop, hop: she jumped to alleviate the sharp sting in her infected toe. *Zakhnaboot*. She stubbed her wound again. It's never going to heal! To check the damage, she stuck her foot out beyond her malnutrition-distended belly. The toe bled; the gash ached anew. *Shoes! I must find shoes ... one shoe? But first, I need food, then a coat ... and then shoes.*

She explored alleys farther beyond the khan, the abandoned inn for caravans that she called home. She needed something to eat before spending the night with the horde of Armenian orphans, all of whom were just like her—scrawny, pathetic, and alone.

In spite of Mannig's petite stature, she dreamed big. Searching for edibles occupied all her waking breaths, but her heart's desire nudged for things beyond. She wanted to read and write, like her older sister, Adrine. She fantasized about becoming a teacher, like Miss Romella, her kindergarten tutor in Adapazar.

A large brick building cast a shadow in her path. A school? She visualized herself seated at a desk, donned in her gray uniform with pink embroidered MB, MangaBardez—denoting kindergarten. "Who can count from one to ten?" Miss Romella's voice echoed in Mannig's head. How she used to squeal, wiggle and raise her hand before the other children to answer the teacher's question first. *I will be number one!*

Her curiosity about the building ended quickly.

Swathed in the dun Kurdish turban and a pair of brown sharwal, a man creaked open the huge mahogany door while pulling up a riotously brilliant jacket over an open necked shirt.

His size, more than his appearance, scared Mannig, and she dashed away as far away as she could. School *musschool*! Being housed with a family like her sister was prevailed over scholarly ambition.

She knocked on a door of an adobe dwelling. "Can I do chores for you?"

"You're too puny," the khatoon shooed her off, slamming the door.

"You're good for nothing," cackled the matriarch at the next house.

"I do the chores here," said a tall orphan who opened the gate of a tenement.

"Your looks will scare the young ones," said the master of the next dwelling.

My looks? Not long before, someone had called her pretty.

She scurried in and out of dirt heaps, evading the littered stones to prevent reopening the wound in her toe. As if sidestepping the poppies in her father's orchard, she skipped here and there. Adapazar loomed … so far away. It stayed fresh with her; she wore her licorice-black shoes. Three long years ago. How foolish to discard them in the desert just because they felt hot and heavy on her feet! The buried pain surfaced and accentuated the throbbing pain of the present. The desert heat between the Tigris and Euphrates Rivers failed to relieve the agony, and Mama wasn't alive to take away her pain.

Entering a side street, Mannig saw her sister, Adrine, fetching water in a goatskin, saddled to her back as if she were a vendor—more like a donkey in the bazaar.

"Why are you lugging water?" Mannig asked, walking backward in front of her sister to face her.

"We don't have a well," Adrine said. "Now get out of my way."

Mannig stepped aside. "Are you a water vendor, now?"

"No!" Adrine's voice rose in irritation. "The khatoon makes me fetch water because the Tigris flows nearby, and she doesn't have to pay a vendor."

Mannig sauntered beside her sister. "Will the lady of the house give you a lot of food for all of this work?"

"Hah!" Adrine sneered. "She gives me only bread." she snorted, raising her nostrils, the sole characteristic of her personality remaining intact. Adrine, bonier and skinnier than Mannig, maintained a radiant, pinkish complexion under the black abaya, swathing her from head to ankles like an Arab woman.

Mannig noticed changes in her sister since the bad thing happened to her. She forgot the word the grownups used for when the gendarmes had hurt her in the middle of the desert. They hurt the big girls, too. Oh, *rape*! Mannig prided herself in recalling a word absent in her daily vocabulary. *Rape, rape*, she repeated silently. They had raped all the maidens on the deportee route. Not Mannig. Why bother with the sooty, ugly, and puny, when older ones whetted their appetites? It hurt Mannig to see how much Adrine had changed. Now she merely existed, a living lump, dependent upon others. She no longer resembled the beautiful, mature girl of fourteen she had been. But she did everything she was told to do. The Kurdish khatoon took advantage of harboring a Christian orphan. She required Adrine to clean the house, wash the clothes, and attend to three pre-teen children. And when the master of the house returned with his caravan, she yelled, "The Sahib is here!"—the cue to collect the camel dung, squash it into patties and lay them on the flat roof of the house to dry. Before descending, Adrine lugged down a stack of the dried-up patties for fuel to bake the bread.

"Can you give me some of your bread?" Mannig raised her voice, swallowing a painful jolt of hunger.

"No!" Adrine yelled and veered aside, the water sloshing on her back.

Mannig rejected her answer. Hobbling close behind her sister, she entered a high adobe-fenced courtyard and snuck inside the mud brick enclosure.

"I told you not to come here," Adrine whispered, dropping the goatskin with relief. She whisked Mannig behind burlap curtains, the family courtyard buffer from the camel shed. "If the khatoon sees you loitering, she will accuse me of stealing food for you."

"So why don't you steal food and give it to me?" Mannig prodded. "I'm your sister."

"Steal?"

"Yes—if I were in your place, I would do anything for my little sister."

"You say such things because you are not in my place," Adrine said.

"If you don't give me bread, I will die like Mama and Baba and …"

"Hush!" Adrine hissed. "Shut your mouth and don't talk of them. Now get out of here!"

It hurt Mannig, too, to remember her parents' deaths. It saddened her to relive the pain of being left alone. But nothing stung as much as hunger. She was willing to exploit every bit of her past for a bite. "You and I are our only family left. If you don't give me bread, I, too, will die … and you will be the only one …"

"Adi? Adi?" The khatoon's voice ended Mannig's doomsday theatrics.

"I'm coming," Adrine said.

Adi? Adrine lost even her own name. Mannig always surmised her sister was given the pretty name because she was the first child in her family. People spoke "Adrine" melodically. Not Mannig—guttural and final. Setrak, her brother's name, was harsh too, but then he was a boy. She missed him so. She wouldn't dwell upon his death in the refugee camp.

"Where are you, girl?" the yelling continued. "Bring five dung patties and start the fire. The dough is ready. Adi? Adi?"

"Now go!" Adrine shoved Mannig out. "Go, before she throws me out."

"I'm going to wait for you outside," Mannig said, leaning against the mud brick enclosure in the alley. "Right here—until you bring some bread for your sister."

"Adi? Adi?" The khatoon's voice was closing in.

Adrine growled low in her throat and rushed back inside the courtyard.

Mannig squatted on the unpacked dust and waited, uncertain of her sister's return. She picked up a dry leaf, shook off its dust, and into her mouth it went.

She looked for more within reach. If only she were sitting among the red-red poppies of Adapazar, instead of stones stabbing her toes and prickly leaves gnashing her bloody mouth. If only green grass grew—somewhere, in the cracks or the mud walls. In Mosul? The parched city? Even the rains avoided it.

Her gaze followed the dust rising at the heels of every passerby. Tiny specks funneled like dirt devils before settling in crannies. There was none of the trees and shrubs in lush emerald hues that she remembered surrounding her Adapazar home.

The high sun above the flat roofs removed the chill of a November noonday. But there was no comfort for Mannig. Leaning against the door, she waited for Adrine's compassion. Would her sister share her daily bread today?

"*Mye, mye!*" The voice of a water vendor wafted over the jingling bells on his donkey's halter. He stopped at the door across the alley and after chanting *mye, mye* several times, the door opened and the trading ensued—a goat-skin full of water for a cluster of dates. He ate one and spit out the pit.

Mannig dashed to the pit and popped it into her mouth. She sucked and sucked on it, following him to the next door, hoping for more. The next payment was a bag of grain, perhaps rice. Not helpful. The waterman tucked it inside his vest.

Anticipating the waterman's next stop, Mannig rushed back to the walls of Adrine's courtyard. She anticipated an exchange of water for the bread being baked in the khatoon's courtyard. She planned her strategy to grab the loaf and run.

To Mannig's chagrin, the waterman bypassed the khatoon's door. He has seen Adrine lugging the water herself.

I wish I owned a goatskin. I could carry its water-weight better than the donkey in the bazaar. No one could brush me away like the fat woman for being so small and useless. Mannig could hear her even now, "Your kind is worthless; you don't do anything, and you eat everything."

Footsteps in the courtyard approached the gate. She jumped up. Adrine? Bringing bread for her?

Her sister stood at the threshold, eyes widening upon seeing Mannig.

Mannig faced her, disgusted at the sight of a pair of empty hands. She is the worthless one. But no one knew that.

"Look, Mannig," Adrine whispered. "Just because we are sisters, it is no reason for both of us to be homeless. Do you want me to lose my livelihood for your sake?"

Mannig worried about her own empty stomach, not her sister. She sniffled and cast a pleading eye. Her insides hurt—her heart as much as her stomach. The day was waning, and her hands were empty. How to end her desperation? She scratched a sore on her chest. The sting brought tears to her eyes.

She noticed a sudden nervous shift in Adrine's stance. Did her sister actually feel sorry for her? Exactly what Mannig wanted. She sniffed more noisily and threw in a moan.

Suddenly, Adrine stood motionless—staring with glassy eyes and rubbing her hands as if she were washing them clean—compulsive behavior that was the result of the gendarme's attack.

For the first time, Mannig noticed how Adrine's hazel eyes lacked expression. The color seeped out of her face and her breathing was shallow. Many of her features were defined by straight lines: quill eyebrows, pointy nose, and narrow lips. But mostly, her face expressed wariness. Much taller than Mannig, Adrine towered over most Armenian girls. The difference between the two sisters made it hard to believe they claimed the same parents. Mannig envied the combed, silky hair and the floral, feminine tunic on her sister's lanky body. Most of all, she wished for a similarly flat belly.

Adrine stood stiff, eyes glazed. She rubbed, cupped, and shook her hands, over and over again.

Mannig really looked into her sister's eyes; she probed deep, thoughtful, and penetrating. Whatever rape was, it must be something horrifying. Its meaning? What explained her sister's strange actions? Those escaped her. She lacked understanding what rape really meant; she only knew that Adrine was harmed in a way that she herself had never been.

Mannig had witnessed atrocities during the deportation, but she had been spared physical attacks upon her own body. She saw her family perish: Baba suffered bastinado lashings on the soles of his feet until he expired; Haji-doo, at 70, slowed the pace of the deportees, prompting the gendarmes to shoot her down; Hagop-Jahn was shoved off the cliff with all 'boys 12 and older'; her younger sister was suffocated in the cattle train, her brother died of typhoid, and Mama, of influenza at the deportation camp in Deir Zor. Mannig relished her luck in surviving the Ottoman onslaught of the Armenian massacre but only understood the pain of hunger. The search for food occupied her whole being. It ravaged her. Only Adrine's lifeless face and impenetrable demeanor surpassed her hurt. *No, no.* She rejected her desire to exchange places. She'd rather remain hungry than have Adrine's memories.

A sudden twinge in Mannig's heart mellowed her thoughts. She leaned forward to grab Adrine's hand. "Stop washing them," she said. "They are clean now. Go in and close the door. I am walking away now. See? I am leaving."

Adrine reawakened to the present. She straightened her neck and held her stance on the threshold of her abode. "Wait!" she said. "Come back tomorrow. Uhm! Tomorrow. When the Sahib returns from his travels. Tomorrow, the khatoon will be busy with the sahib and, and,

and she will concern herself with things other than what I do. Yes, come tomorrow. I will give you … "

Before she finished her promise, Mannig kissed her from face to hands, back to face with uncontrollable zeal. Real tears rolled down her cheeks. "I am so lucky to have you as my sister. I will go away immediately. You say I should come tomorrow? You really want to help your little sister. I will come here only when you want me." Mannig took a breath and, without a second glance at Adrine, vanished among the noonday ramblers in the alley.

Her thoughts ran as fast as her feet. Besides anticipating the morsels in her mouth, her head reconstructed every word and each action that had aroused Adrine's sympathy. She must remember the details—was it her tears? Her face? Voice? Could the touching of hands have made a difference? She must keep these methods in mind, in case she needed to resort to them again.

Children's giggling and the splashing of water lured Mannig downhill into an alley, and unexpectedly, the shores of the Tigris River lay below. Women flocked into the path, some carrying copper jugs, others clay pitchers, filled with water. A few sidestepped down to the riverbank to fill theirs.

Mannig squinted at the glistening river in the brightness of the midday sun. Children's voices swooped in from the opposite shores of the wide river and comingled with the ones on her side. The river flowed low and tawny, its twirling gentle currents dissipating into the water's edge.

Mannig slowed her stride among the babbling women. Most looked like Arabs—dressed in the traditional black abaya. Some attended the children, who dipped in and out of the water with excited voices, while others crouched in twos or threes.

One woman came from behind Mannig, her anklets clinking until she stepped into the water. She slowed her pace, scuffing the bottom of the shoreline to be sure of a steady foothold. Moving deeper into the current, she dunked her jug. When the trapped air bubbled out and the jug was filled, she swung it to her shoulder and carefully waddled to shore and back up the hill, water drops trailing behind her.

Mannig followed her. "That's too heavy for you. Let me carry it."

"I must do it myself," the woman said. "Otherwise, I won't get paid."

Dejected again, Mannig turned toward the river and waded in. She sprinkled a few drops of water on her head. It felt good. She plunged down to her waist, stirring up silt; the murky water swished around her. Cool tingling up her breasts felt even better. She plopped down and wiggled her hips, sliding farther down the slope. She giggled when her burlap dress ballooned up to her chin. Silt and sludge twirled in front of her face and then floated down with the curving current. The cool water against the sores on her chest was like a smooth hand of healing, not unlike the jasmine oil Mama had rubbed on her knee in the Turkish bathhouse. She blinked. Oh Adapazar! Thoughts of childlike carelessness overwhelmed her. Adapazar existed a long time ago, thriving only in her head.

She must care for her wounds. The promise of food improved her attitude and gave her a new outlook on life. She dunked her face and swished it in the water. Realizing moisture made it easier, she whisked her fingers across her eyelids and scraped the crusts off her lashes. Her cheeks came next, but she stopped short at the stinging, red-hot infected lip. With her hand, she cleared away a few floating twigs and took a drink, then another sip. More gulps followed. It felt good to send something to her stomach, cool and wet, even if it were just water.

Upon leaving the river, she felt joy at being alive. She must come back for another dip soon. Energized, she wandered toward the distant echo of another Muslim prayer chant. Water slid off her rag dress, and the sun, still high, dried it as she wandered. Up ahead, the mosaic-tiled dome of a mosque seemed to float in the haze. She knew Islam beckoned the men from their chores to afternoon worship. If they were near water, they washed their hands and feet; if not, they pretended to wash them, almost like Adrine.

Adi. A new name for her sister. Did Adrine adopt Islam? No, no. She pretended to wash her hands. The Muslims in Mosul pretended "cleanliness" of the body and mind, as a symbolic gesture before praying. One man, a few yards ahead of Mannig, spread a prayer rug in the alley and fell onto his knees—in silence. Pedestrians also maintained their silence, perhaps the whole city, inside and out— except for the *mu'adthin*, who climbed atop the slender balcony surrounding the minaret and chanted Qur'anic verses. Mannig stood silent too, listening. Her Christian faith remained in name only, while the Muslim melody elevated her soul. Her spirit soared with the waves of the resonant voice.

Mannig explored one new alley after another, hoping to find something to eat before returning to the khan. She stopped at the outskirts of the city. A cemetery? Her curiosity led her into the furrows and mounds, dug and piled. The absence of markers bearing names and dates didn't bother her. She was unable to read anyway. Even if she had learned, what difference would that make? No one in her family had received any formal burial in the desert between the two rivers. They had perished and died, and her loving family had vanished. She remembered hearing the deported Armenians complain about not being able to breathe under the whips of the gendarmes. How they were mistaken! Now, free from the Ottoman persecution, they breathed normally, but to stay alive, everyone struggled. With an effort, she blocked out the wrenching memories of her loved ones. Why did the painful realities hound her? Perhaps she was loitering at the threshold of a dead-end territory.

She leaped across a shallow pit and sidestepped a mound of fresh soil. On her way out, she saw an old empty grave pit. A dog's bark startled her. It won't see me in the hole! She slid down into it. With dirt, pebbles, and gravel crumbling under her feet, she fell with a thump into the empty grave. She shut her eyes. The dog suddenly yelped with pain as if someone had kicked it on its rear. She held her breath until the barking faded away.

A flash of greenery surrounded her. Not believing such luck, her eyeballs ballooned in their sockets—so much that the muscles around her eyes hurt. Unlike one who has found treasure but in the first moment of delight ignores the find, she feared that every orphan in Mosul had seen the vibrant vision of her green grass. Rejoicing at her solitude, in her private domain, she luxuriated beside the lush leaves! A yellow-yellow dandelion! She plucked it with her left hand. A green-green clover! Picked with her right. With gusto, both slid down her throat. But a limey-lime blade required chewing. *Ahkh!* That required jaw and lip movement—so painful with a split and infected lower lip. To minimize the burning sensation, Mannig held her facial muscles tight and immobile. A continuous supply of grasses, the sweetness of dandelions, the mintiness of clovers, and the tanginess of sumac led to pain in her infected lip and perhaps also to its healing. She broke off one green blade after another in dreamlike bliss, feasting on what belonged to her, and only to her.

What a day! Adrine promised to give her food tomorrow. Her sores pained her less after soaking in the river. The foliage quieted her grumbling stomach.

She wanted to stay in the grave and guard her cache forever.

What if Romella, as promised, came back to fetch her, but found no trace of her in the khan?

2—The Last Link

The old, empty gravesite became Mannig's life-saving treasure. It was dependable. Unlike Adrine's promise for a chunk of bread, often unrealized, her grave always guaranteed greens to pacify her hunger. Romella's promise of a home, on the other hand, remained empty, since she failed to return to the khan after having secured employment for herself.

Mannig knew the grave would never abandon her. On days when she failed to find something to eat, the greens in the pit of the grave guaranteed a lessening of her hunger. Often, when she needed solace from the filth of the khan, jammed with starving orphans, the grave offered a hideaway and fresh air. She guarded her find, never to disclose its location to anyone.

At night, she joined the other orphans in the dilapidated khan. Huddled under her frayed quilt, she dreamed about luxury in her grave. In the mornings, she rose before anyone else. Her emaciated, blanched cheeks accentuated her almond-shaped, large brown eyes below elongated eyebrows. As usual, her bristly lashes were stuck shut by mucous, filth and debris. She scraped off the hardened scum, just enough to separate her eyelids. As soon as she could see, she dashed out to scavenge, long before the other children of the khan awoke.

One day, after foraging the alleys, she was driven by the dry, cold wind to return to the khan for shelter. The dying sun of dusk cast an elongated shadow ahead of her. She noticed a figure leaning against the mud brick wall of the khan. Her silhouette resembled Romella's, except for the stance. This person reminded her of Romella's warning: "Quiet hands make a restful heart, but a restless heart makes busy hands." The figure stood useless as a broken spindle. Head downcast, she leaned one foot on the wall and rested blistered hands across her folded arms. Her olive complexion looked pasty and tired. Her demeanor whispered the pain of one who bore sad news. Unlike the youthful woman in her early twenties that she was, she slumped low with the burdens of the aged.

Nevertheless, it was Romella.

Mannig wanted to dash toward her, to be hugged and loved again by the caressing hands of the one who had become her substitute mother. Yes, she had adored Miss Romella since her kindergarten days in Adapazar, and she knew that without Romella's guidance in the desert, surviving the death march would have been impossible. Mannig craved the motherly love she found only in Romella. Solitude depleted hope. Staying alive wore her down. Surviving in Mosul by her own wits exhausted her.

Seeing Romella after an absence of several months froze Mannig's legs. Something held the girl back from covering her with kisses. Delaying the dissappointed words on Romella's lips sustained her dream of a new life, of being a family in a home and gorging on food without ever stopping.

Romella raised her head and adjusted her scarf. The veins in her eyes accentuated her glazed look. Upon seeing Mannig, she straightened her posture.

Eyes cast down, Mannig shuffled her feet. As each step shortened the distance between them, the pounding of her heart increased. Internal lightning in her head threatened to ignite a thunderstorm within. She dreaded an end to her hopes.

"Cherie! Cherie!" Romella said, with outstretched arms—an endearing gesture Mannig adored, because it reminded her of her mama.

Mannig lurched into Romella's arms—relished the sturdy grip on her shoulders. *She's like Mama.*

"You know what I am going to tell you," she whispered, brushing a kiss on Mannig's forehead. "I thank Jesus for blessing you with such intuition. When I promised your dying mother to take care of you, I failed to foresee how the promise itself became the force behind my own endurance. If you died, God forbid, I would, too. Believe me. I never doubted that you fueled the energy in my life. You still do. My promise to your mother kept me alive, and your presence inspired me to overcome hardships, and … "

Mannig knew bad news lay ahead. People refrained from talking these days. Talking required energy, and hungry people kept silent unless calamity loomed. She concentrated on the pleasantries. When she needed solace, remembering nice comments consoled her soul. *Hear Romella's words … remember them.* In the midst of loneliness, such words become the friends of a lost heart.

Romella listed Mannig's endearing characteristics and delayed revealing the bad news. Praises coming from her kindergarten teacher delighted her. She resolved to store them in her heart. She cherished the moment.

"And you are *jarbeeg*," Romella continued, meaning that she was street smart. "Look at you. How you have grown! I admire your perseverance. You haven't perished like the others because you didn't give up. You are different. You're smart enough to care for yourself. I am sure it will be you, not me, who finds a home for you." Energy flowed in her voice, but there was no luster in her eyes. "I am lucky. I happen to fill the needs of the family I serve." She cuddled Mannig's head against her chest and brushed her hair with her fingers.

Mannig's body tingled. The caressing fingers on her scalp recalled Mama's style. She separated a stringy strand of chestnut hair to the right and another strand to the left. Mannig savored the blissful feeling, especially when Romella traced her widow's peak. Sweetness oozed in her words. "You will become a very pretty maiden one day. And you will be luckier than me, *cherie.*"

"Luckier?"

"Help for the orphans is coming," Romella said, wrapping her floral robe around her hips. She then sat on her heels by the entrance of the khan. "I have heard that important Armenians from Baghdad and Basra are coming to save the children." She tugged at Mannig's burlap dress and prompted her to sit by her. "They're coming to Mosul to collect the orphans. They will surely find you, house and feed you."

"They will really give me food?" Mannig exclaimed in disbelief.

"I am sure!"

"When, when, when?"

"I don't know when. But, they're coming, I'm sure."

Romella's ensuing silence, albeit momentary, allowed Mannig to savor the thought of her stomach stuffed with food.

"In the meantime," Romella continued, "maybe an Arab family will make use of you. Perhaps you can do something for them. Yes, you must find a family and get out of this khan."

"I want to be with you. Won't you take me into your home?"

Mannig mumbled, expecting to be refused.

Romella leaned forward and whispered. "The khatoon of my family is very strict. If things are not done her way, she lashes the servants and then wails sky-high for the whole neighborhood to hear how things aren't done right by her maids. I, myself, cannot seem to do much to her liking." She rolled up her sleeve, exposing a long scar, with the scab still hanging from some parts.

Mannig glared.

"Find an Arab family," Romella insisted, rolling down her sleeve. "Be sure that it's an Arab family. Don't be *tutoum kulukh*, a pumpkin head like me ... by getting into a Kurdish or Turkomen family. Those ethnic enclaves dislike Armenians—they remind me of the Turks sometimes."

No need to explain. The word *Turks* aroused dread in Mannig's heart. Still enslaved by the memory of the horrific treatment at the gendarmes' hands, she failed to erase images of her massacred family. "This is for you," Romella said and removed the brown sweater from her shoulders.

Tongue-tied, Mannig let Romella drape it around her neck. The warmth was instantaneous, the pleasure only over-shadowed by Romella's compliments. Assuming a self-proclaimed grandeur, Mannig raised her head and stood erect; she visualized herself as a powerful person, capable of conquering any calamity.

"Next time I may bring a woolen coat," Romella continued. "I heard that Barone Mardiros, one of those philanthropists from Baghdad, is collecting warm clothing for the...."

Mannig's thoughts hovered over her newly acquired garment. Her flesh and bones relaxed in contentment. She owned a much-needed shield from chills to forage Mosul alleys with confidence. The future Romella described—of a generous man from an unfamiliar-sounding city—was too far from Mannig's reality. She only cared about the present.

"I also brought some bread," Romella said, rising and pulling Mannig up with her. She retrieved a round loaf from the folds of her robe, broke it in half and exposed slivers of dates in its center. "The bread I bring for you next time will contain meat and onions kneaded into it. Definitely. By then, of course, you may be fostered by the philanthropists of the Middle East Relief group. So you won't need anything."

Surprise exceeded Mannig's vocabulary, also her reaction to the bread. She grabbed it and ferociously bit into it. With her mouth full and crumbs sticking onto her lips, she sputtered out. "Will you come here again?"

"It will be difficult to sneak out soon. But I will, sometime. I miss you too much."

Mannig wanted to say, I miss you too, but another morsel of bread took precedence in her thoughts. She devoured the bites so fast her palate scarcely discerned the sweetness of the dates, yet she felt crumbling grains of the crust on her lips. Carefully, her fingertip brushed each grain into her mouth. Then she licked her upper and lower lips clean. Not a single speck must be wasted.

"I must go now," Romella said and approached Mannig with open arms.

Her mouth still full, Mannig remained speechless. She let Romella embrace her goodbye. She could not bear another separation. Repeat abandonment should have overwhelmed her, but the food in her stomach calmed her anxiety.

Romella had not forgotten her, after all. She still cared for her, just as she had done in the scorching desert when everything under the sun melted—everything except the memory of massacred families. For two years, through horror and despair, her kindergarten teacher from Adapazar and she had become partners in pain and misery. Now, in famine-stricken Mosul, they were becoming counterparts in self-reliance.

With half a loaf in her stomach, the other tucked inside the sweater, how *tutoum kulukh* of her to think she was abandoned! Romella had promised to return, and had. A teacher's word should never be doubted! She must remember everything Romella said, especially today, to secure an Arab family for herself until the important people came from Baghdad, loaded with clothes and food for the orphans. Romella named a Barone so-and-so. What was he called? His name floated by while Mannig was concentrating on the food in her mouth—the only thing that mattered to her. She pinched herself. Next time I will focus on the conversation and what's in my mouth.

Romella called her jarbeeg. She must live up to her reputation—become street smart. Tomorrow.

3—Barone Mardiros

Close to midnight, weary Mardiros arrived at Sebouh Papazian's house in Mosul.

The train ride from Baghdad exhausted him. The stop-and-go at each tiny village to disembark and board new passengers tried his patience. The slow train to Mosul frustrated him. *I want to be useful.* The 300-mile trip stole much precious time from accomplishing his mission. At thirty, he faced new challenges in pursuit of his passion to help the orphans of the desert, an undertaking paradoxical to any of his earlier exploits.

What a change from his previous life!

The youngest son of a wealthy family in Baghdad, Mardiros Kouyoumdjian enjoyed a life of affluence. He had returned from Robert's College in Constantinople in 1912, an engineer at twenty-two, and divided his time between social revelries and society gatherings. He knew he was handsome and the most eligible bachelor in Baghdad. Poised and refined, he flattered the beautiful and rich and flirted with the respectable young ladies of the upper class. He chuckled to himself, often infuriating his mother, as well as his sisters-in-law, whose diligence in matchmaking he unabashedly snubbed.

When the Big War broke out in 1914, the Kouyoumdjians became restless. In spite of the 2,000-kilometer distance from Constantinople—the seat of the Ottoman rulers—they foresaw imminent disaster. After all, the education of the five brothers in France or England and business enterprises with Allied nations now against the Ottomans and Germany raised their suspicions. They suffered perpetual sleepless nights.

No Kouyoumdjian foresaw the coming deportation of the Armenian communities from Asia Minor, least of all from Kayseri and Talas, the base of their ancestry. When word reached them that one of

Mardiros' sisters and her family had been deported and then massacred along with all the Armenians in Diar Bekir, rage engulfed Mardiros, contradicting his family's resolve to face fate passively. Realizing the futility of taking his revolver and shooting Ottoman authorities in Baghdad, he devised a secret scheme.

One day in 1916, two years into The Big War, he barged into the Ottoman Millet headquarters in Baghdad.

"I know seven languages, Your Most Esteemed Honor," Mardiros explained to the Sultan-appointed governor. "I can hear things and relate them to you." Switching from Turkish to Arabic, he added, "Your Honor, we all want to know what the Arabs are saying about the British and the deals they are cutting with the French. With my Arabic, I can be your spy in the Diyalah region."

The Governor allowed Mardiros to describe the plan. He assumed allegiance because Mardiros' father, His Excellency Hagop Kouyoumdjian, had been commended and honored with the title of Pasha by the Sultan for his philanthropic deeds and loyalty to the Ottomans.

"Of course, Effendi, you know the British are in control of Palestinian lands," Mardiros said—an optimistic rumor articulated by his family in their own parlor. "The Englaizees, the Fransawees and the locals may be cutting a deal in the territories just west of us—only a few kilometers from your seat, Your Honor."

Encouraged by the governor's attentiveness to facts he probably already knew, Mardiros continued. "Delegate me, Your Honor, as your representative in the western provinces. I grew up in Felloujah, played with the children of the Arabs surrounding our Qasr and farmlands. I can easily mingle with the Bedouin west of the Euphrates. I have good friends in the desert. Let me be your eyes and ears in the field."

The governor agreed to a trial period.

Mardiros plunged into his charade.

He replaced his European clothing with a brown-and-white striped *dizhdasheh* gown and belted his waist with a turquoise-adorned shield for his dagger. He placed a Bedou *aggaal* and *kaffieh* on his head and rode his horse to Felloujah, a Kouyoumdjian stronghold along the Euphrates River. From there, he relayed messages to the Governor in Baghdad telling what he heard from the mouths of his own farmhands. He censored the derogatory utterances and included only the mildest grumblings reflecting the Arabs' dislike of the Ottoman rule over their lands. He didn't want to appear biased in his reporting. Mardiros knew how to appease the authorities.

He rode his horse to Rumadi and Rutba, two Ottoman outposts, at the edge of the vast desert, ninety kilometers northwest of Baghdad. To further establish his credibility, he telegraphed to the Governor every detail he learned from the local Arabs—nothing more, nothing less.

Soon he gained the Governor's full confidence and, upon his return to Baghdad, the Governor dispatched Mardiros to Basra, 600 kilometers south.

"Your job in Basra is to infiltrate the insurgents," the Governor commanded him. "There's a rumor they are cooperating with the British at the Persian Gulf. We think they will invade our territories from the south."

"I will pretend to be an insurgent myself," Mardiros said (controlling a sneer: in fact, he already was one).

Six months into his assignment, Mardiros began sending erroneous messages to the Governor. He distorted many facts to make them appear politically compatible. He intended to manipulate the Ottoman troop distributions and prevent forces from amassing in the South.

"It is only a *rumor*," he telegraphed from Basra, emphasizing the word, *rumor*. "The British, together with Indian forces, are gathering by ship in Basra ...

"We are in control—STOP

"No need to keep one eye open—STOP"

Another message read:

"The Arabs in Basra don't want *Englaizees* on shore—STOP

"The locals will fight if necessary—STOP

"Everyone is geared to crush the enemy—STOP"

The next telegram included more details:

"Some insurgency exists—STOP

"Their number is vastly exaggerated—STOP

"This front remains solidly ours—STOP

"There is no need to worry about Basra, at all," Mardiros repeated. He added a postscript: "I am off to Najaf—STOP

"More insurgents among the Shiites there—STOP"

He rode his horse northwest from Basra, along the Euphrates River, with his entourage of Ottoman escorts. While mingling amicably with the Arabs near Hillah, in the Babylonian region, he recognized his oldest brother, Karnig, also dressed in the tawny Arab garb, cooperating with local insurgents.

After a brief encounter with a British Officer, clothed in the Arab headgear of the *aqaal* and *kaffieh* and known by the Bedouin as Lawrence, the brothers agreed to cooperate in their efforts to deceive the Ottomans full speed ahead.

A Turkish officer in their entourage suspected treason and accused the brothers of being double agents. He spared them instant death in deference to their father's title of Pasha and imprisoned them in an Ottoman garrison between Hillah and Babylon.

Mardiros spent the remaining year of the war in prison. When the Allied forces released him at the end of 1918, he remained demoralized, not only because of his vile prison experience, but because of his brother's death from typhus, the horrible disease that had ravaged the prison population.

With the dissolution of the Ottoman Empire, his father's title of Pasha no longer claimed distinction. Mardiros found himself outside the prison, a great distance from his home in Baghdad. Alone and without money or connections, he walked over 100 kilometers from Hillah to Baghdad.

The sad news of his brother's death overwhelmed the Kouyoumdjians. While the family shed tears, Karnig's widow, Diggin Rose, accustomed to berating others, reprimanded Mardiros, "YOU should have died instead of my Karnig. You have no wife, no children. People like you have no right to survive." She wailed again and again, "Woe, woe to me! How will my four children survive without a father?"

Mardiros, flabbergasted, was defiant. "You talk as if the K-K-Kouyoumdjians are banishing you from the Q-Q-Qasr, our home," he stuttered. "Have you forgotten this big place belongs to all five brothers? The Karnig compartment remains eternally his. Why do you want to leave us?"

Mardiros held his breath, awaiting her reaction.

Her jaw dropped.

Mardiros had succeeded. He went to her, held her hand and whispered, "I can be the disciplinarian of the children, if you like."

The disturbing scene ended right then and there, leaving an indelible memory on all.

Within a year of Mardiros' release, post-war activities in Baghdad society replicated the pre-war festivities. The French and British Embassies became the Kouyoumdjians' playground. Half-hearted, Mardiros resumed participation in Baghdadi society. He fell into the same old habits of fox-trotting with many beautiful maidens to the most recent records revolving on his Master's Voice gramophone. Banquet tables overflowed with European cuisine and cognac. The novelty and flair of mingling with nationalities other than the Ottomans and Germans failed to lure him to a life of fun and frolic.

At one of those palatial parties, Mardiros met Simon Gharibian, an Armenian philanthropist on a fund-raising mission. He traveled to many capitals of the world where large Armenian communities existed, including London, Paris, Sidney, and Calcutta, and he had collected a considerable amount of money to assist the Armenian orphans whose families had been massacred by the Ottoman Turks during The Big War.

Simon Gharibian had come to Baghdad on a similar calling. "There are hundreds and hundreds of orphans," he said, addressing a group of gentlemen in white ties, glasses of cognac in their hands and cigars between their lips. "They are now scattered throughout the lands of the defunct Ottoman Empire. They will perish or they will cease being Armenian. These orphans are our heritage. They are our future. Even if there were only a single drop of Armenian blood in our veins, we must rescue them at any cost."

Something aroused Mardiros. Mesmerized, his gaze riveted on this unusual gentleman as if they were the only ones in the room. Mardiros felt he was listening to a confidante, a friend, a liberator. The man motivated him, spoke to his heart. He foresaw encouragement for his efforts and appreciation for his deeds. Mardiros listened to the gentleman; he spoke a truth and revived in him his deepest values. Of all mankind, this person would believe in him. He could help him achieve his greatest potential.

Mardiros wanted to contribute more than the plain monetary donation the Kouyoumdjians made—though it was a substantial amount. He wanted to be more than a passive donor. Might his involvement include the physical rescue of the orphans? He aspired to finding and saving the children. Work in the field himself? The ground level? He visualized adventures that would fulfill his mission in life.

The two gentlemen, one from Baghdad, the other from Basra,

spent the rest of the evening devising plans to rescue the orphans. When the last of the cognac was sipped and the final cigar puffed, Mardiros volunteered for the first step—to go to Mosul.

With great exuberance, he departed from Baghdad, leaving behind traditional indulgences and not looking back. He smelled his own zeal while packing and tasted his farewells as he bid his family adieu. But the tediously slow train to Mosul tired him, adding uncertainty to his expectations for the coming days.

At least the field granted solid footing. Once in the company of Sebouh Papazian, his host, assigned to evaluate the situation in Mosul ahead of him, he expected great support in undertaking and devising the next steps of locating and housing the orphans.

"I would have met you at the station," Sebouh Effendi said at the threshold of his house, "if I had known of your arrival. I'm relieved to see you here, finally." The two gentlemen from Baghdad shook hands and, due to the lateness of the night, retreated to their respective rooms.

Groaning, Mardiros stretched an exhausted body on the bed. A slender man of 5'8", he wrapped the quilt around his body to combat the coolness of the room. Not the lumpiness of the mattress. If not for the cot, it would have reminded him of the brick floor of the Ottoman prison. For a moment he questioned his sanity. *I must be crazy to leave the comforts of the Qasr.* Why had he? To rescue orphans, of course. His eyes remained open and his heart beat in anticipation. What had aroused such compassion in him? It had never occurred to him to have such empathy. *I'm not knowledgeable about children. Or about homelessness. Far from it.* He understood something about engineering, though only from college textbooks. How could training to survey land and gauge river depths be applied to dealing with refugees?

His host, Sebouh Effendi, had experienced Mosul several days earlier than he. Mardiros would rely on the counsel of this man, who was older and a widower. Baghdadi gossip alleged that the man was raising his little daughter as well as his own wife would have. His sympathy for children boded well for the welfare of the orphans. Working with a knowledgeable person comforted Mardiros.

A fly buzzed in the night silence. He shooed it away and blew out the kerosene lantern. The sun neared its rising time. He rolled over and closed his eyes. What would the morrow reveal?

4—Jarbeeg

Mannig awakened to flies hovering above her face.

She waved them off, but they persisted, landing on the yellow scum stuck to her long eyelashes. *Not on my mouth!* She cupped her mouth, veiling the cut in her lower lip—split in the middle and infected. The sore had begun a long time ago, prompting the habit of holding her lip immobile to ease pain. Because of the never-healing gash, she faced the challenge of chewing and swallowing without exerting lip movement—that is, if she found anything to eat. Food?

Sitting up suddenly disturbed the buzz and stirred the raw smells of dampness. She scraped sticky grime off the folds of her eyelids. A quick scan of the khan bore out a disconcerting mood and the unusual stillness a disturbing notion. Nearby, as usual, the orphans sprawled under their filthy quilts. The sight of them sleeping used to comfort her, for it meant she had a head-start to roam the city for edibles.

Her heart hit bottom.

The sun must be at high noon to filter across the palm branches. Hazy rays bounced off the bare ground. The children's mats rolled up, and the eerie silence warranted quick action. *Vye!* They're foraging Mosul. She was late! She jumped off the hard mat, unable to explain why she had overslept.

Like a second awakening, the warmth on her shoulders thrilled her—Romella's gift. Immediately she reached inside the sweater. *Amahn!* No one had stolen the remainder of her bread! What joy! She wallowed in contentment, a sensation not felt in a long time.

Of course, she had slept deeply. Warmth and a full stomach promoted sleep. She hugged her bread, then hid it under her hard mat. She lay down again. Luck must have come to her. She closed her eyes in awe of the goodness in life. Romella had called her *jarbeeg*.

She sat up again. How could she justify Romella's statement? She must live up to the reputation of being street-smart.

A few stalls beyond her niche, she saw two older girls blowing on bits of hay to sustain flames. Next to food, finding fuel for cooking and heat topped the list. She knew dried animal bones and intestines were grabbed first because they burned slower and longer. Twigs and sticks rated high but had been picked from the neighboring alleys of the khan a long time ago. Firewood, which could always be exchanged for food, might yet be found in unexplored alleys.

She grabbed a gunny-sack from under her mat and dashed out, only to slow down at the sight of a lanky person lingering at the entrance of the khan—a boy, about thirteen or fourteen, wearing a pair of tattered army pants re-belted at his armpits. His eyes sparkling like black olives dancing in oil below arched brows attracted Mannig; she cast a second glance at him. He seemed likable, except for the hungry way he stared at the rolled up bedding where she slept.

"If you steal my quilt," she snarled, "I will yell to the heavens that you are the thief in our khan."

"I don't need your quilt," he smiled, accentuating a square jaw.

"You can say anything," she said. "Speech is cheap. When I return, I better see it exactly where it is now." She took deep breath, questioning herself, *Is that what a jarbeeg says?* "Why are you glaring at it, then?" she growled.

"I am new here," he said. "I'm looking for a free spot to sleep tonight."

Surprised at his consideration for others, she eyed him again. The orphans she knew normally shoved and pushed, grabbed and even displaced each other for a spot to settle in. This boy deserved a second glimpse. Should she offer him a slot next to hers? No! Not to a stranger. It behooved her to stay aloof. She lugged her bag and took a step. I must think *jarbeeg* ... act *jarbeeg*! But how? She swung her bag over her shoulder and glanced here and there, and even at the boy, hoping something might give her an idea. Nothing. He remained, standing tall and peering across the khan.

A *jarbeeg* wouldn't waste time. Out of the khan she flew, in pursuit of her mission.

The wintry dew covered the dry furrows under her bare feet. The pebbles strewn in her path nicked her calloused feet without slowing her pace until she stubbed her inflamed toe. More in anger than pain, she kicked stones and pebbles with her good foot, hurling them hither and yon. The ruckus replaced the surrounding calm as a brindled brown pigeon flapped, squawking a yard above the ground. She chased it; bent and picked up a stone to hurl at it. She pursued, threw stone after stone, aimed closer and flung faster, again and again. She could taste a juicy roasted chick on a spit. Saddened and breathless, she finally gave up. Neither her speed nor aim matched the survival instinct of the bird. *I'm not as jarbeeg as Romella imagines me to be.*

The chase, however, had led her to new paths. Several mosques loomed above the skyline, and one tilted minaret leaned taller than the surrounding tenements. The neighborhood boasted larger houses than the ones near the khan.

Beggars roamed the streets, stretching sinewy arms and muttering, "*Bakhsheesh!* Alms! *Bakhsheesh!*" They called repeatedly, "*Khattir Allah, Joo'aan!* For God's sake, I am hungry!"

Mannig wandered beside the Moslawi beggars, but resisted emulating them. The natives persisted, hour after hour, scouring the less starving quarters asking for charity—a privilege for Muslims, an expression of piety in the name of Allah. But Mama's admonition, "Armenians don't beg," haunted her. Might Mama condone receiving manna in the famine-stricken city?

Loafing about for *bakhsheesh* tempted her. Wouldn't Haji-doo, her grandmother, even from heaven, be chastising her with, "Idle hands are the devil's workshop?" Even Mannig rebuffed laziness. A non-beggar, she felt different from these people, and Romella's sweater gave her a self-imposed pride. Being *jarbeeg* justified stealing, cheating, and fighting for food. Resorting to her wiles, she walked with new purpose.

Farmers drove livestock back and forth in the wide streets. She sidestepped to avoid a tall man in a brown cloak goading his donkey with a stick. When she noticed portly flies feasting on the syrup oozing out of the date-heavy baskets, she dashed toward the donkey faster than a thrown stone. She swept her fingers and her palm across the basket and fled. Only after losing sight of the man did she lick her sweetened hand and all sides of her fingers.

She dodged two mules shuffling their hooves under sacks of barley, but followed the person clad in a black *abaya*—the shoulder-to-toe garb, reminiscent of the Bedouin Arabs. The woman pulled the rope tethered to the cow's neck. Mannig fell into stride with them, ambling in rhythm to the clanging of heavy brass bells dangling from its neck. Mannig stopped when the woman did, at the door of a white adobe two-story house.

"*Haleeb!* Milk!" The woman yelled, rapping at the door.

A young girl, dressed like an Arab maid, opened the door and handed the vendor a metal bowl with a wide rim.

The milk woman squatted, her abaya billowing around her. She set the bowl of streamed milk in her lap with a splash.

Mannig's mouth watered. She must act—quickly. She pulled on the maid's gown. "I am a very good helper," she declared. "I can do many things for you while you rest. Let me come and do some chores for you. You will see what a wonderful worker I can be."

"*Imshee!* Scat!" the maid shooed off Mannig. "I do the chores in this house."

Dejected, Mannig had turned to leave when she spied a bottle under the milk-woman's sleeve. While the maid talked with Mannig, the woman had pulled her abaya close to her body to shield pouring water into the client's bowl.

Mannig grabbed the moment. To be heard by the matron of the house, as well as everyone in the vicinity, she shouted, "She is cheating! The milk woman is cheating! I would never let MY family be cheated like this!" She yelled without a breath, wanting to be heard loudly, clearly and repetitively. "The milk woman is cheating you! She poured water into your bowl! Do you want to pay for water instead of milk? I would never let my family be cheated like this."

She took a breath to yell some more.

The maid overwhelmed her. She kicked Mannig with the back of her heel—Arab custom to scourge a vile creature—and through clenched teeth, snapped, "If you don't shut up, I will turn the dogs on you."

Having made enemies of the maid and milk woman alike, Mannig fled beyond the bend in the alley, leaving them to raise a ruckus of their own.

A group of scavenging boys faced her. Some clutched palm-frond baskets, and others carried gunny sacks like hers. Hearing Armenian, she followed them and stopped when they did. Mesmerized, they scrutinized a horse's arching tail. The instant the dung oozed out, the children dashed to catch the falling dung before it hit the ground.

Mannig knew about collecting dung—camel dung—a chore assigned to her by the Bedouin Arabs. After rescuing her in the desert, they had sheltered her for several months before leaving her in Mosul. The Bedouin teased her as the "best dung collector" of the tribe. Her nimble fingers picked up the excrement intact, without breaking its mucous coating. Her chore began at daybreak before the camels trampled all over their droppings. Within the hour, the Bedou women mixed the pickings with spines of tumbleweed or hay and formed patties to dry in the sun. Dung was treasured as fuel for cooking and keeping the tent warm.

Seeing how the scavengers eyed the dung, Mannig decided to use her expertise. Feigning ignorance, she asked the boy who caught his prize before it splattered on the ground, "What do you do with the *kaka*?"

"I give it to the baker," he boasted, turning his head to reveal a puss-filled boil on his left cheek. "He gives me bread for it."

"Which baker?" she asked, pretending she knew of several.

"Why should I tell you?"

"Because I am an Armenian like you," she said, expecting complete affirmation.

"Armenian, m-Armenian," boil-cheek bullied her. He pushed her aside and tightened his grip on the basket with his muscled arm. "I don't tell. The baker is mine!"

"I am a very good kaka picker. I really am. Will you make me your partner?"

"Partner, m-artner. Nobody is anybody's partner," he sneered and pushed ahead.

Snubbed again, she rejoined the bevy of boys foraging behind animals. She stood apart when the discovery of droppings incited warfare among them. Amid the clamor of barking, braying, and neighing, the bigger boys, overwhelming the little ones, succeeded in grabbing the dung first. The losers scurried for the cow-pies, less precious than the dung of camels, donkeys, or horses.

Mannig schemed over the next pile of droppings. She gathered up the shreds of her garment and girdled them with her rope belt. Hurling herself amid the bedlam of boys over another pile of loot, she shouted like the rest and quarreled for a chunk of the fortune. When she wriggled out of the huddle, she found two boys eyeing her pick. She gasped at boil-cheek, who grabbed her wrist and pushed her to the ground.

He beat her.

She clenched her bag.

He dug his knee into her back.

Her breath stopped under his crushing weight.

She refused to succumb to pain. Having experienced throbbing before, she held her breath. I won't relinquish my dung as long as I live!

A sudden relief from the crushing weight freed her to gasp, cough, and finally inhale. Several successive breaths revived her senses. Who had pulled the bully off? She gaped at two fellows, striking and counter-punching each other, fists landing and heaps of dung flying. Boil-cheek threw a punch at his assailant, who dodged without a blow, and the sustaining momentum landed the bully in the slush with a splash.

Mannig struggled to her knees—covered in manure, smelling of *kaka*. The scavengers were gone, and her rescuer looked at her.

He extended his hand to help her rise.

She was breathless again—this time at his gallantry. Who in these conditions might offer kindness? She took his hand and gazed at him. His black eyes shone below a pair of arched brows.

"You?"

"Yes, me," he said and helped her up.

"And I thought you were going to steal my quilt!" Mannig said with shame.

He grinned. "You ought to restrain yourself from fighting big fellows. It is safer to accompany lions than intrude on foraging boys."

Mannig's heart skipped a beat.

"You are fast, but no match for his size," he said, brushing dung off her shoulders.

Neither word nor sound of breath came from her.

"Promise me to avoid scoundrels at all times," he said, handing Mannig her bag.

"He stole everything I grabbed," Mannig whimpered.

"You can have mine," he said, and scooped a palmful of his collection into her bag.

Amazing! Might generosity survive amid ruined lives? He was different from the others, physically, too. Squashed manure covered muscled arms and greenish masses smeared his hair, further attracting flies. Moist drips sneaked behind his ears, sparkling like stars. And he? He shone like the moon.

"Come!" he said, leading the way. "I know a baker near the river who needs this *kaka*."

"What will I get for it?"

"Bread, of course! He'll give you a fresh loaf, if he still has unsold ones. Otherwise, he will make up for it with two loaves the next time. He is a good man."

Mannig looked into his black eyes with disbelief. This boy shared secrets with her about his baker. Without qualms, she followed him. He even showed her new pathways undiscovered by many foragers. She loved him.

"We should go to the river and wash while the sun is still warm," he said. "What is your name?"

"Mannig. Yours?"

"Dikran."

She followed him to the riverside more from awe than necessity. Her heart beat fast, yet she was not afraid. She watched his gait and followed his pace with assurance. His gallant demeanor overwhelmed her.

By the river shore, he stood coyly behind a rock, guarding the dung bags while she waded in, fully dressed. She splashed in and out of the cold water. Every now and then, she heard him singing, "I am still here and the bags have not gone to Baghdad yet."

She looked toward his hiding place wondering if he peeked at her. Only his voice filled the noonday silence. She giggled. He had earned her trust.

During his turn dunking himself in the river, he slapped the coldness of the surface a few times before swimming a speedy few yards out and back.

How thrilling, Mannig thought. I wish I knew how to swim.

He sat on a rock to dry in the sunshine. *He is like a miracle.*

"You are very pretty," he said, watching her squeeze the water out of her hair. "Cleanliness is Godliness and, in your case, it reveals your beauty."

What an exciting voice! Her cheeks burned. Propriety demanded lowering her gaze, yet her senses insisted on focusing on him lest he vanish like an echo.

He touched her cheek.

Her lashes fluttered up and down.

"Yes!" he said. "Even a little smile reveals a dimple below this cheek bone."

Ah, his touch! Goose bumps tickled her body.

"I found a spot for me in the khan," he said as they approached their shelter.

Her insides stirred.

"I will stay here," he said, "until the Middle East Relief Organization actually opens an orphanage."

Middle East Relief Organization. Hum! Where had she heard the name before?

"We'll see if a Barone Mardiros of Baghdad actually arrives to keep his promise," Dikran said, more to himself than to Mannig.

He had captured her attention a while ago, but talk of an orphanage tantalized her. That night, she lay under her quilt wearing a big smile. *My hero.*

She wanted his happiness as strongly as she wanted to collect dung, seek food, or protect her quilt. Stealthily she brought out the half-loaf of bread from under her mat and took a bite. She decided to save a chunk for him, perhaps share it in the morning.

Before falling asleep, she recalled the clear glow in his smiling black eyes at the khan entrance earlier that day. *Since I'm thinking of him, might he be thinking of me?*

Dikran—named after an Armenian king. Even his name is heroic.

5—Funeral Feasts

The reason for Dikran's support and care for her eluded Mannig. In an environment where only the self mattered, Dikran habitually shared a chunk of bread he found or a bit of dung to exchange for food. Why give anything when he himself owned nothing? Often the two began foraging the city at sunrise, returning empty-handed to the khan before the onslaught of the cold night. In her own niche in the dark, she debated disclosing the location of her grass-carpeted grave. Every morning she woke, uncertain whether to tell Dikran of her treasure, since her grass-supply was dwindling.

While they were searching together for edibles in a new alley, Dikran led her to his baker. "You can give your chips to him today."

Mannig queried his jet eyes. *He's even divulging his food source. Should I tell him about mine?*

She took the disk of flat bread from the baker in exchange for her horse droppings. As soon as she had cracked it in half, she began stuffing it in her mouth, bite after bite. The bread really was filling—more so than the green clovers in the grave. But less reliable as daily fare.

Sensing Dikran's gaze, she stopped swallowing. His disheartened look pressed her to crack another chunk and give it to him while she gobbled the rest. She reached for his hand. "I will show you my hideout."

The cemetery brimmed over with a procession of Muslim-Arab wailers, inching toward the location of her secret grave. Her heart crumpled with the melancholic minor scale of the dirge, and her eyes widened in fear of losing her prized pit. Her soul, on the other hand, embraced the ululating waves wafting towards her. *How beautiful!* Musing over the melody, her body picked up a rhythm, and she swayed wide and short, in step with the procession.

"This is bad," Dikran latched on to Mannig's arm. "Let's get out of here."

"No, no," Mannig freed her hand. "I like their singing. I want to hear more."

"Singing? That won't feed us," Dikran said, grabbing her arm again. "Let's go."

"You go," she jerked away from him. She didn't notice him leave; so engrossed was she in the emotional display of the mourners.

The voices rose as their bodies stretched toward the sky. In unison, they stomped; in succession, they tiptoed forward; light steps accompanied spread arms, which then fell and flapped with the rhythmic lament. Their hands slapped their chests in a regular cadence, twice in a row, and then their cheeks—men, women and children thumping themselves.

With a tempo all her own, Mannig flowed with the mourners. She imitated their long, wavering, high-pitched sound and wondered if she, too, resembled a howling dog. *Of course! Except I can't trill like these professionals.* Emitting a high-pitched voice camouflaged her failure to accompany it with a rapid movement of the tongue.

Mannig watched closely the way women placed right hands horizontally over the upper lips, opened their mouths, and moved the tongue from left to right repetitively. Mannig tried it but produced only a sharp sound, with a variation of her own concoction. She imitated their movements but mostly improvised her own. She exuded agony with her limbs, yet cheerfulness filled her insides; she moaned for the onlookers, yet felt her core rekindling. A heavy footstep changed into an intricate gait and evolved into a graceful leap. She visualized her movements as if in a mirror, floating with surreal fervor, whirling in her yellow dress in the parlor in Adapazar.

At the sound of piercing trills, she opened her eyes—no yellow dress, no parlor. Still in dun sack. She blended right in with the children toddling toward the entrance of a house.

Faces peeked from window slits high in the brick walls. Female shrieks drifted in from a section in the courtyard while a host of tearful women, dressed in black muslin garments, leaned over the rails of the second-floor balcony, viewing the grieving demonstrators.

The procession entered the open courtyard, Mannig in tow. She squatted with them in a circle along an array of potted pink carnations, amid dizzying fragrances.

"So your good mother is like mine," the girl of ten or twelve sitting next to Mannig said, rolling out her Arabic words. Not wishing to violate the respectful silence, the girl covered her mouth with one hand and pointed her elbow to a handful of women lamenting in the center of the courtyard. "My good mother scolds me if I weep with her."

"Did somebody die in your family?"

"No one, good God forbid!" the girl gasped. "My good mother is a good mourner. She wails good; she moans good. When somebody dies in a good family, she weeps in their good house. The good people give her good food. I can mourn just like my good mother and do everything she does—I am good—but my good mother makes me sit and wait."

Surprised to hear of the reward, Mannig asked, "Do you mean people give stuff to eat for crying?"

"Good food and good things." The girl directed Mannig toward the lamenters.

Astonished, Mannig watched the professional mourners strip their top garments to the waist. So many breasts! Bare and bobbing—some up and down, others helter-skelter, each woman's uniquely shaped. The elongated swung from side to side; others, nearly flat, stuck to the ribs; and a couple of pairs were bloated with milk, ready to fill a pail. The women surged upward and bent deep; they picked up handfuls of ash, and strewed it on their long black hair. Their faces and chests, streaked in gray lines, shone with sweat and tears. With shredded mourning sackcloth, they wiped their faces. In deference to the grieving family on the balcony, they wailed great cries—sharp, shrill, and ear-piercing shrieks. They sustained trills, while the women folk of the dead intoned with prolonged ululations.

"The good dead, up there," the girl pointed to the sky, "they appreciate these good lamentations."

Mannig focused her attention on the mouths of the mourners, and her lips mimicked their words. Her shoulders lifted up and down with the tempo, and her head swirled and whirled, repeating the phrases of the rhythmic chant:

> Oh my Hassan—my son, my son,
> Would God, I had—had died for thee,
> Oh my Hassan—my son, my son,
> Gone forever—not your glory.

Mannig nudged the girl. "What is Hassan?"

"Hassan is the good name of the good dead of today," she said. "We change the name of the good dead at other good funerals. Tomorrow my good mother laments for Ibraheem, another good dead."

"Hassan died in the war," murmured a child nearby.

"My father fought in the war," said another. "But God spared his death. He was the one who brought the sad news about Hassan's death. Poor Hassa …"

Two maids appeared in the courtyard. They hauled a huge metal serving tub, taking short, heavy steps. A whiff of rosemary and roasted lamb preceded the servants. Crossing over to the grieving mother, they placed the tub before her.

Chunks of meat steamed atop a heap of pearly rice while the grease-drenched, fried eggplant-wheels shone around the base of the white mound.

Hassan's mother wiped her tears with her robe and motioned to the grieving family to surround the tub.

Mannig's eyes widened; a burst of saliva flooded her mouth at the arrival of a similar tub, heaping with butter-soaked grains of rice. They carried it outside the house to the alley for the cluster of men grieving amongst themselves, without the guidance of professional mourners.

"The men do it differently," the good girl whispered. "They lament for Hassan by bubbling smoke in their water pipes. Every now and then, one man recounts Hassan's excellent deeds while the rest nod with sadness and smoke their *narguilla*. The gurgling stops, and all eyes focus on the maids with the food."

The smell of steaming fluffy rice wafting with the third tub's content brought Mannig to tears, even as the food was placed in the center of the courtyard for the wailing women. She sensed the good girl preparing to pounce when her mother had uttered her last shriek. The professional mourners scurried to form a thick circle surrounding the tub and, with a loud thud, dropped their haunches onto the brick floor in a show of exhaustion. They dipped their hands into the rice and its trimmings.

The good girl darted to her mother, and the rest of the children, tailing theirs, slithered between the bodies to reach the food.

Mannig pretended to be swept along with the wave of dashing children. She hovered around from woman to woman until she found a large person engrossed in her own eating. *She won't notice a scrawny girl huddled behind her.* Mannig extended her skinny arm against the woman's hip, groping for an opening to the tub. Her nose was muffled in the folds of the woman's black robe. *Will I suffocate? How else can I reach the food?* She held her breath, closed her eyes, and pushed her hand farther. *Amahn!* Her fingers touched the moist, warm grains. She cupped a palmful and, clasping her fingers tightly, retracted her arm. She panted a few big breaths before letting the pungent rice slide down her throat.

Then and there, at that very moment, she knew the taste of heaven—a taste that could not be satiated with one bite alone. She pushed her arm in and out, back and forth, and stuffed her mouth with handful after handful.

I must savor this feast of life tomorrow.

6—'Small Wit, Active Feet'

Wailings beckoned Mannig.

As freed soldiers from the defeated Turkish army returned home in 1918, bearing the bad news of those killed in action, lamentations filled the skies of Mosul. To Mannig, crying voices meant a banquet of steamed rice and promised an end to stomach-growling hunger.

As she became a professional mourner, Mannig wept and feasted with them. Grieving families stopped shooing her away as an intruder, and the ululating coterie, in the heat of their emotional outbursts, overlooked her presence. Mannig discovered a steady source of food in homes of the rich, in hovels of the poor, among small families or amid the entourage of clans. Their sorrow ensured her joy; her exuberance, their comfort. Dikran? He provided her solace.

Like the Moslawis, she excelled in wailing and lamenting. Visualizing herself dressed in her yellow organdy dress twirling in the parlor of her Adapazar home, she invented unique moves. Her improvisations blended with the steps of the professional mourners. Soon, she modified their standard routine with distinctive touches of her own. On occasion, she stepped into the lead and gained a front seat next to the tub of rice.

Upon concluding one feast in a new neighborhood, she recognized Romella's house. Stomach full and anxieties lessened, she sauntered toward it. Seeing her kindergarten teacher bent over kneading dough in a tub in the courtyard, she approached.

"Such a long time since I have seen you," Romella said, lifting hands sticky with dough. "Let me hug you with my elbows."

More than the smell of yeast, or the soft folds of the blue, floral tunic, Mannig clung to Romella's breast. In the comfort of her embrace, all tensions disappeared. *Am I in Mama's arms?*

"Let me look at you," Romella said. "The color in your cheeks tells me you are well."

Mannig nodded and followed her across the courtyard to the sunken baking oven—a meter-deep hole dug in the ground and plastered with clay.

Romella crouched beside the mouth of the pit and peered in. "*Oye!*" She pulled up. "The kaka coals are still very hot. I have to wait until the flames stop licking." Resting on her knees, she slapped the surface of the dough, collapsing its puffed-up dome.

Mannig had learned how to bake bread during her stay with the Bedouin. "May I help?" she asked, crouching beside Romella.

"My *khatoon* dislikes others touching her dough," Romella said, scanning the balcony of the courtyard. She pinched a wad of dough, balled it into an orange-sized chunk, and laid it on the flour-sprinkled cloth. She placed six other balls beside it then covered them with a blanket. "They need a short nap."

Seeing a bit of dough left in the brass bowl, Mannig said, "There's enough for another one."

"That is the starter for tomorrow's batch," Romella said, and tucked it into a moist and yellowing cheese-cloth. She picked up a wooden dowel and rolled one of the dough-balls into a large, thin disc.

"The Arabs used their hands to flatten it," Mannig said.

"In Mosul, we are civilized," Romella snickered, waving the slender walnut rolling-pin. "This, you must admit, is twentieth-century progress."

"I'm making progress in my life, too," Mannig said. "I've gone beyond foraging for food. Instead, I go to funeral feasts. They're everywhere." She chuckled and added in Arabic, "The good dead die every day."

"Where did you learn to say such things?" Romella scowled. With a toss of her beautiful copper-red hair, she giggled, inducing Mannig to laugh as if sharing a secret.

Mannig felt a new closeness. Knowing and loving her teacher so dearly stirred a yearning to stay near. Belonging to someone meant staying well and alive. She ached for a lasting bond. It hurt as fiercely as if she were receiving the slaps Romella gave the flattened, round dough she applied to the walls of the hot oven. "Can I live with you, Miss Romella? I promise I will lighten your chores. Fetch firewood for your cooking? Do whatever your *Khatoon* needs to be done. You don't even have to feed me. I can get my own food as long as people die in Mosul."

"I, too, want you to live with me, Mannig-Jahn," Romella said. "The *Khatoon* of this house forbids it." Within a minute, she peeled a steaming golden round of Arabic bread from the pit. She tossed it onto a basket made of date-palm fronds and fanned her oven-heated face. "One day, *Allah Kareem*, as the Arabs plead for God's mercy, I will have my own house, and you will become my daughter. Now tell me more about your—what did you call it?—Ah, the funeral feasts."

"The mourners cry for the dead. That's all," Mannig answered half-heartedly, rolling her shoulders as the mourners did. "I know how they do it. Do you want to see?" Before waiting for an answer, she jumped to her feet, wailing high and low, stepping lightly then stomping her feet. She raised her fluttering arms with a rhythm she had devised, "Oh, my Hassan, my son, my son …."

She glided and skipped, then stomped, more in game than in grief. She wailed like jackals, screeched like ostriches, exhibiting sorrow while rivers of tears flooded her face. She whirled past Romella and twirled around the oven, making sure to sidestep the basket of bread. She danced around the oven again, unaware that she had attracted the household. Deaf to the hilarity and blind to the amusement of the onlookers on the balcony, she allowed her body to express her joy.

Pretending exhaustion, Mannig paused, then collapsed dramatically to her knees. She took exaggerated breaths. Only then did she become aware of her audience—women and children leaning along the railing and admiring her antics.

Fearing repercussions for disturbing the peace, she dashed over to Romella, now on her feet and staring into the smiling face of the approaching *Khatoon*.

"That's amazing," the Khatoon said, tickling Mannig's chin. "You devil, you! Where did you learn all that? You're a *sheytahn*—a clever girl. I like your Bedouin accent—it is so amusing."

"Do it again. Do it again." The children from the balcony chanted.

"Yes. Repeat everything," the Khatoon nodded. "And I will give you a loaf of bread."

"Thank God your funeral imitation was not disrespectful," Romella whispered and gestured to Mannig to comply. She piled the wood chips in a heap and drew the bread basket aside, making room for the entertainment.

Mannig stepped forward, but hesitated at sight of so many onlookers.

"Do it! Don't anger the Khatoon," Romella insisted.

Mannig timidly paced her rhythmic movements in a circle. She felt awful in her baggy burlap dress and uncombed chestnut tresses. Her knees locked; her torso froze. Taking tiny steps, she proceeded in log-like stiffness.

"Dance like you did earlier," the *Khatoon* yelled. "With your arms … and your shrieks … yes … more gyrations …."

Dance? Was I really dancing? That label and the smell of freshly baked bread triggered Mannig into her monkey-like antics again. Within seconds, she improvised twitches to novel jerks, pulsating howls accompanying the rhythmic applause of her audience.

The Khatoon caressed Mannig's face and handed her a disc of bread. "You are very, very, devilishly amusing. I'll give you a second loaf if you promise to come tomorrow and dance for my friends."

Mannig sought Romella's nod of approval before she accepted the offering.

"Come tomorrow," the Khatoon repeated, "and you can eat your fill."

Romella led Mannig outside the courtyard. "Be sure to show up. Don't you dare let me down," she insisted, hugging her farewell.

Mannig departed as the sun blinked behind the courtyard. A few minutes beyond, a cluster of hungry boys lurked at the far end of the alley. If those starvelings saw the bread, they would tear her apart. Instantly, she bent in half as if she foraged for edibles. *Dikran! Where are you? I need you!* To safeguard her bread, she resorted to tactics learned during the many times she had foraged for food.

Stooping down, she pretended to poke at something by her feet then put it in her mouth, all the while sneaking the loaves inside her garb. Next came elaborate choking, noisy spitting, and grunting to make the final act more disgusting. Her show paid off. Assuming her predicament no better than theirs, the scavengers rounded the bend and left her alone.

She cracked the discs in half and swiftly wrapped them in the folds of her burlap skirt. The crispy edges pricked her abdomen. *I'll be at the khan shortly.* She scurried down the path, skipping over stones, wary of assailants.

Approaching her baker, she slowed down to a loitering gait. The rays in the sky faded, casting thick shadows on him.

"Hey, Maria," he called, his version of Mannig, and stopped lowering the legs of his bread-stand for the night. "What's this? Don't you have chips for me today?"

"No," she said. "I don't think I will collect dung anymore."

"What's this? Have you become rich?"

"No, picking *kaka* is hard work," she said gazing into his eyes, seeking confirmation.

"Ha! All work is hard," he shook his finger.

"My grandmother used to say, 'Small wit, active feet,' " Mannig said, surprised to hear herself quoting Haji-doo's proverb.

"What's this? Have you become a philosopher?" he guffawed. "You keep your new smarts to yourself. But tell Dikran to bring chips tomorrow. You hear?"

"I will," Mannig said, and moved on, hugging the two half loaves. One for me; one for Dikran.

Dance. Mannig smiled. The *Khatoon's* word. She also liked my performance. Why else would she have labeled her *sheytahn* and repeated 'clever' and 'devilish' so many times?

7—Under Her Wings

The following day, Mannig enthralled Romella's khatoon and her lady friends.

Youthful and elderly spectators joined Mannig in the center of the courtyard, imitating her and howling with laughter at their own clumsiness. The giggles, carefree faces, and silliness of the afternoon energized her all the more to perform audacious and innovative steps. Leading the circle, she danced as long as their hearts desired.

To catch their breath every now and then, the ladies crouched on woven mats made of date-palm fronds. They sipped tea, nibbled sweet *ghourabia* cookies, and chatted about the girls, holding hands and following Mannig's lead. The line circled the gurgling fountain and snaked from one end of the courtyard to the other.

Romella cut into the chain of dancers and held Mannig's hand. "It's your lucky day!" she said, touching shoulder to shoulder. "One of those khatoons wants to shelter and feed you. You don't have to sleep in the khan anymore."

Mannig wanted to screech with disbelief, but was short of breath. She panted, "Really?"

"Let's take a break." Romella pulled her aside. She wiped Mannig's face with her sleeve and finger-combed her hair. "Look at the khatoon in the shiny-striped tunic—she is rich and has many servants. But she wants someone small like you to do tiny chores. I promised to take you to her *Qasr* tomorrow."

Mannig held her breath. The attention Romella gave to her appearance felt more precious than her words. She imagined Mama touching her locks. The gesture was not only comforting and familial, but it was a luxury to experience one of non-essential aspects of being alive. "Will I stay with a family? Where? Can I come and see you?"

"Of course, you can! I'm staying in this house. These people are good to me. I'm sure your khatoon will be the right person for you."

"*Y'allah! Y'allah!*" The covey of chirping females begged Mannig to return to the line and lead the dance.

Romella belted Mannig's baggy burlap dress with one of her own scarves. "Roots and leaves need not quell your hunger anymore, my *jarbeeg*-Mannig. Smartness brings luck. And you are *jarbeeg*. Now go and entertain them."

❧❦

The next day, after telling Dikran of her good fortune, Mannig met Romella at her house. The two headed to the woman's *qasr*, perched on the highest point of the city's northern section. Built like a castle, with upper and lower domed courtyards, it surrounded an open patio flagged with white stone. *I'm lucky, indeed.* She glanced at Romella. *She's impressed, too.*

At the entry arcade, the door-maid greeted them in Arabic, "*Salaam Aleykum*," and pointed Mannig to a tub to rinse the mud off her bare feet.

"Speak only Arabic, here," Romella warned, following the maid toward a tall, heavy sycamore door. "If you have anything to say to me, don't speak Armenian. They'll look at us with suspicion thinking we're gossiping about them. Do you understand?"

Mannig nodded.

The maid pushed the door open onto a lower courtyard surrounded by a balcony. From the cast-iron railing of the gallery, black-eyed and long haired children stared at Mannig. Their gazes felt as cold as the geometrically laid stones under her feet, while the meaning of their silence was as obvious as the gurgling fountain. She marveled at the in-house cistern, potted poplar trees, yellow rose bushes, and orange geraniums. *Is this paradise?*

The maid stopped at an ornately carved cedar door and, looking down the steps to the sunken area, sing-songed, "*Y'abnayya* is here."

The coarse Kurdish carpeted stairs pricked Mannig's bare feet as they descended into a dim room. Turkish finely woven silk hangings of various sizes decorated the walls, and a glut of Persian rugs covered the floor. She held her breath and tightened her shoulders at the dark, weighty, chilly ambiance. *How should I behave?* She wanted Romella's advice concerning appropriate decorum, but she knew she shouldn't speak Armenian, and speaking Arabic would broadcast her ignorance.

"Take a *minder*," said the maid, pointing to paisley-cased pillows cushioning the carpet corners in riotous colors. Mannig waited for Romella before sitting down. Indeed, Haji-doo's precept echoed in her head: "When a girl dies, the ground must approve; when alive, the public must. Sit on your legs and be civilized."

Mannig sank inside her baggy burlap dress. It tented her crossed legs and bodice, leaving her stick-thin arms exposed. Romella had stitched the armholes to smaller openings, and her fear of exposing her maturing breasts had vanished.

A bulky curtain, coarsely woven with checkered designs of brown camel-down and spotted black goat-hair, divided the room in the center. The maid slid it to one side and anchored it to shiny brass rings on the wall. From the latticed windows, high up near the domed ceiling, sun rays streaked in and bounced off a golden tooth in the smiling mouth of an elderly face. *I saw that glitter among the spectators in Romella's house.*

The woman was sprawled amid the giant-sized *minders*, displaying the bottoms of her feet. How uncouth!

"Let me look at *Y'abnayya*," the mistress beckoned, waving wide-cuffed long sleeves—a style depicting the wearer's scorn for labor.

The maid pushed Mannig forward.

She resisted the momentum several pillows away.

"You say she's ten or twelve?" the mistress jeered. "More like a thirty-year old creature."

"She is an Armeny orphan," Romella said. "She is without a family and has suffered much."

"She will not suffer under my wings," the mistress said, and waved at the maid. "Bring chai and *kleecha* cookies. Let's put some life into her face."

The maid set the *manqqala*, a brazier filled with faintly glowing charcoal, by the bare feet of the mistress. She positioned the cobalt-glazed tea pot in the embers, placed the cookies and three clear glass cups on the circular copper-tray table and prepared to serve.

"I'll pour the chai," the mistress said, pulling herself up and rolling her sleeve up to her elbow. She poured a glowing Ceylonese tea into the slender and handle-less glass cups.

Mannig's eyes riveted on the tea-serving routine.

Unlike the beverage in a china cup in Adapazar, the crimson drink blushed in clear glasses. The mistress held a silver spoon and swirled sugar granules into each serving. The jingling of metal on glass tantalized Mannig; the smell of cloves made her mouth water; the ceremony induced a faux taste of days gone by.

The mistress handed a saucer with a radiant glass of tea to Romella, and another to Mannig.

The glowing warmth fulfilled all expectations.

"This will comfort her flesh and the *kleecha* her stomach," the mistress said to Romella. "Don't fret over her. I shall see that she is well fed every day. She may even say the bread came from Allah." She eyed Mannig with a chuckle. "What is your name *Y'abnayya?*"

Bewildered in the midst of unfamiliar quarters, Mannig stayed silent, her eyes demurely cast down.

"Your name, girl? Is your tongue as mousy as you, girl?" the mistress insisted, holding a cookie to Mannig. "Take this *kleecha* and speak up. So what is your name, *Y'abnayya?*"

"Mannig," she whispered, reaching for the cookie.

"What?" The woman guffawed. Her smiling lips betrayed having already heard it correctly. "What did you say?"

"Mannig."

The mistress broke into a side-splitting laughter, tears running past her golden tooth and dripping onto the quivering flesh of her neck. "I am glad I'm the only one to hear it." She straightened up, pretending to be serious, but uttering her words between spurts of laughter. "Such a name will disgrace my son's house. His wives live here, and my grandchildren live here. We cannot have anyone working for me named *manyook.*"

"It's Mannig, not *manyook*," Mannig protested.

"Mannig, *manyook.* They sound the same. That is a bad word and it refers to males; I forbid you to roam my house with such a name."

Mannig's eyes pleaded.

"I can't understand how you Armenys survive in this town without learning proper Arabic," the mistress sneered, "or how to articulate gender differences."

"She speaks good Arabic," Romella defended Mannig. "She lived with the Bedouin before coming to Mosul. She spoke with them all the time. But she lacks knowledge of lewd words used in the streets or classy speech like yours."

"We use clean Arabic in this house," the mistress said. "We will

call you *Y'abnayya*. That means, 'hey girl'. That's that." She picked up
her glass of tea and signaled them to sip, also.

I can endure a new name.

But not the ravenous thirst for the tea. She gulped and scalded her
mouth. If I spew it out, *I may be discharged even before I get hired.* She held
the hot liquid, hoping no one noticed the tears in her eyes.

"*Mal'ooneh!*" The mistress swore. "I see I have to teach her how to
sip tea." For the first time, she pulled her feet under her seat. "Watch
me carefully, and you'll never burn yourself again." With great zest, she
grabbed the rim of her glass cup with her thumb and forefinger,
fanning out the other three digits. Then she held the saucer the same
way and daintily poured the steaming tea into it. Between sloshing and
blowing at the deep red liquid in the saucer to cool, she slurped a sip.
Immediately after, she replenished the saucer with more droplets.

When Romella swallowed her final bite of *kleecha* and sipped the
last drop of the tea, the mistress pulled colored candy from her robe
pocket and gave her two handfuls. "We are settled now," she said,
signaling an end to the meeting. "I like *Y'abnayya*. She stays with me.
You may come and see her as often as you like."

Romella embraced and patted Mannig. "I will visit you, soon." She
followed the maid out without glancing back.

Mannig kept her seat, facing the mistress. With Romella gone,
loneliness gripped her. Eeriness closed in, darkness drenched, and
smells dulled her senses. *What is my job?* She remembered that the
mistress intended "to take her under her wing." But no one had
spoken of her chores.

❧❦

Past the hours of sunset, the maid returned with a basket of
cooked wheat kernels. The leafy fingers of the palm-frond basket held
the tender, fluffy grains in a mound. She set it beside the *manqqala* of
glowing coal.

The mistress searched for her pocket amid the folds of her floral
linen gown and again brought out some colored candy. She cast the
sweet and sour drops of translucent yellow, green, and pink on the
heap of puffy golden wheat and said, "Dip your hand and eat." Then
she reclined on her *minder* and, straightening her knees, once again
exposed the bottoms of her feet.

"Well, *Y'abnayya*," she said, watching Mannig pick the last grain hidden in the recesses of the basket. "This is a treat just for you as long as you work for me. Did you like my son's food earlier? You can eat a whole lot more while you live under the roof of his *Qasr*."

Mannig had joined the family for a lavish supper in a room opening into the courtyard. A white tablecloth, spread on the floor for the meal, reminded Mannig of the first time her family had gathered for a meal on the deportation route. Mama had flipped a bed sheet on the ground and explained, "We will have a picnic, like the Americans." *Did she mean like the Arabs?*

Unlike the scant nibbles on the deportation route, the *Qasr* cooks displayed an array of several communal platters brimming with foodstuffs, scattered across the cloth. The smells of rosemary and sage dizzied Mannig as much as the display of heaping serving dishes dazzled her. Not even Adapazar claimed this many specialties. She crouched in a circle with fourteen other children, ages two to sixteen, boys and girls of one father and four different mothers. Supper time gathered the Qasr families who dwelt in separate compartments to eat their meal collectively.

Emulating the others, Mannig broke off a chunk of the flat bread and dipped into the platter of roasted eggplant sloshing in a stew of tomatoes, onions, and sage. She gulped several bites until the rosemary aroma wafted from the platter of garbanzo and lamb stew. She stuffed herself until her stomach brimmed. She eyed the leftover food. *Vye! Wish I could run with them to the khan for Dikran.* She missed him and hoped he traded the daily dung for a bite of bread from the baker.

Darkness trickled in and the sky domed the courtyard with a plethora of stars. The children retreated with their mothers to their own compartments on the upper veranda, and then gradually the lanterns in the rooms were blown out. The blue of the horizon deepened into a distant black, becoming as aloof as Mannig's grasp of her worth—no one had assigned her chores or a place to sleep. Earlier a woman had scrubbed her clean and dressed her in a blue gown. While she prized the soft floral cloth caressing her skin, she insisted on keeping her burlap dress—its smell reminded her of Dikran and its tawny color, the *khan*. She roamed in the courtyard at will throughout the day. No one informed her of her duties or asked her to dance. *Surely, the mistress wanted me to entertain the children.* Of course the Qasr dwellers would join her theatrics. She wiggled her hips. *They'll want to adopt me.* She assumed her performance would exhilarate everyone. But when? The deep hour of the night engulfed everything and her full stomach induced drowsiness.

"*Y'abnayya?*" The maid's voice summoned her to the mistress's chambers.

Finally!

Mannig scurried over with great anticipation to learn about her job. *I can do any chores. I am a hard worker. Romella called me jarbeeg.* She must promise the mistress to work from dawn to dusk.

Light from the hurricane lamp flickered on the mistress, now slouched in bedding where earlier she lounged amid an array of *minders.* Mannig held her breath and stood by the brass curtain rings on the wall. A brown lace-covered quilt lay over the mistress from neck to ankle, and pink satin sheets draped to the floor. A jarring element in the soft atmosphere, the woman's feet were thrust out at Mannig. Seeing the woman's starfish-like sprawl, Mannig held her breath. *Is she dead? Amahn! My luck ends here.* She tiptoed toward the head. When heavy breathing raised the pretty quilt up, Mannig relaxed.

"Did *Y'abnayya* eat enough?" the mistress snorted without uncovering her face.

"She ate more than any two broods put together," the maid said, and shooed Mannig aside while she drew the mid-room curtain and fastened its loose edge to the opposite wall. "The *ibriq* of water and the bed pan are in the usual corner."

Mannig glanced at the spot. *Aha! My job is to empty the bed pan.* How easy—after all, dung collecting was her expertise.

"You can leave us alone, now," the mistress grunted, waving her hand at the maid. When the door squeaked shut, she groaned, "Get in."

That doesn't make sense. Mannig stood still.

The mistress opened her eyes. "Where are you, *Y'abnayya?*"

"Here," Mannig responded even though she disliked having lost her true name. She leaned her head within the mistress's view.

"*Y'allah, y'allah.* Get in," the woman insisted, flapping the sheet and exposing plump nude legs. "What is the matter with you?" She sat upright, her bare breasts dangling over the satiny pink. "Do I have to drag you in myself? Crawl under my quilt!"

Mannig retreated two steps back, smack against the lantern.

"Get in! Why do you think I wanted you? You must do something for being fed and sheltered. Don't you like my food?"

Mannig nodded.

"There will be a lot more for as long as you remain in the *Qasr*—that depends on how you pleasure me." The mistress reclined on her pillow and wiggled her feet. "Get in, under the quilt!"

Mannig sneaked a look at the closed door, wondering if she should scat like a cat.

"Get under the quilt next to my feet," the mistress ordered. "Scratch the bottoms of my feet. I want you to scratch my soles. *Y'allah.* Get going."

Scratch the bottoms of feet? Mannig's eyes widened, for the strangeness rather than ease of the chore. She remembered being stranded in the desert without shoes. *What relief after Romella poked a needle to pull the thorns out of the soles of my feet!* The mistress needed similar respite, except she said 'scratch.' *I'm so lucky to get food for merely scratching feet.*

"I cannot sleep at nights unless someone scratches my soles," the mistress moaned—resignation and pain resonating in her voice, but also with a hint of anticipation. "Lie down on the mattress by my feet and keep warm under the quilt. Then scratch the bottoms of my feet. Scratch, scratch, scratch! Until I fall asleep. Begin!"

Mannig crawled up on the mattress and timidly touched the woman's foot with her fingers.

The mistress suddenly sat up and grabbed Mannig's hand. "I will show you how I want it done, *Y'abnayya*. Use your fingernails, gently but firmly. I want your fingernails to creep up and down—each hand on a foot; five fingers on each sole. See? There is nothing to it. Now, you do it. That's it, girl. Don't worry about hurting or tickling. Yes! You are good. Press more. Poke in deeper. Don't skip any part—along the toes, the edge of the heels … Oh, you are a good one … Ah, that's exactly right."

She dropped her head on the pillow with a moan of great relief.

When Mannig saw the mistress closing her eyes in ecstasy, she pulled her hands away.

"What are you doing?" the mistress yelled. "Scratch, scratch. Until I am asleep. Do you hear?"

"Yes," Mannig said.

This will take longer than I had expected. She crouched on the mattress and pulled the end of the quilt over her. She scratched nonstop while the mistress grunted "Ah" and "Oh." After ten minutes, a drowsy voice whispered, "You are good ... I certainly picked a good maidservant this time ... You are the best ... Ah ... Don't you dare stop."

Thirty minutes later, the woman seemed as still as a mountain.

Mannig stopped. Before she could relax her cramped fingers, the woman snarled, "No, no. I am still awake."

Curled up at the foot of the soft mattress, beneath the warm, soft quilt, with a full stomach and scratching the woman's soles without falling asleep before the mistress did, became torture in eternity—purgatory and hell wrapped into one.

Sometime later, past the deep midnight, Morpheus captured both of them simultaneously.

❧

For her stomach's sake, Mannig tolerated the entrapment for several nights. Throughout the day she agonized over her wakefulness at the woman's feet. She cringed at the accumulated crud in her fingernails and suffered a crook in her neck. She couldn't block out the feel of the sweat oozing from the khatoon's thighs. *Peece-kezi!* The woman unabashedly blasted *kaki hodair*, putrefying inside the quilt with intestinal gases. Mannig poked her head out only to be whacked by belching halitosis. The audibility of bodily noises was a double-edged luck—they alerted Mannig to escape the fetid assault by poking her head out and, at the same time, perpetuated the woman's wakefulness deeper and longer into the nights.

Throughout the day, Mannig wondered about her predicament. What's wrong with royal meals of fresh milk and honey? She hop-scotched, jump-roped, and giggled with the children in the daylight, but at night, she prayed for a plan to extricate herself from the mistress.

At dusk, the mothers called in their children, leaving Mannig alone in the courtyard. She accepted her separation from the household siblings as the norm, a routine befitting an orphan of her status. One evening, the sight of familial hugging and caressing tormented her. A twinge in her heart defined her desolation. *I'm irrelevant in the Qasr.* Not so in the khan. She longed to huddle with other orphans. *I miss Dikran! Khan, sweet khan—my home.*

The sky in its distant endlessness appeared closer to her than any

55

person within this palatial abode. She fell on her knees and prayed loudly in Armenian so God would hear above the storm engulfing her from within. "Haji-doo, my Haji-doo! You said God listens to children. Tell Him … tell God … that I am praying to Him. He is on my mind. He is in my heart. And His name is between my lips. Dear God, release me from this job."

"*Y'abnayya? Y'abnayya?*" the maid called from the lower courtyard.

Work beckoned. She dawdled on the stairs to delay the loathsome chore. So what if her patron were deprived of her ritualistic nightly pleasure for a few more moments? *I don't care.* But what was the alternative?

When she opened the dividing curtains, the mistress, sprawled on her mattress, waited in her domain. Mannig crouched by her feet and proceeded with the "gentle but firm" scratching with "five fingers on each sole" routine. She performed her job dutifully, consistently, repeatedly, over and over again, and again, and again until lulled by her own ministrations.

She fell asleep.

Not for long.

Kick, kick, kick! Mannig was rudely awakened by the mistress's thrust of feet. Kick, kick, kick—blows on her head, nose, and temples—relentless. The insolence angered Mannig, who was disgusted by the woman's cruelty. The question, "What is wrong with this?" transformed into, "Nothing is right." *A strange household I am in*, she thought. *They call me Y'abnayya here and Hey Girl, there. They stripped me of the one and only heritage I claim—my Adapazar name—and they cast me at the bottoms of their feet.*

Her free spirit stirred. The need to be *someone* rather than to have *things* finally answered the question. Everything was wrong at the *Qasr*.

The mistress who had promised to take an orphan under her wing had instead thrust her under her feet.

Mannig hurled the quilt off.

Her feet took wings; she flew away.

8—Beyond Staying Alive

Mannig dashed from the malodorous, gawky feet of the rich toward the stale smells of the *khan*.

Soft breezes that sighed along the curved roads combined with the moldy scent of the grungy burlap dress rolled under her arm. The *khan* silhouetted against the early rays of dawn. Her heart stirred. My palace. The fantasy of a life she had abandoned two months earlier drew near.

She entered the dilapidated building with great expectations. Dank air chilled her, then motionlessness baffled her, but it was the silence that reawakened her sensibilities. Everyone is still sleeping. The sight of a curled-up body in her own prized niche disheartened her. How about Dikran's place? She moaned at the sight of the vacant mat until she spied his favorite blanket tucked under it. *He's already foraging for food.* Caressing his bedding, she sprawled on it. *He'll be so glad to see me.* Her inner peacefulness and the surrounding quiet lulled her into a deep sleep.

"What are you doing here?" Dikran awakened her a few hours later, his face and voice unsmiling. He questioned her sanity for giving up the security of the *qasr* for subsistence in a hovel. He stroked her shiny, clean hair then touched the hem of her floral dress. "You could own pretty clothes for the rest of your life and never worry about tomorrow. Instead you're gambling with staying alive."

Sweet voice! More so, she relished his arms, warming her all over. "I wanted to be here, like this, always. Nothing there seemed worth it."

"I missed you, too. But sentiments have displaced your good judgment."

"The mistress hurt me, inside and out," Mannig whimpered. "I wanted to be like you—to stand tall, proud, and unafraid. I would rather take my chances finding food in the alleys than stuff myself at her table. She stripped me of my name! I could not stay and still call myself an Armenian."

"Are you mocking me?"

"No. I am admiring you—but only for a moment," he said, pinching her arm. "The mistress put real flesh on your bones. It won't be long before hunger twists in your stomach, haggardness paints over your pink cheeks, and filth coats your skin. Let's see if you can garner wisdom then."

"I'll eat with the professional mourners again," Mannig protested. "Can even bring some for you."

"Not necessary," Dikran stood with a sudden air of confidence. "I eat with the men at the church."

"What men? Armenian church?"

"I stumbled upon them last week." He described approaching several men, speaking Armenian and clothed in western suits, huddled in the courtyard. "They hired me to locate Armenians hidden in Mosul's nicks and crannies. At the end of the day, I inform them of my discoveries and they invite me to eat with them. I go to church every day." He paused to make the sign of the cross. "Their mission is to save the orphans."

Orphans? "Did you tell them about me?"

"No, because you were lucky to live at that *qasr*," Dikran said. "I don't fully understand everything they talk about. I've heard them speak about arabization in deference to the Muslim families who harbor us. They say communities throughout the world have finally recognized the extent of the Armenian massacre. So they're showing concern for the great tragedy. Some say saving the orphans will save humanity at large; others hope to re-establish the monarchy on our ancestral territories. The intelligentsia wishes to repatriate us in a homeland, somewhere, sometime in this year of 1920."

Mannig only understood *home*. "Can I go to Adapazar?"

"Don't build up your hopes," Dikran's voice lost its sparkle.

"Where will I go? My Mama died ... they all died."

"These philanthropists have grandiose plans," Dikran said. "But, so far, all they've done is raise hope like a mountain above the haze."

"What will happen to me?"

"I don't know," Dikran continued, accentuating arched brows above wide-open jet black eyes. "Whatever these important people do, I hope it will improve our lives. I've heard them say they ought to register the orphans and enroll them into a *vorpanotz*."

Vorpanotz? A new word for Mannig. But *Vorp* meant orphan, so she surmised it meant a school for children.

From the time she was plucked from her normal life and deported across the Anatolian Plateau, she dreamed of returning to her kindergarten class in Adapazar. She visualized sitting at a desk, raising her index finger to answer questions her kindergarten teacher, Miss Romella, posed to the pupils.

Mannig couldn't wait for Dikran's gentlemen to start the school. *I will learn everything. Answer all questions. Even get a diploma like Miss Romella.* She remembered how her teacher, unable to carry her trousseau along the deportation route, discarded satin-embroidered linens in the desert, salvaging only a yellowing rolled parchment tied with a pink ribbon— her diploma. Mannig became obsessed with that scenario and the importance of education.

Her thoughts churned with a torrent of plans for entering the vorpanotz. I must get registered. Right away. While my hair is clean and shiny, and dress, pretty.

"Will you take me to the church?" she asked.

"I will also speak to them about you."

In her delight, she teased him, "You mean you want to get rid of me?"

With a sad look, he said, "Never. My dream is to own a *qasr* of my own one day and share it with you." He then finger-combed her chestnut hair, brushed it behind her ears, and, tracing her widow's peak, added, "Your mistress must have been really good to you. Your beauty, um, *spirit* has become visible. Even your lower lip is not split or festering." Pointing to the wooden *gabgobs* on her feet, he added, "You will not nick your bare toes on rocks anymore, either."

Touched by his knowledge of her ailments, a pang of guilt filled her heart. Should she forsake him for the sake of schooling?

During that restless night, his concerned voice echoed in her head—soon to be vanquished by visions of a classroom.

❧

When Dikran stopped by a mud-brick fence the next morning, Mannig remembered foraging the neighborhood not far from Adrine's place and reprimanded herself for failing to notice that it enclosed a church.

Seeing a mob of milling children in the courtyard, Dikran gave a surprised look and then stepped forward with Mannig in tow. He shoved to the left and scooted to the right, jostling his muscular and tall physique above the figures of the emaciated orphans. The sun grew high, and rancid moisture mingled with the fusty smells of poverty.

Two *effendis* sat at a small table in front of the carved, tall mahogany entrance to the sanctuary, each jotting names in a ledger.

An orange-and-black-spotted butterfly fluttered and perched on the shoulder of the hatless one. He slanted a tender look at its quivering wings, stroking its tiny head. His honey-colored eyes below a wide forehead attracted Mannig. He looked like a favorite person in her life. But who?

"The butterfly is good luck," she heard him whisper, barely moving his lips, lest he startle it. Nevertheless, it spread its wings and flew out of sight into the sun. "She'll bring good luck to someone else," he said, his thoughts seemingly in flight, too. He dipped his pen into the ink well and narrowed his gaze at the ledger. "Who's next?"

"Good morning, Barone," Dikran said.

Surprised, he asked, "Shouldn't you be searching for lost orphans in Mosul?"

The second effendi scanned the horde of children and slanted his chin to the right. "You think we need more?"

"Every one of them, lest they perish."

"Here's an orphan from my khan," Dikran said, positioning Mannig in front of him.

The effendis scrutinized her from head to toe. Each puckered a curious lip. The man with the receding chin spoke first. "Your khan must be a palace and she the princess."

"Healthy, groomed, and well-fed!" asserted the Barone, in a voice matching the gentleness of his honey-colored eyes.

Dikran stuttered, "She has no family. Nobody. Nothing."

"Look at them flocked in the courtyard," chided the first *effendi*, and thumbing rapidly through the ledger, he slammed its black leather jacket closed. "Our mission is to save the abandoned, the strayed— before evil grips them. Can't you see how well off this girl is under your care? She is clothed, fed, and certainly safe from being converted to Islam. You make us Armenians very proud. We need more fellows like you." The *effendi* then motioned to Dikran to move aside and, shaking his head, added, "She does not qualify under our mission guidelines."

He then pointed to the next girl. "What's your name, child?" He prepared to enter it in the ledger.

They want her—not me!

Mannig's heart sank into a suffocating pit. She wanted to rebel, yell, and hit; to beg, tug, and plead her case, but she froze, except for glaring at the next girl's raggedy garb, tangled hair, and stink-veiled face.

Dikran pulled Mannig aside. "Things work out for the best," he said, shooing her off to the khan. "I will bring food for you when I finish my work."

Mannig wept all the way back to the khan. Her eyes still shone with tears when Dikran returned at dusk. "The Barone noticed your disappointment and gave these raisins to comfort your soul." He stuffed a handful into a pocket bread and broke it in half. Before he bit into his share, he said, "I am sad for you, just as much."

Barone! That meant *Mr.* in Armenian—easy to remember. Was he the one with honey-colored eyes? He looked the kinder of the two. She bit into her sandwich, but each swallow induced more tears. They rolled down her cheeks. *Will I ever go to school?*

"The *vorpanotz*," Dikran consoled her, "would resemble a khan anyway, and like this one, will be crowded." Glancing up at the ceiling patched with reeds and corrugated tin, he added, "Perhaps it will have a real roof."

"Where is it?"

"There isn't one yet. The Barone is searching for a building to house the homeless children," Dikran said, handing her a few more raisins he had found clinging in his pocket. "I was surprised at the masses of vagabond children who mushroomed at the church! You and I are fortunate in our *khan*."

He unrolled his mat for the night. "I feel secure working for these gentlemen," he said, and lit up a cigarette. "The Barone gave me a whole pack." He inhaled a few puffs and faced Mannig, who lay on her mat, knees to chest and whimpering. "Don't cry. Before long, a good Armenian man will come along and marry you. Unlike me, he will provide all the beautiful things you deserve."

You don't understand, she thought. All I care about is schooling. The children at the vorpanotz will learn to read and write while I'll be imprisoned at this khan. She pulled her quilt over her legs. The crescent moon peeked into her stall through a displaced plank on the

roof and shone in her teary eyes. The amber rays may be beaming on
the sky-piercing minarets, touching the neighboring flat roofs, but not
shining on anyone as unhappy as she. *No one suffers my pain.* Tears lolled
her to sleep.

She awakened to a bright day that buoyed her gloom-filled spirit
despite the familiar surroundings. Buzzing flies clouded piles of grime;
manure patties lined up to dry gave off a familiar reek. However, living
with Dikran ensured the end of loneliness. She preferred this to the
comforts of the *qasr.* Still, something troubled her soul.

They said I don't qualify.

"You're alive because you scrambled for your own air," her
mother's words fanned her thoughts like fresh breeze. At one point
during the deportation, the Armenians were crammed into a cattle
train. Mannig scooted, crawled, and slithered through legs, feet, and
squatters in the people-packed box-car to poke her nose into a hole on
the wall. Her own efforts secured the breath of life; otherwise, she too,
would have suffocated like Sirarpi, her younger sister.

Today must unwrap itself like a precious gift, she thought. If I am
to be happy, it is up to me. She raised her hand and firmly wiped off a
remnant of a tear. Her scheme emerged before the khan dwellers arose
to relieve themselves in the water can.

She was sure that being clean and wearing a new dress had barred
her from the *vorpanotz.* Dikran's protection further prevented her
enrollment.

Lest anyone sense her movements, she held her breath while she
slipped into her grubby old dress. Pounding in her temples flushed her
whole body, but the heat wasn't enough to blunt the coldness of the
burlap against her skin. More than anything, she wanted to pee and
tuck herself back under her quilt. Then what?

She hid her pretty dress under the mat and slid into the rising
summer haze. She ran so fast that not even the dogs had time to bark.

The smell of rotting vegetation signaled the nearness of the river.
She battled a cloud of mosquitoes fluttering over a stagnant puddle,
sloshing through the cool mud along the weedy shore and displacing
the brown frogs that puffed their bellies like bellows.

She clutched a chunk of mud and squashed it all over herself,
clotting her hair with muck and tangling it in strings across her face. *I
wish my lower lip were still split and bleeding.* She tore her dress seams knee-
high, unraveled the hem until it hung in shreds, and dangled one sleeve
off the shoulder down to her elbow.

Soon women trickled toward the river. Robed in black *abayas* and balancing water ewers on their shoulders, they gazed at Mannig's antics—caking her legs with sludge. She persisted until she stunk of filth before leaving the privacy of the riverside to the *Moslawis* attending to their daily routine.

I am ready. She ran up the alley, past the two-way donkey trail, and onto the dirt path toward the Armenian Church.

Bees buzzed their thin shimmering wings around her, and a company of butterflies flickered in a riot of colors ahead. She concentrated on finding a way to nick her toe without too much pain. Each time she tried to kick a rock, her instincts prevented her from exerting the necessary force. *A bad idea, anyway.*

A few steps ahead, unknowingly, she stepped on a spiny hedgehog curled up in a ball. The painful sting immobilized her. *Zakhnaboot!* With contorted face, she flaked off the caked mud and pulled out the needle. The oozing blood elated her. She bent in half, squeezed the puncture hard, and dripped red over her finger. She smeared droplets on her lower lip, then her thighs, knees and legs. *I hope the stain stands out over the grime.*

The sight of the church slowed her to a shaky pace. The noonday yellow warmed the reddish hues of its brick walls. A low tone of babbling children in the courtyard induced a big calming breath and the necessary courage.

She entered the courtyard, limping on one foot.

The two effendis were writing names again. *Will either recognize me?*

The one with the receding chin removed his red felt fez, exposing a sweaty bald head shining like a mirror. She feared a bad omen, should it reflect her image. *His brain may tell him my identity.* She stepped backward and snuck a glance at the other. The *Barone. He won't tell me apart from the others.* After all, sticky hair covered her face, and the pretty dress lay in the *khan.*

Clothed in a European-cut suit, he reminded her of her father. *Might this man be as kind?* Unlike Baba, he wore a healthy mustache, trimmed and uncurled.

Exaggerating a phlegm-choked cough, she hobbled toward him, and barely a step away, stopped to pant. She lowered her eyes to just below his heart and, deliberately enunciating the word *chojoukh*—Turkish for *child*—and *mahhal*—the Arabic for *place*—she stuttered, "Why so many *chojoukhs* here? Is this *mahhal* for orphans?"

"Well ... yes," the Barone answered, as if pleased to be talking with someone instead of just registering names.

His deep voice sounds like Baba's.

"*Anny joo'aaneh*," she expressed hunger in Arabic, and then continued dotting similar words into Armenian syntax. "I'm an orphan. Can I live here? I have no *mahhal* to go to."

"What do you mean no place to go? Where did you come from?" the Barone asked.

"*Fül shari'at*," she waved toward the street. "I saw the *chojoukhs* ... and I followed them."

"Are you Armenian?"

"Yes. I think so," Mannig hesitated. Her thoughts darted back and forth like a squirrel, but she focused her eyes on the ground before she spoke in perfect Armenian. "I've lived among the Arabs for so long I'm confused who I should be."

The *Barone* stood up, and his voice rising in suspicion, he asked, "Where's your own family?"

She stepped back, forced a tear. "The Turks massacred them." She sniffled for added antics and pretended painful cold standing barefoot on the courtyard stones.

"Who do you live with?" he asked, searching for truth in her eyes.

He suspects my lie. Compelled to continue with the act, she lowered her gaze to the tip of her nose. "An Arab family. They took me in, but they beat me now. See the blood? They say I must become a Muslim like them."

"Don't you want to?" he said, restraining a smile.

"Oh, no! Haji-doo, my grandmother in heaven, will cry if I become arabicized. Please, Barone. You must save me. I cannot fight for food in the streets safely, and the awful khatoon ... she beats me every day."

"Impossible!" he said. "I have not heard of any Arabs mistreating little Armenian girls. Who is this monster? You must show me her house."

She succumbed to a wave of terror. Was her lie discovered? *Vye! All my efforts in vain!* She cried—real tears. "No! I won't go near that house ever again. You can go if you want. It is over there. But I will stay away ... I am scared ... they will beat me."

"Where is the house?" the Barone insisted.

Mannig stared at him through the strings of her hair and noticed the tips of his mustache rising a bit. *Is he teasing me?* She refused to let the tide of her lies go out and reveal the rock. He must not get the best of her. "Barone," she said. "Are you sure you want to see the hovel?"

"Let's go."

"It is far from here. The cut on my foot hurts a lot. It will take a long time to reach it. What about all these children in the courtyard?"

"They can wait," he said. "They will be all right until I return. Are you going to show me the way?"

"Barone … I will try to walk. Oh! Ah! It is so painful … those stones are so rough. The house lies this way. You follow me." Seeing her entrapment, she led him toward the gate of the fence, hobbling, limping, coughing once, pulling her leg with both hands, stumbling once and moaning spasmodically. She wrinkled her face with pain. "Barone, the sun will disappear before we get there."

"That's quite all right. I can find my way back," he murmured.

Oh, heavens my God! What am I going to do? Take him to the khan? I'll be a dog for there are no Arabs there. I must take him to Adrine's—her khatoon hates me anyway. Oh, Haji-doo. Will God hear me? I need help, dear Jesus. I promise not to lie again.

"I guess we have gone far enough," she heard the Barone say.

When they approached the gate of the courtyard, he grabbed her ripped sleeve. "I admire your determination to enroll at the orphanage. I refuse to crush your enthusiasm. Let's go back and get you registered."

"Really, Barone?" Mannig squealed. "Thank you. Thank you. I will always remember your kindness. You will be in my prayers every day. My dreams will be of you for the rest of my life." As these last words tumbled out of her mouth, the courtyard seemed to transform into a happy place housing flocks of birds singing with one voice. The church walls shimmered in myriad colors, the reds blazed like flickering flames, the yellows pure like amber, and the blues, a thousand times clearer than the sky.

I must show him my gratitude beyond words.

She took the Barone's hand to kiss it first, then to raise it to her forehead.

He pulled it back before she placed her lips on it. "You should only kiss the hand of a priest. And I am not a priest."

"But you are more wonderful than a priest," she exclaimed.

"What is your name, you little *jinn*?" the Barone asked.

9—It Shall Be April 1, 1906

"Her name is Mannig." The Barone directed his partner to register her in his ledger. He watched him dip the pen in the inkwell, tap it, and with a flourish, spell M-a-n-n-i-g before he scooted into his chair to register the orphans lined at his side of the table.

Mannig leaned forward, wanting to see what her name looked like on paper, sandwiched between the other scribbles. *How beautiful!* The elaborate calligraphy attested to every advantage she assumed schooling promised. The hollow darkness in her heart vanished and a bliss-filled flavor swelled her imagination. *I, too, will learn to pen my name.* Her spirit soared like the vibrant butterfly in flight she had seen earlier.

"What is your surname?"

The man's voice grounded Mannig.

Surname? What does the word mean? Her head felt empty, her memory blank. She peered into space in as deep a silence as the quiet growth of a weed. What must I say? A wrong guess might deny entrance to the orphanage. Think. Remember. Invent. The bread baker had called her Maria.

"Maria?" Her raised voice betrayed self-questioning. Then quickly, she camouflaged a sigh of relief when the registrar dunked the pen in ink and scribbled in the next column.

"Mannig Maria," he said, without looking up at her. "Now tell me your surname."

"*Yab-nayeh*," she whispered, hoping the mistress's label sufficed.

"That's Arabic for girl," he said. "Family name ... family name." He studied her face. "I need your surname."

Mannig drowned in ignorance. Confusion suffocated her. *I've flunked the school's first exam.* The mistress had stripped her of the only name she owned, while these Armenians required more than one! Her eyes lost focus as she stared at him, her heart pounding tearfully.

67

"You do have a last name, of course," the registrar repeated, holding the pen in limbo. "Don't you know it? I must enter it in the next column."

Hoping to distract his attention, she squealed, "The pen. The pen," and pointed to the drop of ink about to drip on the ledger.

He swung the pen and shook a drip into the ground. "Have you forgotten your family name, child?"

"No one told me anything," she replied honestly. She remembered everything she'd seen or experienced but nothing beyond surviving the massacre. What she never heard of didn't exist. Wherever she went, they took her at face value and no one had inquired about her identity. Might Romella know? Adrine? Mentioning them or their relationship would surely jeopardize her orphan status. She kept mum.

"Do you know your parents' names?" he asked.

Of course! "My mother's name is Mama and my father's, Baba." She breathed confidently.

The *effendi* shook his head.

I failed again. How could her parents' names be wrong?

"*Kheghj aghcheeg!*" Resting his chin in his palm, he repeated, "Pitiful girl. I suppose you don't know your birth date, either. Do you know how old you are?"

"I don't," she mumbled, tears streaking her cheeks over her ignorance of anything the *effendi* asked. How was she going to succeed in school? *Obviously, I'm NOT worthy of the orphanage.* Without a surname, ignorant of her parents' identity and uninformed about her age, she lost heart over ever making anything worthy of her life.

Not entirely.

She cranked up her wits for another chance. "I remember going to kindergarten in Adapazar."

"Aha!" exclaimed, the *effendi* "That's good. We will call you Mannig of Adapazar …"

Thank the Lord for His goodness. Haji-doo's words echoed in her head.

"Unless we've already registered a Mannig from Adapazar," the *effendi* said, sliding his finger up and down across several pages of the registry.

Her breathing had stopped, hearing blocked, and sight veiled. What will happen to me if I am not Mannig from Adapazar? Fear of another rejection paralyzed her.

"Well, Mannig …" the *effendi's* voice eased her muscles' stiffness, "you are, from now on, formally registered as Mannig of Adapazar. Unless …"

Oh, no. Not another rejection.

"Unless, of course, you tell us your surname. Actually, you're the first survivor from that town. You are the one and only Mannig of Adapazar."

The one and only. Mannig squeezed her eyes shut in delight— almost glad not to have a family name. What responsibilities did owning a unique name entail? She'd do anything to live up to it.

"You don't know how old you are," the *effendi* resumed, "but you say you remember going to kindergarten. Right?"

Mannig nodded and then choked, dreading he'd find more faults in her.

"Well, you must have been four, five, or six years old," he continued, looking at his partner. "Barone Mardiros, do you know the date when the Adapazarians were deported?"

"In the spring of 1915, I believe," the Barone answered. "Its citizens were the first to be purged by the Turks." He then glanced at Mannig. "Adapazar—so that's where you're from—nice affluent community across the Bosphorus from Boleess (Constantinople)."

"We rode the train to Boleess!" Mannig squealed, excited at how the conversation between the effendis triggered the memory of her past. She relished this moment that had revived a bit of her history. She saw herself in the train with Mama, Baba, and her four siblings, all dressed in new clothes traveling to visit her uncle.

"I know her town," the Barone said, facing the *effendi* but casting a calm and reflective glance at Mannig.

Mannig honed in on his face and finally knew who he resembled. *Baba!* Her father too, had had honey-colored eyes and wore a similar expression when he handed out sweet-and-sour candy in the train to pacify the children in their seats.

"When I was a student at Robert's College," the Barone continued, "my friends planned an excursion to Adapazar, but I thought I ought not to interrupt my training for the Olympics. But when my coach insisted I take a break, I enjoyed the town immensely and its beaches at Izmit."

"What shall I write down for age?" the *effendi* asked. "How old do you think she is?"

The two men eyed Mannig—up and down. They asked her to spin and checked her from front to back, all around—from mucky hair to bleeding toe.

Their scrutiny disconcerted Mannig. She fidgeted and heard her heart pound but did not hear their comments about her shape and height. She remembered tearing her armholes before coming to the church and instinctively pressed her arms against her bodice to hide her nipples. She decided to tolerate anything as long as they admitted her.

"Let me figure it out." The Barone rubbed his forehead. "This is 1920. If, five or six years ago, she was six or seven, I guess she must be eleven or twelve now." He looked at her again and instructed, "Write down 'thirteen.' "

The calligraphy of being thirteen in the ledger fascinated Mannig.

"Would 1906 be the year of her birth?" the effendi asked. But, seeing the Barone engrossed with another orphan, he wrote "1906" and mumbled, "As we have done with others like you, today will be your birth date. This is the month of April, and today is the first day of the month. So Mannig of Adapazar, if anyone asks you about your birth date, tell them you were born in Adapazar on April 1, 1906. Will you remember?"

"Yes, *effendi*," Mannig said, wanting to thank him, but he waved her aside and indicated that she should move on toward the sanctuary where the registered orphans waited in twos and threes, squatting down on their heels.

In the quiet courtyard, under the setting sun, they looked thinner than she. Hunger dulled their eyes, and ragged clothes revealed skin and bones. Despite suspecting how much better off she was—setting her apart from their condition—she crouched like them.

It had been declared aloud as well as in writing that she owned two names—Mannig and Maria—an official age and a birth date. It didn't matter how they had concocted her identity. What mattered was that she belonged to the orphanage. She felt as beautiful inside as those names sounded, even without a surname.

Mannig's eyes veered from the sunlight across the courtyard fence toward the shadowy silhouette of the registrars. The Barone was immersed in his writing; his bronze complexion sparkled. *He is handsome*. His partner called him Barone Mardiros. The name sounded melodious and masculine. Even more, its uniqueness pleased her, for she knew no one else by that name. *I won't forget it.* She wondered if he had truly been convinced of her destitution or her overwhelming need of the orphanage. Either way, he must be a gentle man, one fitting Haji-doo's sayings: 'If it is written in the heart, it will be written by the hand.'

She gazed at the sky, scantily clad in clouds. The last rays of light formed a halo of silky yellow cords intertwined with satiny-crimson. She felt born today, created anew. Today was, after all, her birthday. Her heart stirred. Sitting upright, she welcomed this new beginning.

10—The Telegram

Mardiros returned to Sebouh Papazian's house in Mosul at midnight—exhausted but unaware of it, hungry without craving anything, disheveled but not grimy.

The day had fulfilled all his expectations. Grouping Armenian orphans in the northern region of the Tigris River in three days had indeed required his engineering skills. Collecting and resettling them into a building energized him. Coordinating means for their survival recharged his ego. *Is this really me?* The sweeping changes in his lifestyle invigorated him.

Working in Mosul put him smack where his volunteerism meant something. *The poor orphans.* He housed as many as 200 children in a nearby *khan*. He must send Dikran on a search-and-rescue mission again. There must still be a few astray. He scrutinized his image in the mirror of the garderobe. Rubbing his three-day whiskers, he noticed smile lines near his hazel eyes. Notwithstanding his age of 30, he exaggerated a few deeper grooves around his mouth. God's gift to me—for guaranteeing the children's future. He grabbed the joy of the moment. Being accountable refreshed a hidden need, unbeknown to him.

"Barone Mardiros?" Sebouh knocked on the door. "This telegram came for you after you left this morning. I carried it with me all day, but our paths didn't cross."

Mardiros read the enlarged black letters on the yellow paper. Without changing his demeanor, he stared at Sebouh, who obviously had read the same message himself. "We expected this, but it came sooner than I hoped."

"Come have tea with me," Sebouh said, and led him downstairs, holding the lantern in one hand and wiping his forehead with the other. "We both need a respite."

"Let me have cognac, instead," Mardiros said, grabbing the half empty bottle off the nightstand and following him to the parlor. He had brought the snifter from Baghdad for his host, but Sebouh preferred to abstain; Mardiros refrained from his nocturnal pleasure in deference to his friend. Tonight might be his last in Mosul.

He sat on a carpet-covered divan in the parlor and shifted a few satin covered cushions behind his back. He noticed Sebouh caressing a lacy pillow on his settee. *He misses his late wife. Anyone would, in surroundings replete with a woman's touch.* Sebouh's wife of barely two years had died while giving birth to their daughter, Stella, but her feminine imprint of comfort and cheer had graced the house soon after the Big War ended, even with the limited resources available in Mosul.

Mardiros filled a glass tea cup with cognac for himself and watched Sebouh swirl an extra fourth spoon of sugar in his tea. They both preferred their drinks strong. Neither said anything. The jingling spoon in the tea cup and the sniffing of brandy filled the silence for a few minutes. Their daily work for the past month had satisfied them both, especially since they had secured a *khan* to house the orphans, the primary function assigned to them by the Middle East Relief.

They were too exhausted to eat the *gatta* Sebouh's housekeeper had prepared before going home. As agreed, she had taken Sebouh's little girl with her for the night, not knowing when he might return from his field work. Occasionally, he walked home at noon to see Stella, eat lunch, and 'rest the legs of a forty-year-old man.' He wished younger fellows would appear on the horizon to carry on the dedication to ethnic survival, but he often complained to Mardiros about the coming generation being too engrossed in themselves to see the long term benefit of rescuing the Armenian orphans.

For Mardiros, the house was a place for the two adults to sleep. Since Mardiros often arrived late at night, he saw the little girl on rare occasions.

"I see they need you in Baghdad more than I do here," Sebouh said, breaking the silence soon after each sipped his beverage. "I wonder if they're aware of the magnitude of effort needed to do the best for the children in Mosul. I don't know how we'll manage."

"You will, I am sure," Mardiros said, offering Sebouh a rolled cigarette from his silver case. "You know this town inside and out. And there's no doubt in my mind they will send me back to complete our mission."

"I shall miss your company, and I shall miss the luxury of smoking your *Englaizees*." Sebouh used the Arabic endearment for English cigarettes. He leaned over the burning coal in the brazier to light it. "Rolling our local brands is becoming difficult. My arthritis gets worse every day."

"You can have all of mine," Mardiros said, emptying his silver case, engraved with his initials, M.H.K. He set the rolled cigarettes on the glass-top table and dropped the case back into his vest pocket. He watched his friend inhale, as if observing him for the first time. The man's brows closed on small beady eyes in a longish face; his bulbous nose nearly brushed the cigarette cuddled between thin lips. "Barone Simon Gharibian alerted me that I will be a roving emissary. I will be back, and I will bring as many packs of cigarettes for you as I can." They smoked in silence.

Mardiros liked Sebouh, not just as a colleague in the fields of orphandom, but as a friend. Staying under Sebouh's roof eliminated the solitude within the four walls of a hotel or the tenant-guest formalities of a pension. Being with a like-minded compatriot rejuvenated him. Silence about shared experiences and tired limbs filled the emotional void, and neither needed to expound on his day's work. Otherwise, there was not much in common between them—Mardiros came from an aristocratic family whose father was a Pasha, while Sebouh was a shrewd businessman trading carpets with the Kurds, the Turkomen, and the Persians—a self-made man.

With the ending of The Big War and the revelations of the Armenian massacre, social distinctions had faded, and the two gentlemen's philanthropic goals meshed into one. They plunged into the business of preserving their ethnic heritage. Mardiros sensed a rebirth of energy for a life of service by escaping the decadent, self-indulgent boring life of Baghdad. Sebouh needed an involvement beyond his own self-pity for the death of his wife. In helping the orphans, they saved themselves from becoming apathetic toward other people and cynical about life in general. Mardiros realized that in meeting the needs of the orphans, they had met their own needs as well.

Both Mardiros and Sebouh dedicated their lives to rescuing the children, and both received tacit acknowledgement for their deeds. Their friendship flourished in the absence of the affluent life in Baghdad. Mardiros knew Sebouh would do absolutely anything for him, and he would do the same for Sebouh.

Mardiros referred to the telegram again. "Aren't you surprised how orphanages are needed in locations besides Mosul?" He resumed reading it. "I'm unfamiliar with Ba'qubah or Nahr El-Omar."

"Ba'qubah is near Baghdad." Sebouh exhaled rings of smoke. "It prides itself on its citrus groves. But Nahr El-Omar—I don't know it, but I suspect it is somewhere close to Basra."

"Why? Why down that far south ..." Mardiros checked the telegram again. "Oh, I see. The British are donating their military tents in Nahr El-Omar. Their forces were centralized in Basra."

"It is a curious telegram. What do you think is the overall plan of the World Relief Organization?"

"I suspect funds are scarce, but I will learn more in Baghdad, of course," Mardiros said, flipping his shoes off and propping his legs up across the divan. "I'm sure we'll continue the search and rescue children and," he raised his brandy, "learn how to pitch tents! That is, after we get acclimatized to Iraq's southern region. Aren't you astonished at their claim that there are hundreds of orphans in that area?"

"I suspect the high numbers account for their urgency ... that's why they are summoning you."

Mardiros sat up, held the telegram to the lantern and read aloud:

COME TO BAGHDAD stop
SPECIAL MISSION FOR YOU stop
NEED FUNDS stop
HUNDREDS OF ORPHANS IN BA'QUBAH AND NAHR El-OMAR stop
TO BE HOUSED IN DONATED BRITISH TENTS stop.

Signed: Simon Gharibian

"We have almost 200 orphans here," Mardiros said. "There may be twice as many in the surrounding areas whom we haven't collected yet. Apparently, there are more in the south than in Mosul."

"The high number of children is both good and bad," Sebouh said. "The good is—the Ottoman butchers failed to annihilate our race, and the bad is that we are now compelled to rescue many more."

Mardiros stood and stretched his arms. "I must leave first thing in the morning. I hope there is a train to Baghdad." He killed his cigarette butt in the green ceramic ashtray. "If there's a train at all! Without established departure and arrival schedules, we are at the mercy of whim. Initially, I wanted to drive my automobile here, but I debated over the availability of petrol. When I return, I will drive up and see that we complete the Mosul project."

Sebouh nodded. "I'm relieved you recruited a few Arabs to supply basic foodstuffs to the *khan* on a daily basis. But we are short on older girls to cook for the children. Many of the grown-up survivors are working for Arab families, and it is impossible to entice them to give up on their employment for the sake of Armenianhood."

"That's just a temporary setback," Mardiros said. "I fear locating teachers a bigger problem."

"I've asked my merchant friends to inquire among their customers," Sebouh said.

"Good!" Mardiros stepped out of the parlor. He stopped by the door and looked at his friend. The flickering rays from the lantern accentuated the man's tired demeanor. "I am leaving you with awesome responsibilities. I'll see that the powers-behind-the-throne in Baghdad realize your perseverance."

11—Dunk the Chunk
and Sip the Soup

As soon as the children began the trek from the Armenian Church toward the orphanage, images of the kindergarten in Adapazar flooded Mannig's head. *Going to school! Going to school!* Visions of chanting the alphabet, playing arithmetic games, and skipping rope in a stone-tiled courtyard in the shadow of the Armenian Apostolic Church, twirled in her head and energized her lively gait. Above all, she saw herself happy, seated at her metal-framed desk, copying the teacher's marks off the blackboard hanging on the adobe wall. *I must recite all of Miss Romella's lessons for our vorpanotz teacher.* She wanted to be admired, affirmed, and validated once more.

She remembered being praised for reciting the alphabet. She mouthed *Ayp-Pen-Kim-Ta* ... the first three letters—but stopped short. What comes next? *Meg-Yergoo-Yerek ... No! Those are numbers! What about the rest?* Everything she learned in kindergarten, she had forgotten. She drifted with the flow of orphans like a grain of dust, oblivious to the wind and rough ground that made hiking the alleys of Mosul toward their new home such an arduous task. *Why did I forget?*

The caravan of children shuffled at lava's pace, neither its head nor tail visible in the debris-tossed footsteps. An hour into the trip, the Mosul *Mu'adthin's* noonday chant of "*Allah u-Akbar*" filtered through the air; the caravan listened to the chanting in respectful silence. Mannig skirted rocks and stones. With great deference, she swerved around patches of animal droppings—someone in Mosul needed the dung. *Not I.* Muck-grabbing scuffles belonged to the past; only brain-training days lay ahead. An orphanage would be a place for better things. Schooling.

"There's our *khan*." The guide pointed straight ahead.

The typical building with a flat roof and tawny bricks by the banks of the Tigris River stirred oohs and aahs and muffled the shuffling of the staggering children.

Mannig shoved and pushed past the others, flailing her arms with excitement, rushing to reach the orphanage first. Unable to handle the narrow uphill path, she stumbled and dropped her rolled-up bedding. She groped for it, panicked at the memory of losing the bundle with her yellow dress three years ago.

She remembered being perched atop the bags on the wagon with Mama and Baba and her family of eight, 'the day they deported us from Adapazar.' The wagon barely squeaked across the narrow bridge on the Sakarya River, agitating the load and riders. Frightened, she clung to her mother. In the shakeup, her bundle of clothing had rolled off and vanished into the gurgling water. The memory of that loss gripped her heart with pain. *I could have lost this, too.* She clutched her bedding and fell back in line.

The lofty oak gate of the *khan* squeaked open and scraped the gravel-strewn entrance; Mannig felt that it was welcoming them. The sprawling courtyard full of chattering youth fit her notion of what a school should be—a big tangle of joviality. She loved the sight of clusters of girls hugging their new friends and boys bonding. It did not matter that she was by herself and no one looked for her; she sought no one either. She did not feel left out or isolated. Nothing mattered more than the happy children congregated in one building, looking forward to schooling as much as she did. The air, the cheery voices ... just the idea of being within the boundaries of the *vorpanotz* ... everything seemed perfect. *My dream is becoming a reality.*

The smell of spices surprised her. She didn't remember eating in kindergarten. Food in the orphanage? The idea of sharing a meal with classmates delighted her like syrup on baklava. She scurried toward the aroma wafting from a steaming caldron only to be stopped by a firm grip on her left arm. The screeched "Watch out!" prevented her from tripping over the steaming stew.

The woman's sinewy hand tightened before she released Mannig. She scanned the orphans in the courtyard and smiled, revealing a toothless mouth. Her gaze lingered as if she were counting her blessings.

She wrapped the skirt of her tunic around her belt and picked up a wooden ladle.

She scooped broth, grease floating on top, into a tin cup and handed it to Mannig. "This container is yours; you will need it for all your meals. Don't lose it." Pointing to a heap of wedges of barley bread on a towel, she added, "Take one, child. Dunk the chunk and sip the soup. Move on, now."

Mannig's mouth watered at the warm cup in her palms. She squatted and relished the aroma, even though it was unfamiliar to her. The broth—hot, greasy, salty—was exactly what her stomach needed. After quenching her raw hunger, she bit into the barley bread. *Akh!* Her teeth wouldn't cut through the thick, rock-like crust. She set the tin cup by her leg and, while anchoring her teeth into the chunk, she pulled it with both hands. Still, she failed to break it down into morsel size. She licked the crust for flavor before giving up. She resumed slurping the soup when she noticed the orphan crouched next to her, sucking her bread after bringing it out of the cup.

Aha! So that's what 'Dunk the chunk,' means. She copied the technique and devoured the softened bread, chunk after chunk. The stew of alfalfa roots, apple cores, and herbs steeped in boiling water would have been enough to satisfy hunger. Dunking the barley bread transformed the meal into a feast.

After the last sip of soup and bite of bread, she sat in silence, gazing into space. Life was good, and its goodness made her drowsy. By and by, she climbed to the second floor balcony and unrolled her bedding. Contented, she fell asleep.

಄

She awoke to swooping and darting swallows. Birds. Singing non-stop. Happy sounds. She rolled over and watched a beetle scurrying on and off the edge of her quilt, groping for a path—the liquid luster of the violet and magenta of its shell surged beyond the crimson and auburn. Bewitched, she marveled at the joyful birds and brilliant creepers.

I'm in paradise.

Surprised to see a person next to her, she jumped up. Her bed-partner lay asleep, her long black hair covering her face. Her frail frame shifted. *In my space?* In the Mosul shelter, orphans selected a niche to settle in, free and separate, never sharing the same sleeping spot. She glanced at the rows of sleeping bodies sprawled along the balcony floor on either side of her. Two or three, all shapes and sizes, slumbered on a shared mattress. She peeked through the railing at the courtyard below. Dune-like forms lay asleep there, too, from one wall of the courtyard to the other—no one stirring. On this first morning at the orphanage, Mannig became aware of its confined environment. She was not alone anymore, but bound by its strictures. Only the fountain gurgled freely. Beyond the stone-lined pool, the bubbling water flowed across the courtyard and out the huge entry door. What happened to the sparkling water outside the walls of the *khan*? She dared not speculate. Residing in the orphanage mattered the most to her. Her heart fluttered like the erratic flight of the swallows in and out of the overhead awnings.

It must be time to prepare for school. What about a uniform? She stroked her chest in search of the satin stitches of M and B for *MangaBardez*—meaning kindergarten—embroidered in pink on her gray smock. Her fingers stopped tracing the coarse burlap hanging from shoulders to knees. Adapazar existed a long time ago—three years? Five years? *Did Mama pack my uniform? Even so, the gendarmes forced us to discard all bundles in Eski-sehir, except a jug of water per family.* Her mama had cried at leaving her Singer sewing machine behind, and now Mannig's tears threatened to gush for want of that dear outfit—but more for the distraught mother she vaguely remembered.

Surely, the Barone will hand out the required clothes soon. But where was he? Engrossed in the prospect of life at the orphanage, she had forgotten to look for him during the walk.

Seeing no one else awake and not knowing what to do, she slid back into her bedding and peered around the courtyard and at the several doors facing the fountain. *Which one opens to my classroom? Ayp-Pen, Kim-ta* ... She recited the beginning of the alphabet and as it had yesterday, the rest vanished from her memory. Remorse thumped in her chest. Disappointed at having neglected her studies during the deportation, she withdrew inside her quilt to hide her ignorance.

I'll remember everything when I enter my classroom.

When will the school bell ring?

෨෪෨

The giant door swung open for a new batch of orphans led by Dikran.

Mannig dashed to hug him. "I feared I might never see you again."

Dikran backed away, freeing himself from her embrace and confronting those who witnessed Mannig's demonstrative welcome with a shrug of his shoulders. Seeing the courtyard full of children, he spoke with confidence. "The batch I just brought is the last. The Moslawi poor will no longer have to compete with Armenians scavenging the alleys." He locked the gate behind him. "I've completed my mission. Finally, I can actually do the essential chores of the orphanage."

Mannig lifted the loose end of the bundle he dragged and stepped behind him. Using the term of endearment, she said, "Dikran Jahn. Please tell me, when will they ring the bell for classes? The sun is so high, and it must already be midday."

"What classes?"

"Classes for school, of course," Mannig raised her voice in disbelief. How can Dikran not know about the place and purpose of the orphanage? "When will the teachers call us to our classrooms?"

"What teachers?" Dikran asked, raising his thick eyebrows the way older men often did. "Mannig, Mannig! This place is not a school. It is a refuge for homeless children. This *khan* is only to shelter us, provide food, and protect us from getting lost."

Mannig swallowed a lump of disappointment. She had already lived in a shelter in Mosul; no harm had befallen her and she had never gone astray. She had counted on the orphanage to educate her. But now her friend had quashed her hopes.

Reality hurt.

Tears stung her eyes and her heart felt crushed. Disappointment made her short of breath. She fought against crying—she had shed enough tears when the gendarmes closed her school in Adapazar. She had resisted tears even after discovering her mother's dead body beside her at the deportee camp in Deir Zor. *I won't cry now, either.* She lowered her gaze, sighed, and dragged her feet behind Dikran.

"You are sad?" Dikran touched her arm. "Take my advice, Mannig Jahn. 'No expectations, no disappointments' is my philosophy. Be thankful for our lives."

"But ... but ..." Manning whimpered.

"Listen to me," Dikran stopped, facing her. "Be grateful—we escaped the massacre by the gendarmes—we survived. Be thankful—

we're not scattered among strangers—we're with Armenians. Be appreciative—people like the Barone have found a place for us to live together—we're ..."

"What about the Barone?" Mannig interrupted. "Can't he make this place a school?"

"I suppose he could do many things," Dikran said, putting his bundle on the ledge of the fountain. "Actually, he has returned to Baghdad for more assistance and supplies. There are hundreds of orphans across the lands between the two big rivers."

"What two big rivers?" Mannig's curiosity had been piqued. Might Dikran become a teacher?

"The Tigris and the Euphrates Rivers ... but that's not important. What's important is the size of the area. The Barone will be very busy collecting children and settling them in orphanages; I wonder if we will ever see him in Mosul again." Dikran splashed his hands in the gurgling cold water, cupped his palms, and slurped. He slouched, leaning against the gray granite wall of the fountain. "I must rest ... I know there are many chores to be done ... now go! Find out why all the girls below the balcony are squealing."

Craning her neck above the group, Mannig saw a shiny pair of scissors in the hand of the supervisor cutting a girl's hair short to the scalp. The spectators cringed and squirmed at each click. The victim was her bed partner, whose tears rolled down her pallid face more profusely than her black locks dropping onto the red bricks. "What's her name?" Mannig nudged her neighbor.

"Garina."

"What did she do to deserve such punishment?" someone whimpered.

"It's the law of the orphanage," another whispered.

The moaning and sighing rose higher when the supervisor applied the hair clippers to Garina's head, leaving little but fuzz. Mannig watched placidly, but noticing the girl to her right coiling her curls as if fearing a permanent loss, she nudged her. "It will grow again." She caressed her own long locks. "Once my mother hacked my hair ... with a butcher's knife ... in Deir Zor. See how it has grown?"

"Ooooh!" The girl squirmed and chewed on her hair. "Did your mother hate you?"

"Of course, not. There was a deadly sickness at the deportee camp and my mother said long tresses would promote it. She was right. She cut mine and I didn't get sick. I didn't die."

A tall girl behind Mannig leaned forward. "The supervisor suspects lice because the girls were scratching their heads." She straightened, continuing with authority. "We'll soon all look alike ... but eventually, it will grow long again. But no one knows what color it will be. It may even grow curly!"

Mannig swung her straight hair before her eyes. *Was my hair chestnut color in Adapazar? Curly?* Everything had changed in Deir Zor. A lump rose in her throat. *No one in the* vorpanotz *knows how I looked before the deportation—not even me.*

Mannig took her turn without apprehension. She relished the zippy fingers and scissors across her head, almost like Mama's pampering hands tying a ribbon. Had it been yellow? The memory of her yellow dress swelled her eyes with tears.

"Up!" the supervisor pulled Mannig by her sleeve. "Follow those girls and wash your head."

Reawakened, she stood up. Was it finished? Daydreaming had distracted her from the sensation of human hands on her scalp. Nevertheless, the clippers' touch must have stirred nostalgic memories, making the mundane magical. The fuzz tickled her palm. Wash? A bathhouse?

Mannig stepped into a roofless, brick-walled enclave in the courtyard. How unlike the steam-filled and jasmine-scented *hammam* in Adapazar! Instead of the prattle of playful children scampering in the nude, this cacophony of shrieking orphans, still clothed in their rags, stunned her.

The girl ahead of her rubbed a bar of soap onto her naked scalp, eyes shut to avoid stray suds; then she leaned forward, groping for the ladle in the bucket of water hauled from the courtyard spring. Any luxurious images of bathing Mannig had acquired prior to the deportation evaporated at the orphanage.

A tight pinch on her arm startled her.

"Scrub thy head with this." Garina handed her a brick-size-soap. "Scrape with its edge and lather every bit of thy scalp, like I have." She dropped to her knees and ladled water onto her head. "A-a-a-akh! Co-o-o-old." She screeched, shaking her head and spraying droplets every which way. "This is colder than the springs of Van."

The coarse edges of the soap bar grazed Mannig's scalp. She endured its abrasiveness but not the iciness of the water. She shrieked like Garina, and shook off the clinging water in the manner of a dog.

At the exit, the supervisor handed Mannig a *yazma* from a stack of multihued scarves. Mannig's eyes focused on the yellow one topping the pile.

"You can have that one instead, if you like," the supervisor said, smiling at Mannig's delight.

Across from the spring, the boys received a similar head-shaving from the Old *Effendi*. There were only twenty or thirty male orphans. Even so, Mannig gave up trying to recognize Dikran. She squatted against the wall next to Garina.

"They all look like turnip-heads." Garina snickered at the boys and faced the sun. "Only the girls get a *yazma*. On this occasion, we have an advantage. But what is the use?" She sighed as tears glistened down her broad cheeks.

Touched, Mannig reached out and grasped her hand.

Garina squeezed back, then holding one end of her scarf, she blew her bulbous nose. "I came to the orphanage for nothing, anyway. Without hair, my chances are zero anywhere in the world."

"I am sad, too," Mannig said, "but not for my hair. This place is not a school."

"School?" Garina probed. "Who cares about that?"

"Don't you want to learn anything?"

"What I want is to marry an Armenian man," Garina said, scanning the courtyard. "If I were in Van … if any Van men survived the massacre … if only …." She wiped her cheeks and gazed afar. "I came to the orphanage to find a man. The only one here is the *Effendi*, and he's married to the supervisor. I should have stayed in Mosul and married an Arab." She sighed, gesturing toward the bunch of boys huddled for warmth. "There's no hope among them … they are so immature … naive about Eros."

Mannig ignored the unfamiliar word "Eros," assuming it to be part of Garina's lazy dialect, common to Armenians of Van.

Haji-doo's image appeared, admonishing finger-wagging-sloppy enunciations with, "Put your tongue to work—you are not a *Vanetsi* peasant." After a moment, Mannig nudged Garina: "If they made this place a school, the boys could learn all about it."

"Schools don't teach such important things."

Mannig stared at Garina. Yes, this older girl, maybe fourteen or sixteen, claimed worldliness, but what would a *Vanetsi* know anyway? Peasants, Haji-doo called them. Mannig closed her eyes with sadness.

This building was neither a school nor a nurturing home. The courtyard walls curbed the freedom she enjoyed in the old khan; the regimented hair-cutting and bathing impinged upon her free spirit, and the dwelling was confining. *This place is worthless.* She agreed with her *Vanetsi* bed partner. Feeling a chill on her shoulders, she pulled at her neckline. "My dress got wet in the bathhouse."

"Let me take care of it for thee," Garina said, grabbing the ends of Mannig's *yazma* and retying them into a tight knot. She slid the fringy ends inside the neckline of Mannig's gunny sack. "This will separate thy skin from the wetness. Now turn thy back to the Mosul sun—it dries everything to the bone."

Mannig relished the silky patina of the *yazma* on her neck, but more Garina's attentiveness. Someone cared for her. She glanced at her, and the two exchanged smiles.

"Two hundred girls in one place," Garina said, shaking her head. "Thou wilt soon find out how the supervisor puts us to work. Remember my words. We'll cook and sweep and collect firewood … while twenty childish boys will get pampered … just because they're boys. They will sit and do nothing. They will be the princes of the orphanage, and we their slaves, and …" Garina abruptly stopped speaking and rose from her squatting position. She stretched her neck and squinted. She leaned forward, honing in on her find.

"What is it?" Mannig yanked at her sleeve.

Garina held still; her thick-lashed brown eyes sparkled with intensity.

"Tell me, please!" Mannig insisted.

Garina remained silent. Her nostrils flared with short breaths, enticing Mannig to rise and see what held her attention.

At the far end of the courtyard, the boys crouched. *They're orphans, too.* Next to them, smoke plumed from the smell of dry droppings. Nothing special. The supervisor stirred the smoldering soup cauldron. Hardly worthy of attention. The woman was talking to the tall, lanky fellow beside her while pointing at the gate with her free hand. He nodded his turnip-head in consent.

"You must be very hungry," Mannig said, looking at Garina again. "Soon she will call us to dunk the chunk and sip the soup."

"Soup?" Garina snickered. "Who cares about food? That boy next to the woman … he looks like a man. *Amahn, Amahn!* My luck …" She adjusted the *yazma* around her face and dashed toward the duo.

Mannig focused on the boy listening to the supervisor. His attentive silhouette reminded her of another tall and thin fellow. Finally she recognized him, despite his bald head. Dikran.

12—Do This ... Do That

For several weeks, Mannig performed chores she had never imagined doing in a school. The routine required a whirlwind of "doing this and doing that." She liked gaining new skills, not necessarily for the increased dexterity they gave her but for the novelty of the experience. Self-sufficient, the *vorpanotz* prized itself on how it used its work-stations to teach life skills. But these were not the skills she wanted. *I'll never learn to read or write.*

"Pull!" Garina ordered. Mannig was helping her operate the hand mill for grain. The two sat in the red-brick courtyard facing each other, alternately pulling and pushing the upright handle, rotating one circular upper sandstone slab sitting atop another. The supervisor had assigned the two girls the task of grinding barley for the daily bread flour—the grinding sound often being the first to greet the ear in the morning.

Mannig appreciated the novelty of the chore, but she knew Garina resented it because she did not respect the supervisor's authority. "Who does she think she is?" Garina grumbled in an undertone after each command. In retribution, she called her *peece gunnig* behind her back, meaning 'filthy woman.' When the two eyed each other, Mannig saw venom darting from Garina's gaze.

"This is nothing but a hissing task," Garina said. "That *peece gunnig* better assign others to this Whirr and Purr task."

"That's a perfect tag," Mannig said. This was yet another label Garina had given to the various work-stations in the courtyard. "I like the sounds of whirring and purring. The humming is murky—not musical—but it comforts me like Mama's lullabies."

"Go on, be the sentimental one, if thou must. In Van, it is the work of a servant. To me, this is hard work demanding a man's strength. The *peece Sup* (for supervisor) could have commanded the big boys to assist us."

With her free hand, Garina poured a palm full of barley into the funnel-shaped opening for the pivot. She gauged the flow of the golden-hued seeds from her hand while the upper slab rotated about the wooden hinge fixed in the center of the lower stone. "Thou, too, must pour in the grain," she said. "Thou ought to get used to the 'feel'—when to feed the hole and how much."

"I'd like to," Mannig said. "But we're out of barley."

"Aha!" Garina smirked. "I told the *peece Sup* we needed more grain, and that the sack is too heavy for you. This week, I can't carry weight. I have the curse."

Aha, Mannig thought. As usual, this *Vanetsi* had slurred her lazy tongue over another strange word.

"I hope she delegates the strongest and oldest boy to haul some."

Her words were barely spoken when Dikran approached with a gunny sack on his back.

Instantly, she re-framed the fringes of her *yazma* and finger-brushed her eyebrows. Her eyes shone brightly, and the corners of her lips turned slightly upward. She sprang to her feet just before he set the sack down and coyly touched his hand, supporting the bag. "You're so sweet to do this manly job for us frail girls." Touching his arm more than the sack, she assisted him with sliding the weighty bag beside her feet.

Dikran glanced at her, tilting his head to one side, grinning and cocking his left eyebrow.

What an unusual facial expression. Was he surprised or unaccustomed to assistance? Garina, too, slanted a look of delight at him. Shrugging his shoulder, he bent and pulled the sack closer to the mill before emptying it on the ground between the two girls. He swung the empty burlap sack onto his shoulder, floating dust every which way. Straightening up, he asked Mannig, "How do you like the *vorpanotz* now?"

"I'm always doing this or doing ... " Mannig began, but Garina's anxious gestures stopped her.

"We're very happy," she said confidently, her eyes warning Mannig not to declare otherwise.

Mannig couldn't help but drop her jaw in amazement at how deftly Garina lied.

"Because thou art with us," Garina sweetened her voice and stepped closer to him. She wrapped her palm around his biceps, inside the rolled-up sleeve of his khaki military shirt. "We're happy because thou art under our roof. We depend on thee. We need thee to protect us, always. Thou art so strong. So grown-up …"

"That's good to know." Dikran freed his arm. "I shall relay your comment to *Sebouh Effendi* in Mosul. Such news will be encouraging to Barone Mardiros, too." He turned his back to leave.

Garina pulled on his shirttail. "Wait. The Sup isn't anywhere nearby to see thee befriending me … us. Stay here and talk to me … us."

"I have many chores to do."

"Thou could do things for me … us," Garina smiled into his eyes. Then she pointed to the sheepskin around the mill stones and the heap of the issued flour. "I want to carry it with thee to the Fiery Front."

"Where?" Dikran asked open-mouthed, looking at Mannig.

"The *toneer* at the baking station."

Dikran smiled, shaking his head. "Not to worry." He kneeled and scooped the flour into the white muslin sack.

Garina knelt, too, her knees touching him and her hands brushing his. She whispered a word or two into his ear, but mostly they filled the bag in silence, until a fine layer of flour remained around the mill.

The supervisor's voice, chastising the workers in the Carding Cave, brought the two to their feet.

With no further ado, Dikran slung the bag on his back and departed.

Garina's gaze followed him, and gradually an invisible veil dulled her eyes. Her sad eyes lingered on his departing figure as he dropped the white bag at the bakery area. Her gaze chased his silhouette until the huge entry door of the orphanage closed behind him. She then plopped down to resume pushing the handle and pouring the grain with her free hand. "Do this," she said, louder than the hissing grain being pulverized into flour and faster than the white powder running from between the stones. She poured a second handful and regurgitated the phrase, "Do that."

More than the granular sensation in her palm, the golden kernels cascading through her fingers attracted Mannig's attention. "It's beautiful."

"Beautiful?" Garina grunted through tightened lips. "Boring!" She looked at the door again. "Where did he go?"

"Who? Dikran?" Mannig said, without taking her eyes from the speckling flour dust.

"Is he called Dikran?" Garina squealed. "What a sweet name. Is he from your town?"

"He never told me," Mannig said, still spellbound by the bewitching, fine particles.

"How old is he? Come, tell me."

"I don't know," Mannig said, puzzled at Garina's flashing eyes.

"What is his family name?"

"I have no idea," she said, giving her an incredulous look. *How would I know when I don't even know my own?*

Garina stopped pushing the handle. "I want to know everything about him, and thou must tell me," she insisted, looking at the entry door again. "I wish I knew where that *peece Sup* sent him."

"To Mosul," Mannig mumbled, pulling the handle and focusing on her task.

Flour for bread.

Being linked to the chain of food preparation exhilarated her. Baba. The memory of her father's flour mills in Adapazar vaguely surfaced in her consciousness, yet his complaints shortly before the deportation echoed clearly in her head. "The gendarmes confiscated my oxen," he seethed in their parlor in Adapazar. "We've had to resort to using donkey-power to turn the millstones." His image faded, and Mama's words clung in Mannig's memory: "At least you didn't have to hand-crank the mill."

Might Mama suffer if she knew my own fate?

The drone of the grinding stones and its hypnotic hum, like the smell of life, lulled her to relax. She closed her eyes.

"Wake up!" Garina yelled. "Idle hands are useless. Pull. This job requires cooperation. You ought to sweat, too. I refuse to do a man's work by myself."

Sometimes Garina yelled louder than the supervisor, echoing across the courtyard. Mannig promptly alternated pushing and pulling the handle.

A woman's work? *What about Mama?* She baked her specialty baklava for Easter; otherwise, Nazlu, the maid, prepared the meals, and Baba's handyman ran errands. Haji-doo resented even soiled hands. Mannig remembered her grandmother's scorn at seeing her pick green walnuts off the tree in their orchard. "Shame on you! Ladies never stain their hands."

She had depended on her childish wits to survive starvation and loneliness in Mosul; at the *vorpanotz*, not only was she told to 'do this or that,' but every effort required specific techniques. "What is a woman's work?" she asked, searching Garina's eyes for hidden clues.

"To stay in the courtyard! NOT to be entrusted with errands like Dikran is!" Garina fumed. "That *peece Sup* could have sent me along. No-o-o-o! She controls us females in this confined space, keeps us separated from the boys every chance she gets. Thou hast seen her gather the boys by her skirt when we eat our meals; she chastises stowaway girls in the boys' quarter and segregates us during rest time. What is a woman's work, you ask? Just look around ..."

She then listed the spots in the courtyards, beginning with the make-shift station of basket weavers. "Dikran's fingers are as nimble as the girls' in the cluster; but that *peece Sup* won't let Dikran lace the palm leaves. Instead, she sends him on errands. Men do exciting things; whatever it is, their work is never boring. I wish he sat in the Weaver's Web, next to us. I'd be having a tête-à-tête with him."

Garina's sweeping *odaar* vocabulary often tantalized Mannig. Before she could ask about one unfamiliar word, another one trickled from between Garina's lips. Often, their assigned chores separated them—not necessarily due to the supervisor's dictates; Mannig suspected Garina sent herself on contrived errands, even when claiming, "The *peece Sup* told me to "do this" and "do that.""

"Same thing at the Teaser Gazebo," Garina continued, pointing to another station she tagged. There, the girls separated grit from a lock of wool using an iron comb—a womanly chore according to Garina. Farther across the courtyard was the Carding Cave. Mannig had attempted to fluff the wool, but nicked her fingers on the spiky wire-toothed brush, bloodying the pale wool.

When Mannig had been assigned to the Spindle Dingle to twirl the small wooden instrument to make yarn, she had become exasperated. The craft demanded patience and quick fingers, neither of which Mannig possessed.

Managing the spindle proved a complete disaster, prompting suggestions from experts in the Dingle. "Dance your arms," one said, flailing skinny limbs. "Twirl the spindle up in the air and drag it down," added another. Mannig failed to simultaneously move her upper extremities and loop her fingers on the spindle. The thread broke, and the wool never transformed into lovely ivory-hued thread.

"Some spindle-dingle, thou art," Garina snickered. "I dislike it, too. I prefer the Sheep Flip."

Mannig knew why—flipping sheep and shearing the wool required manly strength. The supervisor assigned the task to the boys, designating a location just outside the orphanage door.

Once Garina sneaked past the courtyard door and slipped inside the station. Seeing Dikran flipping the sheep flat on its side, she grabbed the rusty shears and scurried to him, preparing to clip the wool.

"That's not a woman's work." The supervisor shooed her off. "Get out of here!"

To avoid confrontation, Garina retreated—but only after she rubbed shoulders with Dikran and flashed white teeth at him.

Startled, he lost his grip, and the sheep scampered away. Under the stern gaze of the supervisor, he started the process again from the beginning—grabbing a sheep, forcing it to the ground, tying its legs, then picking up the clippers to shear its wool.

"She hates me!" Garina seethed in the courtyard. "I am bigger than most of the boys. The woman is determined to keep me apart from Dikran. I'm sure about it ... she is saving him for herself. She is jealous. Just watch me show her—I am destined to be with Dikran." She retreated into the courtyard and plopped down by the Spindle Dingle. She spun the wool violently—grimacing, scowling and sulking.

Mannig picked up a spindle, too. Her elbows undulated like a swan's neck but, instead of in a smooth wave, the instrument swayed in and out in a jagged arc. The jerky swings broke the thread. The spindle dropped to the ground. Mannig halted the twirling momentarily and then resumed rippling her fingers on an imaginary tool, swaying her arms in a surf-like motion. Without the demands of string tension at the tip of a spindle, she moved about with greater ease—elevating arms, lowering them, her body flowing in synchronicity. The whirring of the other spindles sent a rhythm to her feet. Completely oblivious to her surroundings, she felt transported to a higher domain. Mannig twirled and whirled, her hips replicating the soothing motions of a spindle; her legs and feet, the stance for shearing wool. She added arm movements, imitating carding and fluffing wool, hands and fingers spinning yarn on a spindle, pantomiming the chores conducted in various stations within the confines of the Spindle Dingle.

A roaring applause awakened her to reality.

"Mannig is dancing. Look at her!" the girls cheered. "Again. Do it again! Yes, yes. You entertain us with your Spindle Dance, and we will do the spinning for you."

"That's a good solution for boredom," Garina said. "Dance for them." She used the distraction to sneak away.

Garina's erratic nocturnal habits piqued Mannig's curiosity most. Even though the two shared the same bedding, Mannig often fell asleep without her bed-partner, only to wake up in the morning just as Garina slipped under the quilt.

Several weeks later, Mannig caught Garina crawling into bed at sunrise. "My stomach hurts," she murmured. She wiggled her body under the quilt without apparent pain and, raising her eyebrows, added, "I'll stay in bed ... do not tell that *peece Sup*. You cover for me at the Teaser Gazebo or wherever the *Sup* commands."

What is really the matter with Garina?

13—Weeping Meeting

Unable to understand Garina's behavior, Mannig focused on improvising dance routines at the Spindle Dingle. She created wiggles and mastered footsteps to music in her head, twirling and spinning at the cost of improving her clumsy spinning skills. When the supervisor checked the progress of each orphan's handiwork, one of the spinners snuck a refined ball of yarn into Mannig's hand and whispered, "It'll prevent the anger of the supervisor. You keep on entertaining us, and we'll do the spinning for you."

Mannig felt flattered. *All this, and no one has ever shown me how to dance.*

As one week rolled into another without schooling, the onslaught of winter storms froze her shattered hopes for education. *Could I read and write without a teacher?* No one owned books at the orphanage. She neither saw a pencil nor heard the rustle of paper anywhere, even while blasts of air-borne debris from the earth-packed neighborhood roofs floated into the courtyard and the doors of the rooms flapped and squeaked with the racing winds.

The rain beat as assuredly as Mannig's heart had pounded when she first heard of the orphanage. Her head spun, and her mind replayed fantasies of a classroom. An occasional wish for the Barone*'s* appearance flickered in and out of her thoughts; his speech and stance hinted at mentoring, and his mere presence promised formal lessons. *Where is he?* No one spoke of him.

Visions of studying, which had once set her aflame, now filled her with apathy. Her enthusiasm had been dampened little by little, without her realizing it. Staying alive did not require tasting life, just swallowing it. Her current dwelling was not her choice. She no longer enjoyed the simplest things as if they were gold or treated gold as if it were a simple thing. Mere subsistence dulled her enthusiasm. The orphanage had become a purgatory, providing food, shelter, and security, but no excitement or inspiration. She was going through the motions of being alive, like a twig drifting down the Tigris.

A havoc-threatening sky of black and weighty clouds gathered over Mosul. Darkness fell, and a terrible clamor arose. Squalls screamed across the open sky. The girls rolled up their bedding and rushed off the veranda for safety, crowding as many as twenty to each room, upstairs or down.

Mannig peered through the wood-latticed window at the idle Spindle Dingle, the deserted Teaser Gazebo, and the dormant Mystic Bath used for dyeing yarn. Courtyard ramblings had ceased, but not Dikran's chores.

He herded the sheep from the Sheep Flip without much goading, sending them scampering into the courtyard. But he struggled with the lofty oak gate. The wind assailed him from every side. Garina dashed downstairs and pushed at the gate he was approaching, only to be suddenly shoved aside by the supervisor. After exchanging a few words, the two women rushed out and pushed the gate against the blustery weather. Dikran bolted the metal latch; one sheep "baa'd" nearby, and others echoed it, responding to the sounds of the storm. The supervisor hurried to her quarters, and Garina, back up to the veranda.

The branches of the myrtle tree by the fountain staged a dance of their own. They twisted in the erratic gusts of wind, relaxed, and then intertwined, competing for attention like clowns. Protected in her niche, Mannig enjoyed the entertainment provided by the natural phenomena.

"*Amahn! Amahn!*" Her roommates screeched and leaped with excitement when Garina brought in the brazier. *El-manqqala*, the portable metal pan with burning coal, traveled to a different room each night. "It is our turn. I can't wait to tell my story."

Mannig, unaffected, glanced at the girls dashing to surround the heater. They sat on their feet beside Garina and raised their arms like a steeple to catch the rising heat.

The steady glow in the *manqqala* stirred her emotions. *Why is my throat throbbing?*

She crouched with the smaller girls in the back, behind a tight circle of the bigger ones who blocked out the glow with their bodies and the rising warmth with their stretched hands.

Lala, a recent enrollee at the orphanage, sprinkled a few crystals of incense into the flames. A clean scent of pine cones dissolved the pungent odors of many bodies confined in a small room. This was part of the ritual in front of the brazier.

Wisps of smoke from the burning dung-ambers soared above their heads.

A girl stirred the coals with a twig.

"Stop poking up the fire!" Lala yelled, stunning everyone. Her voice crackled as her sunken jet-black eyes blazed with fury. "We must end our insane Armenian obsession with fire!"

Silence sank into darkness—the smoke-grimed walls, the glowing coals, the crackling flames, the blowing wind outside—every sound faded out of Mannig's surroundings. She scanned the faces of her companions—unbroken stillness, uninterrupted melancholy, lifeless expressions. She choked, tongue anchored to the roof of her mouth. *Why does no one speak?* Pressure in her temples signaled a command coming from within. She forced a tiny voice. "What 'insane obsession'?" she murmured with a camouflaged cough.

"You are scaring us," another gasped.

"Is not the thunder frightening enough?" a perturbed voice echoed within the flickering shadows of the damp room.

Lala inhaled deeply. "My father, my poor father, God bless his soul," she said, an unshed tear glinting in her eye. "He ... he ... he unwittingly betrayed his own Armenianness when he poked up the coals in the brazier. He died for it."

"Stirring the fire?"

"We must stop doing that," she shouted. "It's a clue to identify Armenians."

The circle of girls stared at her.

"Don't you know it is an Armenian trait that the Turks use against us?"

Turks? The mere utterance of the word stopped all breaths, transforming the room to a tomb. Deathly stillness veneered horrifying images. As intense as the thunder rolled outside, the silence inside sank deeper. Lightning cut through the shadow-dimmed courtyard, while Lala's voice patched bits of memories with pieces of pain.

"When the gendarmes *ChaBOOKed* us out of Erzerum," she said, "they goaded the doctors outside the town walls on the pretense of needing their services at the Russian front. They shot them all—except my father. His perfect Turkish accent hid his ethnicity. They held him in a cell to observe him for many days. Then one night a brazier was brought into his cell—very much like this one, only filled with burning coal. Real coal, not dung. My father found a stick and, being a good but naïve Armenian, could not keep his hands from poking up the ashes—just as you did, a moment ago. He stirred and swerved the ambers throughout the night. When morning came, they hung him … by his feet … from the arch of a bridge."

"But everyone pokes up cinders."

"Not according to the Turks," Lala whispered. "They know Armenians do because, once upon a time, we used to worship fire, like the Zoroastrians – stir the fire and say a prayer. That was before we became Christians. The Turks believe that sooner or later, the true nature of people surfaces under duress. They caught my father in the act."

"They took my brother, too," a lonely voice drifted from a girl, glaring pityingly into space. Dark circles under her eyes showed age beyond her years. "He was only fourteen," she lamented. "They separated him from us … tied his feet to his hands, then raced their horses over his body. They crushed his skull. My mother buried him. We wept. Everyone moaned to no end. So many bodies were crushed …"

Lamentations rose and tears flowed while the wind whined and the rain crashed against the door. The gushing water on the veranda plunged onto the bricks of the courtyard floor. The sky loosed a torrent outdoors, streams of tears indoors.

"The gendarmes made us walk to Diyarbekir," Garina's voice rang above rising sobs. She gathered the folds of her tunic between her legs preparing to squat for a long session. Unlike her hasty speech, her expression matched her grieving posture. "They shot the men in our group," her phrases chimed like a tolling bell. "They accused them of swallowing gold coins … forced my mother to cut open my father's stomach … I was petrified. She stabbed my father's chest. I screamed. She handed over the golden pieces. I howled. The gendarme forced me to hold a knife. 'Open him up!' He kicked me while pointing to my brother.

'Nooooooooo!' I yelled.

"My mother blocked my mouth. 'They'll kill thee, if you don't.' I got down on my knees; my brother was not dead yet! He murmured my name ... his voice tore at me. I threw away the knife. Before it hit the ground, a slash from a scimitar hit my chest."

Garina tore open her tunic to show the horrible scar.

"I was forced to open him; my own blood flowing from my breast." Garina's tears drenched her face. She covered her chest, eyes squeezed shut in shame.

Shivering seized Mannig's back; fear pierced her cold body. She trembled, held her breath in disbelief. The torture, death, and torment her family had suffered paled in comparison to the atrocities inflicted upon the families of her roommates. *Do they hurt more than I?* Mannig hid her pain in the recesses of her brain, a feat she assumed would make her capable of leading a normal life. These girls, too, endured their pain, conquered their suffering, and strove for regular lives, even though the deep furrows on their faces were revealed by the glow from the coals. *How could they speak of such tragedy?*

She pulled her knees to her chin, covered her ears with bent arms, and retreated into the fortress of her thoughts. *What makes me different from them?*

Garina fanned the blinking embers with a frond of palm leaves. Her swift movements revived inflamed passions and hidden pain. The girls prayed and wailed, groaned and retold the tales of their massacred families. "They drowned my brother ..." one girl wept. "They beat my uncle to death ..." another sniffled. Lament followed lament.

Time after time, when the brazier of coal found its way back into her area, Mannig tried to turn things over and over in her head, fixing her eyes on walls blackened with cobwebs. She resisted being swept down the slopes of her own tragedy.

What was the purpose of this orphanage? Why survive the massacre? Mannig curled up under her quilt, while the rest memorialized their loved ones. She wanted to hear their stories but resented the details. Even though she thought she'd heard everyone's accounts, she prayed they'd speak of them again.

It never occurred to her that the orphanage had evolved to gather survivors in one place to commemorate the massacred. It pained her to revive the memory of her family—it was enough that the others were consumed by their agony. She wanted to remember hers only wrapped in the splendor of Adapazar. Were the orphans really honoring the memory of their loved ones?

She sat apart but remained a part of the weeping meetings. The dreamless voices of crosses and losses poured into her ear, but refused to run out the other.

Mannig re-awakened to a blinding insight. Her sadness, too, deserved a place of recognition. She must honor her family's harrowing narrative. Inflamed with passion, she, too, immersed herself in all-encompassing agony. *Ah! The loss of beautiful Adapazar!* Did she really have a home? Where? As far away as the lives of seven precious members of her family. Mama and Baba, Setrak and Sirarpi, Aunt Anna and Agope-john, grandmother Haji-doo ...

The images of her massacred beloved—private, personal and hidden in her memory until now—poured into the orphanage. Her eyes beheld torture; her nose, the whiff of death. Her ears heeded agony and hands felt pain. The taste of being alive soured against their misshapen corpses. She shared their suffering but coped with their memory alone. Their legacy belonged to her now. Bearing the pain by herself overwhelmed her. Might talking about the tragedy lessen the burden? She felt compelled to preserve their identity. *What is my responsibility?*

A cold draft blew in. The flames leaped to the height of hands domed above the brazier, then flickered down. Ashes fell silently upon ashes while rain splashed in big rapid drops. Voices and eyes drowning in grief wrung Mannig's heart. Tears warmed her cheeks and wet her chest. Although her suffering emerged more awful than bearable, she felt a deep inner peace.

Mannig let herself become immersed in the weeping meeting.

"They deported us from Adapazar," she said. "My sister, Sirarpi, suffocated to death—too small to fight for air in the packed train. Haji-doo fell off the donkey on the deportee route—the gendarmes shot her for slowing the caravan. They whipped the soles of my father's feet until he bled to death because he traded his coat for bread to feed us. The guards called for "all boys twelve and older," which included Agope-jahn, and shoved them off the cliffs into a big river. My brother, Setrak, died of typhoid in the tent city of Deir Zor; Aunt Anna of influenza. Mama, too, died in Deir Zor—I'm sure more from sorrow than disease."

"Are you the only one still alive in your family?" a tearful voice rang in the back.

"Adrine ..." Mannig gasped at her own utterance and appeared dazed at the here and now—no longer trekking the deportation route, but in Mosul, where the orphanage provided refuge and tears, tender solace. How could she remember every dead member of her family yet forget the one and only surviving sister?

Adrine! Adrine! To be alive had a purpose, after all. She jumped to her feet, shouting, "I have a sister among the Arabs ... they call her Adi ... my own sister! She is my family. She should be in the orphanage. She is Armenian."

14—A Sister among the Arabs

The stormy sky cleared into a gentle, hazy pink—washed clean and blushing.

The sun lipped the horizon's rim, and a wisp of mist rose with soft, crackling noises from the courtyard. Mannig awakened filled with optimism—every bit of herself aroused and driven by purpose. Her eyes, ears, hair, and skin, even nails and nipples, as much as her pulse and consciousness—every cell in her body focused on reuniting with her sister.

I'll be with family again. How strange the word sounded.

The two siblings, four years apart, had never been close, even in Adapazar. Mannig had resented how Mama and Baba doted over their oldest child and bragged about her achievements in school. After the slaughter of seven members of their family, the sisters had escaped death independently of each other and subsisted without each other's support. Following the war, an Arab family hired Adrine as a live-in maid—a great fortune in famine-stricken Mosul. Mannig accepted that it was her fate to forage the alleys. *Nobody wants me. I'm not like her—tall and strong.* Mannig had fought starvation for nearly two years with her own wits and with Dikran's heartfelt attentiveness—he had cared for her more than any blood relative. She had even contrived her own entry into the orphanage. Why the sudden desire to reunite with Adrine now?

The intensely emotional weeping meetings at the orphanage had changed her outlook. The nightly gatherings of the children, mourning the mass murder of their loved ones, released Mannig from the sadness pent up inside her.

She awakened to the amazing fortune of having a family member.

My own sister is still alive. Sharing a future life linked her with her legacy.

Mannig leaned pensively against the balcony railing as the orphans' chattering signaled the start of the day. Babbling voices mingled with early morning smells. Dikran piled up twigs to start the fire for breakfast tea. The scent of flowers filled the air until fumes of burning dung filtered through the myrtle tree's pink and white blossoms.

The supervisor threw a handful of tea leaves into the boiling water and *voilà!* A simple, instant meal was ready. The spiraling blue wisp of the ginseng tea twirled above the deep amber beverage bubbling in the same black caldron she had used to simmer last night's soup.

Everyone craved extra sweet tea. Someone always diverted the supervisor's attention so Dikran could scoop his tin cup into the sugar sack and dump it into the steeping beverage. Then innocently, he would ask her, "Khatoon Supervisor, did you put in sugar?"

"Yes, yes, yes!" she replied, shaking her head, jingling the decorative coins sewn to her white head kerchief. "Taste it."

He scooped a ladle full into his cup and took a noisy sip, nodding approval.

The supervisor then created the opportunity for his subterfuge by turning her back to him, pretending to straighten something on the ground. Dikran quickly scooped his hand inside the sack and dumped a palm full of sugar into the caldron. She would continue to stir as though nothing had interfered with her recipe. The game was repeated every morning like a ritual, to the hidden delight of all.

While the orphans received their ration of tea and a chunk of bread for breakfast, Dikran squatted against the wall and lit his pipe. He dragged voraciously in a non-stop series of puffs.

The supervisor stirred extra sugar into Dikran's cup but not into her own. She sat beside him and rolled her own cigarette, confident that a serving of sweetened brewed tea with a chunk of yesterday's bread would fortify the orphans to improve their skills in various crafts.

"The priest is coming! The priest is coming!" Dikran chanted like a town crier, from one chore station to the next, making sure everyone would have time to groom themselves and tidy up their rooms. The priest visited the orphanage intermittently to give communion, bring supplies, and enroll a new batch of orphans rescued from Mosul.

Unlike on previous occasions, his visit excited Mannig. She combed her hair and belted her sack-dress with braided cord she had salvaged from discarded yarn at the Spindle Dingle. Her heart fluttered, and like many resident girls, she held her breath and observed the group who trailed in at the priest's wake, awaiting the arrival of her lost sibling.

The priest was hunched over as his horse passed through the creaky gates and click-clacked into the courtyard. The supervisor's *effendi* followed him, leading a donkey laden with one gunny sack.

No one else trailed in.

Mannig dashed outside, searching for stragglers in their dusty path. Disheartened at not seeing her sister emerge, she dawdled back into the orphanage, sulking.

Resigned, she watched Dikran pull on the rein to steady the horse while Garina placed a wooden crate beside it.

To dismount, the priest swung his right leg toward the horse's rump and cautiously set his foot on the crate, exposing a hairy leg. *Do priests wear undergarments?* He freed his other foot from the stirrup and stepped onto solid ground; quickly, he drew together his black priestly robe, gathering his dignity. He reached inside his vestment, pulled out a glittering cross that hung on a chain around his neck, and then brought out a plain black mitre for his semi-bald head. The tip of his head cover matched the end of his healthy black beard. *Does he tuck all that hair under or above his quilt at nights?*

The supervisor dashed over and, kneeling, clasped his hand to her lips.

"*Asdvadz orhnayl,*" he murmured.

Mannig knew *Asdvadz* meant God. How about the rest? Must be *Grapar*—the ancient Armenian of the Bible, seldom studied by non-clerics.

The children hovered around him like a swarm of crickets, touching his robe and kissing his hand. *He loves their adulation.* Mannig approached him, too, more swept up in the courtyard mood than prompted by her heart. Beside the gurgling spring, he swung the incense vessel, tinkling and spewing curls of gum fragrance. *Delicious.* His robust Gregorian chant vibrated off the veranda from the four sides of the open courtyard. Were these the sounds of the Adapazar church? She had seldom gone into the sanctuary with Mama and Haji-doo, but played in the church-courtyard with her school friends, not far from Baba and other men smoking and discussing big people's affairs. *I wish I knew what they talked about. Even more, I wish I had sat next to Mama.* Her mother had donned a wide-brimmed hat and heels and, corseted like Europeans, wore a fitted ankle-length ensemble. She had modestly sat next to Haji-doo, who in her brown tunic and headscarf, had proudly observed how everyone looked at her daughter-in-law with admiration.

Mannig guessed the orphans observed the priest with similar wonderment. Were they entranced by the liturgy? They watched his mouth opening and shutting beneath the straggly hairs of his moustache while he signaled for everyone to repeat after him. Stirred by his baritone, Mannig mouthed the refrain in the wake of his reverberating voice. *What do the words mean?* The children kept their eyes cast down, heads covered and reverently bent low like a band of early Christians gathered furtively in the hinterlands to renew their faith.

Mannig held her place beside the clump of myrtle, her eyes darting every which way, fidgeting nervously with the fringes of her head kerchief. Her thoughts about Adrine smoldered like the cloudy incense, rolling aloft, curling upward, its mysterious aroma escaping into the open air. Images of a real family replaced the incomprehensible incantations she mouthed with the orphans. Her thoughts wandered; then conscience pricked. *Am I wicked in ignoring Asdvadz? I'll be religious when I grow up.* She longed for her sister. Her thoughts dwelt on her. But now, how could she, among 200 others, get the priest's attention?

He, meanwhile, wet his hand in the stream, let a drop fall on one child, and crossed the forehead of another with his right thumb before sprinkling the final drops across several heads. He warbled sing-song phrases, pleasantly melismatic but unfamiliar to Mannig's ears. Signaling Dikran to approach, he said, "Hold two corners," and handed him a lustrous purple cloth while the supervisor held the other two edges. "It will catch the communion wafer should it fall."

The priest held an aged and stained chalice of olive wood in one hand, while with the other he dipped a white chip of *lavash* bread into the wine and put it into the mouths of the orphans, who kneeled before him one at a time.

Mannig salivated. Would there be enough for her? The pile of *lavash* beside his elbow would suffice, but not the wine. Unless he diluted it with water. More than his blessings, she needed his attention today to approach him about Adrine. She shouldered her way ahead of a few girls. As soon as she knelt by the edge of his black robe, fear sealed her throat. Her legs trembled, stomach churned.

The priest's hand reached her face. He put the mass in her mouth. She choked. Tears rolled down her cheeks.

Garina whacked her back.

The wafer flew out—landing on the purple cloth that Dikran and the supervisor held.

The supervisor patted her. "Are you all right?"

Mannig nodded, looking up at the priest. Heart, head, and throat together, she croaked, "Venerable f-a-t-h-e-r ..."

"*Asdvadz bahe kezi*, my child," he said with a smile and motioned her with a wave of his sleeve for the next orphan to kneel and receive communion.

She felt like a kindergartner on her first day of school, and her own boldness terrified her. Not knowing what she intended to say or do, she stepped aside, yielding to his hand gestures. The trace of wine soured in her throat. She put on a mask of indifference, swept past him with bowed head, and retreated to the scented myrtle. She tossed a pebble into the running water. Clouds of tiny insects rose to the sky, dove down, scattered over the courtyard, and hovered like meandering clouds along the shores. The coughing and choking left no more of an impression on the priest than a dunked fist would make in a bucket of water. He'd never notice her.

Gurgling water often filled time to think. What a wasted day! And all because a little puny fear had tied her tongue! What frightened her? Unable to pinpoint it, she recalled Haji-doo saying, "One who is afraid cannot be saved." *Is that my fate?*

Even after her death, Haji-doo's admonishment sparked fire in Mannig's belly.

She dashed ahead, preceding the priest to his next ritual—the blessing of the rooms. Like a sentry, she waited for him at the head of the stairs.

"Venerable-Father, your grace," she said, pulling on his flowing sleeve before he stepped onto the threshold of the veranda. She placed passionate kisses all over his hand. "Your grace, I have a sister among the Arabs."

"*Asdvadz bahe kezi*, my child," he said. Freeing the kissed hand and swinging it behind him, he sauntered into the first room, holding the cross off his necklace with the other.

He did not hear me.

While he blessed the air, waving his cross, Mannig shoved aside a few girls surrounding him. "Venerable-Father," she said, brushing a quick kiss on his sleeve. "I have a sister among the Arabs."

"*Asdvadz bahe kezi*, my child," he repeated—monotone.

He's either esh (donkey) *or doesn't understand my Armenian.* She eyed him, then the supervisor. Neither changed their expressions.

Mannig remained deaf and mute but engrossed in any movement the priest made. When he was midway across the balcony, she stepped in front of him. "Venerable-father, I have a sister among the Arabs."

"*Asdvadz bahe kezi*, my child," he responded—same voice, same pitch.

I wish I spoke his language.

She dashed downstairs and waited at the landing for his descent to bless the rooms at the courtyard level. She pressed on his hand while it was still on the banister. "Your grace," she raised her voice, and in one breath, assailed him with a string of declarations. "My sister is among the Arabs. Her name is Adrine. She is my blood family. Sisters ought to be together. You must bring her to the orphanage. You're the only one who can save her. Venerable-Father, you must save my sister. Venerable-Father? Please … She is Armenian."

"Restrain yourself, child," he said, catching Mannig by surprise, actually uttering words of her language.

"Forgive me, your grace," she said after a loud breath. "I do have a sister among the Arabs."

"Impossible, my child," he said. "We collected all the homeless orphans. Everyone is here now. My scouts scoured every alley and many abandoned *khans* in Mosul. All parentless Armenians are in the orphanage."

"But my sister is NOT here. I know where she lives. She is a maid for an Arab family."

"Well!" he pontificated. "She is lucky to have a job and a roof over her head."

Mannig remembered how at first the registrars at the church denied her admittance to the orphanage because she looked clean, bright, and self-sufficient.

Tears ran down her cheeks. "The Arab family treats her very badly. They beat her when she speaks with Armenians … they forbid her to share her daily piece of bread with Armenian orphans. You must bring her to the orphanage before she is lost. She is a pitiable Armenian orphan."

"She cannot be," he said, brushing his robe past her. He held Mannig at bay and then signaled to the supervisor to lead him to the next room.

Mannig waited in the courtyard for his exit. She darted to him, crying, "Believe me, your reverence. I do have a pitiable sister in Mosul, and she is an orphan. If you don't bring her here, she will become a-a-a-Arabicized. She will perish."

He ignored her again, and facing the horde of orphans, said, "God bless you all, my children. I am finished here ... until next time." He held his cross to be kissed by the supervisor. "My job of collecting orphans is finished. Now I can do the normal business of God's work." A few 'Amens' from here and there made him pause. "I have neglected my regular flock in Mosul too long—many funerals, much weeping." Groping inside his robe, he retrieved a frayed Bible. His lips touched its leather cover before he flipped a few pages, in preparation for his final blessing. The reading sounded more like incantations than reflections upon the passage.

Everyone's eyes became fixed on the movements of his lips again.

Mannig remembered how Adrine read from a book in Adapazar and how her parents praised and admired her fluency.

"Venerable-Father, I must tell you one more thing," Mannig's voice screeched in desperation. She quickly lowered her pitch with a cough. "My sister knows how to read. She can read the Bible to us in the orphanage while you are doing God's work in Mosul."

"My child, my child," he said, shaking his head at her persistence. "No one can read the Bible, except of course another priest, if any survived the massacre."

"Your grace. I have heard my sister read. She is very good in reading and in writing. She ..."

"My scouts have collected everybody we could find in Mosul. None encountered anyone who can read the Bible. So as of yesterday, we concluded our search. I disbanded my scouts and sent my report to Baghdad." The priest finished his speech while stroking his beard.

"Our gracious, reverend priest," the supervisor's rattling words rang above the low hum of orphans' voices. She cleared her throat and wiped her mouth with the edge of her head kerchief. "All my life, your graciousness, I have wanted to hear God's words—I have wanted to hear Him in the morning when I woke up and then again before I went to sleep. We owned a Bible in our home in Adana ... but no one knew how to read it. It remained wrapped in its velvet bag. Before my mother died in Deir-Zor, she made me promise to guard it with my life. I have. Now I lay my head on it every night and pray in the darkness in my own way. How I long to hear the Lord's words coming off those precious pages in the morning and then again in the evening!" She wiped her tears.

"My sister will read the Bible for you any time you want," Mannig said. Then added, looking at the priest. "She'll read for us, too. Everybody in this orphanage wants to hear the words of our *Asdvadz*."

"My prayers will be answered," the supervisor pleaded, choking over her words and glancing at the priest, "if only someone could read God's message to us every day."

"I don't have the time, assistants, or money to look for someone, somewhere, who is supposed to know how to read the Bible," the priest said. "I have more important issues at hand." Before he turned his back he added, "That's final." He slid his cross inside his vestment and tucked his mitre in his pocket. "Until next time. I shall return and we shall take communion together again."

Dikran untethered the horse, and Garina lugged the wooden crate.

The priest mounted up quickly and, clicking his tongue, kicked the horse's sides. He tilted his head and exited the orphanage without hearing the chorus of adieux he'd received from the children on previous visits.

Dikran put his hand on Mannig's shoulder. "Do you really know where your sister lives?"

Mannig nodded.

"Tomorrow you show me the way."

"After we have tea that's heavily sweetened," the supervisor added. "That donkey hauled a sack full of granulated white sugar."

15—Things that Matter

What mattered to Mannig emerged unexpectedly.

The way Dikran commanded the supervisor's compassion opened Mannig's eyes. For the sake of family ties, they dropped the requirement to "do this and don't do that." Mannig realized that depending on her wits alone, even with a strong will such as hers, could fall short. Despite the refusals and protests of the priest, Dikran's boldness and the supervisor's kindness had paved the path to reuniting her with her sister.

Finding Adrine's house proved to be complicated. Mannig had assumped that she knew the location of Adrine's abode. Haji-doo's warning, 'You can't cook pilaf with words,' hung over her. At first, trailing Dikran from the orphanage into the outskirts of town and then into Mosul seemed to lead them in the right direction. When they entered the noonday *sooq* following a mule laden with baskets of produce, she experienced self-doubt. The babbling of hagglers, the ripe odors of roasting lamb from vendors' braziers, and cardamom spices of bakeries disoriented her.

"Let's not go that way," Dikran said upon exiting the market. He pulled the waistline of his army pants above his belt and veered away from the alley of the Armenian Church. "Where is your sister's house from here?"

Donkeys carrying gurgling water in goat skins reminded Mannig of the jug Adrine carried on her back for her Arab family. "She lives near the River." They followed the animals into yet another strange neighborhood. The fetid sewage odors weighted her uncertainty to a level denser than a camel's hump. Am I lost? She glanced back to check Dikran's expression but saw only his back. His feet were anchored on the sides of the open drain while he urinated. She giggled, then continued to lead. They departed from one bazaar crowded with

113

quibblers, entered an alley void of pedestrians, and trudged another path amid children playing jacks. She wanted to hesitate by another cluster of young ones playing *marmar* with real marbles—a grand game compared to the game of pebbles she used to play with the Bedouin children. Knowing her priorities, she pushed on to find Adrine's abode. She'd assumed she knew her way around, but there were thousands and thousands of inhabitants in the mud-brick walled city.

Dikran's prolonged silence worried her. She had never witnessed his frustrations in the face of pursuits not of his own making. Might he get angry? Could she lose this chance to reunite with her sibling? Better to cut off the legs of pretense before they could lengthen further.

She grabbed his arm. "Could we go back to our old *khan*?" she pleaded. "I really know the way from there—I promise."

"We'll do it your way," Dikran said, changing directions.

They drifted into a district of large houses, with a palm tree or two topping the surrounding high protective walls. He hesitated—glanced ahead and beyond the bend. "This is not the short-cut I intended to take." He gauged the location of the brilliant sun in the faint blue sky. "I thought we'd be back home by the time of late afternoon sun."

"These houses look familiar," Mannig said, pulling his shirt-sleeve. "Adrine's place must be here."

"Your sister lives with the rich?" Dikran shook his head. "We're wasting our time. She'll not stay at the orphanage."

"She will and she must," Mannig insisted. "I'm depending on you to persuade her. You and the supervisor should do everything you can to keep her ..." she stopped, held her breath. After scanning the neighborhood, she said, "Wait! Adrine doesn't live with the rich. Her house is not one of those big ones. But it has to be nearby—I can smell it." She hurried ahead of him, hopping across the open sewer run. She peered left and right, dashed more often than halted to check the façade of several courtyard walls.

"There it is," she yelled, pointing to a building with a corrugated roof and recessed inside a stucco-walled courtyard. She pressed her nose and chin through the slit between two planks of the gate and called, using Adrine's adapted name, "Adi! Adi!" After a moment, she yelled in Arabic. "*Iftahi el-baab*, Adi! Open the door."

Hurried click-clacking of wooden-soled slippers across the stone courtyard shushed Mannig. If the khatoon opened the gate, she'd be a dead donkey. Two steps backward and Dikran's full-size man's physique became her shield.

The gate creaked open. A surge of breeze fluttered the edge of Adrine's floral smock, and crouching, she peered at her sister. "I told you not to come here," she chided in Armenian, cupping her mouth to mute her voice.

"We have good news," Mannig chirped, facing her. "They have opened an orphanage. Dikran and I are already in—with many orphans. We came for you. Let's go. It is getting late already. It took us so long to find your place. Hurry ..." she pulled on Adrine's sleeve. "Come."

"Leave me alone," Adrine panted, freeing her arm. "And shush! Orphanage, m-orphanage! Get out of here! You will get me in trouble again." She swung the gate, but Mannig squeezed one foot in, the other on the threshold.

"You'll never get in trouble at the orphanage," Mannig said. "Everyone there is Armenian. The supervisor is Armenian. The children are Armenian. The priest says the orphanage is our future and our fortune. Come, let us go ..."

"I will NOT leave my Arab family," Adrine said, fluttering her nostrils.

Mannig nudged Dikran. "Tell her about our place."

"We are lucky," he said, after clearing his throat. "There is food for everyone and a quilt for each. There's a roof over our heads and a supervisor who protects us."

"I have all of that right here," Adrine said, trying to shut the gate.

"It's our destiny," he said with a higher pitch than before. "Whatever work we do, it is for us and not for some landlord. We face problems together, and we share our joys with everyone. We are as one tribe under the same tent, so to speak. In the end, our efforts are for the sake of preserving Armenianness."

"And we talk in our own language all day long," Mannig added.

"I don't care," Adrine screeched with reddened face. "Leave me alone!" Startled, she jerked her neck and gazed toward the balcony.

She must still be fearful of being observed.

She shoved Mannig out, shouting in Arabic, "*Imshee*! Get out of here, you vermin!"

"Who are you speaking with?" The khatoon's voice preceded the shuffling of leather *babooj* slippers.

"No one," Adrine said. "She is gone." Facing the approaching khatoon, she stretched her hands to her rear, signaling the duo to scat.

The woman gasped at the mature young man towering by the gate. She swerved sideways and reached for the black chiffon veil that draped under her chin—she pulled it over her nose, up to the circles below her kohl-lined dark eyes. Her henna-polished fingernails secured the ends of the veil behind each ear. After turning around, Dikran discreetly retreated to the street.

Mannig craned her neck and in Bedouin Arabic—the assertive dialect she learned in the desert and later on used in famine-stricken Mosul—said, "We have an order to take her, your maid, to the orphanage. Our ... our ..." She intended to say *our priest* but did not know its synonym in Arabic. Our *mullah* hovered on her tongue, but that denoted a Muslim cleric. Even describing him in a black robe, beard and Bible, seemed too complicated for her vocabulary. She feigned a cough and continued, "Our *leader!* Yes—our leader insists we take your maid to him. We must obey the command of our worthy leader. He insists Adi obey him, too. We will take her to him. She must leave your house."

The khatoon's eyes narrowed as with a smile and she faced Adrine. Emphasizing some of Mannig's unusual vocabulary, she said, "If the leader insists, then you must obey."

Both sisters stood aghast.

"You'll let her go?" Mannig asked.

"But, Khatoon-Hannum," Adrine pleaded, shoving Mannig aside. "I am very happy here. This is my home. You are my family. I only want to obey you." Her voice wavered and tears glistened in her doe-shaped hazel eyes. She lifted the hem of her tunic and blew her nose. "Please, Khatoon-Hannum, don't send me away. Keep me here. I want to stay with you. I will work hard ... harder. I am so grateful to you, please. I am happy here. You can ask me to do anything, but please do not send me away."

"Your contentment is not my concern," the khatoon said, the veil fluttering with each syllable. "It's my *effendi*—he wants a Muslim girl in the house."

"Then I will become Muslim," Adrine said, confident in voice and glance, taking a step toward the woman.

"Many Armenian girls have done that," the khatoon said, shaking her head. "The *effendi* has already decided ... " she choked, and then sighed as if for the impending relief from divulging more information. "He's bringing in a second wife—to MY house!"

"I will do anything she wants to be done, too," Adrine rushed her words.

"You don't understand. All he thinks of these days is his *zub*," she pointed to her crotch. "He has the gall to fornicate with two wives in one house," she sputtered angrily inside her veil. "Allah should punish him for breaking the 'one woman, one tent,' tradition. He can't afford a separate house for his slut, so his foolish desire is to activate his *zub*—I plan to see that he fails—the *ser-seri*. As the first wife, I will make that new girl the maid of the house. He has no idea what's coming, believe me. I will put her to work like a slave, tire her so much that he won't get satisfaction in bed no matter how young her *kuss* is."

Silence cut through her pain like ice.

The lewd vernacular flabbergasted the sisters.

"I must let you go," she said. "Your *mattraan*" (Arabic for bishop) … she coughed, casting a mocking look at Mannig. "I mean, your Leader—if your Leader insists on your presence, who are you to disobey? I also say, you must GO. You may take those slippers with you. Now go bundle your other tunic. Go!"

Adrine's head dropped below her shoulders. Lowering her face, she shuffled her *gabgobs* across the courtyard.

In spite of Adrine's flowing tears, Mannig's heart swelled with gratitude. Her sister's ache aside, joy of success thrilled her inside and out. She wanted to kiss the khatoon's hand. "We will leave immediately," she addressed the khatoon while waiting for Adrine. "Our *mattraan* will be pleased. He will remain grateful to you and—"

"*Usskutee*! Shut-up. Enough jabbering, you imp!" the khatoon uttered, tearfully.

Upon Adrine's reappearance, holding a small bundle under her arm, she gestured toward the clothes Adrine had washed that morning and hung to flap dry in the sun. "Take a *kaffieh* to cover your braid. Modesty pays in Mosul; its streets crawl with *ser-seris* like my husband."

Adrine pointed to a mustard scarf with lavender paisley designs and asked the khatoon, "This one?"

"Any one," the khatoon yelled. "Take them all, if you want." She held the gate and shooed her out. "*Imshee*. Take care of your sister."

Mannig blushed. How did the woman know her identity? Adrine had always kept her outside the gate when she came scavenging for bread. One had never faced the other. Mannig had once spied a silhouette on the balcony—a female voice ordered the shooing away of that 'useless sister.'

117

The khatoon's lifestyle reminded Mannig of the Bedouin. Abu Jasim, the head of the family who rescued Mannig from perishing in the desert, had had three wives, each established in a separate tent with her children. The first wife's dominion extended to the activities of every one related in Abu Jasim's tribe. The other wives catered to her wishes and hovered around for her comfort.

Unlike the Bedou, Adrine's khatoon considered Mannig useless. *She should have seen me doing things for the first wife.*

Being recognized flattered Mannig. "How did the khatoon know me?" she asked Adrine as they departed the premises. "Did you tell her?"

"I said nothing about anything," Adrine sniffled while walking between Dikran and Mannig.

"That woman knows everything," Dikran said. "She looks worldly, grasps what goes on around her. She knew about Christian clerics. She acknowledged the fate of Armenian girls. Well, Mosul is like that. People know everything. Word of mouth repeats itself faster than an echo." He glanced at Adrine as she wiped tears from her long lashes. "She must have been a good khatoon for you."

Adrine gave him a fetching look. She bawled.

Dikran fidgeted with discomfort and quickly added, "You two sisters are very beautiful—even when one of you is crying, the other exultant. You don't look alike, but you are both pretty."

Mannig ignored the flattery; she wanted to prevent Adrine from lingering on her loss. She ranted about a perfect future at the orphanage—how it was not just a place, but had a mood of its own, making the orphans proud, confident, and passionate. Seeing her sister's passive demeanor, she entreated Dikran to confirm her words: "Tell her about the weaving, crocheting, and other crafts—the all-Armenian traditions."

Dikran waited for two mules pulling a cart loaded with large, oval watermelons to stop braying. The three stopped, honing in on a horde of black flies devouring a half-cut of a lusciously red melon on top of the heap.

He cast his gaze on Adrine, "And no longer do we sleep with one eye open."

Adrine swerved her long neck toward him and snickered. "That will never be true," she choked. She rubbed her big hazel eyes—deep pools of liquid pain—and wiped her calloused fingers on the small bundle in her hand. She clenched her teeth.

Mannig rejoiced—not only at the family reunion, but at the sight of her sister no longer suppressing her emotions. Even though Adrine sauntered in sad silence, Mannig knew she had regained the sister of Adapazar who angered quickly and laughed easily.

Alive and together, they headed toward the orphanage—Adrine between Dikran, the tall one, and herself, still shorter than her sister who had towered over her in Adapazar. She had graduated from craning her neck to looking eye-to-eye—once a physiological impossibility. Mentally, they walked the path as far apart as the Tigris flowed from the Euphrates.

"Dikran? Is that you?" A voice from behind made Mannig and him turn around. Unaffected, Adrine stepped forward.

"*Sebouh Effendi!*" Dikran said, startled. Finger-brushing his thick brown hair, he walked back to the man standing on the front porch of the apartment building of his house. They shook hands. "I know, I'm supposed to be at the orphanage."

Mannig grabbed Adrine's arm. "Wait. We must wait for Dikran."

"Is that his name?" Adrine said, glancing at the two men engaged in animated conversation, then focusing on *Sebouh Effendi*.

"I think I've seen that man at the church," Mannig said. "He was registering the children with the Barone." She didn't urge her sister to get closer to the duo for fear of being recognized as the girl who had tried and failed to enroll at the orphanage. She held her stance beside her sister who gazed at him unblinkingly. Seeing that something about the man attracted her sister, she asked, "Do you know him?"

Her query hung in the air unanswered.

Should she obey her curiosity and ask again? *I won't risk any more prodding, lest it revive my sister's memories.* Adrine's gaze turned glassy, and Mannig feared the return of her sister's bad memories. She had just gained a sister; she refused to let her be replaced by a zombie. "Let's go."

"Wait for me!" Dikran called out as he ran after them, dodging late afternoon striders. "What's the rush? *Sebouh Effendi* was really pleased at how we saved another orphan. He asked your name, and all I could say was, 'Adrine, sister of Mannig of Adapazar.' Do you know your family's name?"

"Dobajian."

"Really?" Mannig shouted in disbelief. "Dobajian? Oh, that is such a beautiful name! I love it."

❧❧

Owning a last name made Mannig even more ambitious—made her want more than just being with her sister. She saw herself as grown up. Hadn't Adrine's khatoon eyed her with deference? *I am not useless anymore.* She smiled inwardly and turned to Adrine. "The orphanage will be a school soon," she said, more a statement of hope than fact.

Dikran stopped her. "Who told you that?"

"Well, the Barone collected us all and put us together. He must be bringing teachers and everything."

"Sure," Dikran said, pointing back at *Sebouh Effendi,* who was still standing at his threshold. "He just told me Barone Mardiros was sent to Singapore to collect funds for the Armenian orphans all over the world. That man will not have time for us."

Dikran spoke the truth. The last time she had seen the Barone, he was supervising the registration of the children at the old Armenian Church in Mosul. Still hopeful, she asked, "He intends to come back, right? And ... and then, we'll start school."

"Stop driving nails into the sky," Dikran admonished her and stepped forward.

Dikran doesn't know. Mannig ignored his cynicism and focused on being in her sister's company. She replaced the desire of her heart with gaining a family. *Maybe Adrine will become the teacher.* She managed a smile until they entered the orphanage.

The supervisor's exuberant welcome failed to evoke a reaction in Adrine. She reached to hug her, but Adrine tightened her narrow lips, lowered her face, and leaned away. Quickly, she squatted beside the gathering of children for the evening meal. "You must be starving, my poor child," the supervisor said, handing her a large bowl and a big chunk of bread. "We prepared stew—especially for you."

The word stew in Armenian sounded foreign to Mannig. She gazed at her ration in her tin cup—squash, onions, and tomatoes surrounded a chunk of meat. Meat! She bit into it—as succulent as her meals at the matron's, whose soles she scratched. *Good riddance.* She sniffed the pungent garlic. "Is this called stew?" she said, slurping a mouthful of the thick gravy. "It tastes like the *murga* I ate with the Bedouin. Adrine, taste it. It is delicious."

Adrine's hazel-greenish eyes ignored her portion; she stared off in the distance.

"Here's more," the supervisor interfered, adding a ladleful to Adrine's already brimming bowl. "You can have more after you read from my Good Book." She looked up at the dimming sky as the last sun rays withdrew from the balcony awnings. "*Ahkh!*" she sighed. "It is too late today. It's already too dark to read anything. We lost another day without hearing the Scriptures. I shall ask the priest to bring a lantern on his next visit for bedtime devotionals. But now you must eat, my child. Tomorrow, I will make time for you to read from the Bible."

Adrine cocked her neck in surprise. "Read from the what?"

Her sister's astonishment troubled Mannig. The supervisor wanted someone to read, and Mannig had volunteered her sister. Why else had she given her blessings and sent Dikran to find her? If she could read in Adapazar, she could read here. Mannig closed her eyes. She felt compelled to divert attention. After forcing several phony coughs to override Adrine's question, she spoke: "My sister is very confused." She added other excuses. "Don't you see how tired she is? She cannot even eat this wonderful stew." Mannig paused. "Tomorrow Adrine will realize how lucky she is to be here, and we will learn how lucky we are to have her among us."

"You can sit on my rock," Garina said, relinquishing her prized location to Adrine. "You can also sleep in my slot." She scooted over next to Dikran, a sly smile on her lips. "I will find a new place."

Her words collided with Mannig's impressions of her bed-mate. The girl seldom slept the whole night through on their mattress, and Mannig never questioned the older girl's nightly shenanigans. While the other girls confided in their bed-mates, Garina hardly said anything. She often elbowed between the girls at meal time so as to sit next to Dikran, assumed work assignments near him, and otherwise followed his movements literally or with her eyes. Why Garina's sudden interest in accommodating Mannig?

A mischievous sparkle in Garina's eyes alerted Mannig to how speedily she bundled her belongings and darted downstairs. She seemed to be searching for a place for the night, yet she headed determinedly toward the boys bedtime enclave.

Near midnight the orphanage chattering faded to an occasional cough, a sporadic snore, and the shuffling of a sleepwalker. Mannig reached across her sister's resting body beside her, wanting to cuddle and whisper about her joy in their reunion. Receiving no reaction, she carefully rested her arm across Adrine's shoulders lest she disturb her sleep.

Poor Adrine! Being plucked out of an established home and cast with a bunch of needy children loomed as depressing a future as she had ever envisaged. The whole day must have jolted her. Why else snub the kindness of the orphanage people and ignore the joy of family togetherness?

Cautiously, she peered at her sister's face, still asleep peacefully but for a slit-opening in one eye. Was she feigning sleep? Guarding against rape? The violation had happened a long time ago, somewhere in the middle of the desert. The war had ended a while back. The Ottoman gendarmes had vanished since. The Armenians rejoiced at the end of physical harm. Why Adrine's continual fear? The ensuing years had failed to bring her sister back into normalcy.

I wish she felt as safe at the orphanage as I.

Why had Adrine been surprised to her talk of the Bible? Mannig felt assured that once she held the book and read from it, the qualities their parents had admired—her intelligence, knowledge, and helpfulness—would be restored.

What mattered was being together.

16—Ousted for Sex

Sun rays glistened off the balcony's tin awnings. The daily clatter was far from approaching when a big commotion disturbed the entire orphanage.

Mannig jumped up and rammed into Adrine, already out of bed and leaning over the balcony rails.

The supervisor yelled and screamed, "You, immoral fornicator! Woe to me." She snatched Dikran's quilt off his bedding, exposing two naked bodies. "Woe to all of us! You have ruined my sanctuary."

Dikran rose to a sitting position, while the supervisor kicked the curled-up nude girl next to him.

"Immoral fornicator! This place is NOT a brothel! You have defiled my orphanage!" she ranted, pulling on the arm of the balled-up exposed form.

"Gari ... Garina! I should have known you'd defile our reputation. You useless one. You filthy girl!" She shook her hand as if getting rid of germs. "As an older girl, you are supposed to set an example for my innocents. *Vye! Vye!* My poor children," she pounded her hands on her chest like a mourner. "Is this your style now—fornicating in front of my children? You defiler of my orphans—that's what you are." She held a moment's silence, looking skyward as though hoping for guidance from above. "Out with you and your lewd self! Get out of here! Fornicator! Fornicator! Out! Out! Out!"

"What is a fornicator?" Mannig asked, nudging Adrine.

"It is in the Bible," Adrine said, her gaze riveted on Garina.

"Garina is in the Bible?" Mannig asked.

"Don't you know anything?" Adrine grunted and pulled away. Like her old self of long-gone Adapazar, so familiar to Mannig—smart, knowledgeable, and intolerant of stupidity. The courtyard happenings had thrown Adrine into her know-it-all mode. What had caused this change? Mannig wondered how her sister's pre-deportation character had emerged recognizably normal.

Stumbling over a garment on the ground, the supervisor grabbed and cast it over Garina's naked form. "Scat! Out that gate before I slash your lecherous *vohr*. May the Lord not hold your sin against us. Out the gate, fornicator!"

Mannig raised herself on tiptoe and whispered in Adrine's ear, "Is Garina a bad girl?"

"Bad?" Adrine seethed through her teeth, blood rushing to her face. "That supervisor should scream at HIM! Gendarme or Armenian—men are the fornicators. He is the bad one."

"What is a fornicator?" Mannig asked again.

"He used his thing to hurt her," Adrine sputtered, getting redder with each word.

"What are you talking about?"

"He is the fornicator ... men have a tail between their legs and they make it like a stick and drive it into girls ... it is horrible." Adrine shifted her gaze from Garina to Dikran, to the supervisor and back again; she honed in on the threesome with the intensity of one utterly familiar with the experience.

"Are you banishing her from the orphanage?" Dikran talked back to the supervisor, pulling up his baggy *shalvar*. "If she goes, then I must go too."

"You stay," the supervisor ordered, wagging her finger at him. "We need you here, even if I must become your sentinel from now on. Go! Do your chores."

"I cannot let her leave without me," Dikran objected.

"Don't you see she's ruined our orphanage?" the supervisor screeched. "Only God can absolve us from her sin. She must depart immediately. SHE goes. YOU stay."

"I must go with her," Dikran said. He rolled up his quilt, and with lowered head, added, "She needs my protection. She is heavy with my seed."

"She is pregnant?" the supervisor said, slapping her own cheeks with her hands. "Such fornication has been going on under my nose and I only discover it today?" She dropped on her haunches, her black tunic billowing in her wake. "She cannot stay ... she cannot stay here ... I cannot allow debauchery amid my innocent children ..." She shook her head and grimaced in desperation. "Then, we must manage without you. Get your things and get out of my sight. Both of you ... get out!"

Dikran gathered his belongings into a gunny-sack. Eyeing Garina, he rolled his bedding speedily. Then he rushed to her side and helped her knot the corners of her *yazma*, now full of her clothes.

"Out! Out! Out!" the supervisor shooed them—pushed, shoved and kicked in their wake until they exited the orphanage. She latched the gate behind them and fell into a body-shaking, crying torrent.

"She is a good woman," Adrine said. "She ousted the man. It is his fault. He is the bad person. I will go to console her ... I can do the things he was supposed to do—all of his chores." Down the stairs she darted, tripping on a lose brick. She stood, rubbed her ankle, and hobbled down to touch the woman's shoulders. "I can do the things you need done."

The supervisor raised a wet face and, for a few seconds, held her breath. Pointing to the caldron, the firewood, and the gunnysack of bread, she burst into tears. "I had other plans for you ..." She wiped her nose with her sleeve.

Mannig relished her sister's enthusiasm.

Adrine charged from one chore to the next. She almost danced, proceeding from the task of piling chips and wood, then starting the fire. She favored one foot while carrying the caldron to the brook and hobbled back to the pit. In no time the tea water bubbled. Instead of hobbling, she shuffled her hurt foot to the bag and dumped a few palms full of tea leaves. She sniffed the aroma and asked the supervisor, "Do you have more of the thyme I tasted in the stew yesterday? It gives tea a unique flavor."

"We all need something special," the supervisor replied, pointing to the storage shed. Still sobbing and casting glances at the latched gate, she added, "You can also throw extra sugar into the tea."

Adrine dropped a few sprigs of thyme into the boiling tea, then the sugar. She squatted and broke off chunks of bread, piling it onto the burlap sack.

By the time the tea boiled to its rich, ruby hue, the orphans congregated around the fire pit. Adrine called on two of the tallest orphans, "One of you can ladle the tea; the other, hand out the bread." She then hobbled to the gurgling spring and dangled her legs into the stream.

Mannig took her ration of tea and bread and scooted beside her sister, near the myrtle tree. Handing over her breakfast, she said, "I will get mine later."

Despite their four-year age difference, Mannig appreciated how Adrine was living up to her Adapazar reputation—clever, expedient, and as thoughtful as an adult. Scooting next to her, she dangled her legs beside her sister's. Unlike Adrine, whose ankles were submerged in the water, Mannig could barely touch the surface with her toes. Even so, chilly gusts of air crept up her legs. She jerked them out, disturbing a swarm of thin-legged insects that rose up and settled a yard away. "Did you hurt your foot?" she asked.

"It is nothing," Adrine said. "Cold heals everything."

She truly knows a lot. Mannig took comfort in emulating her sister without dunking her feet in the icy water. She focused on an insect sitting on a blade of grass; a long, steel-green mosquito, gleaming alluringly.

"Tell me more about a fornicator," she whispered.

17—Another Language

L ife without Dikran shaped itself into a routine.

At midday, the smells of the orphanage lifted high. Summer scents mingled with the sharp odors of dung fires and wood-smoke. Adrine charged from one responsibility to the next, assisting the supervisor, often directing the older girls to carry wood, lug water, or help reorganize for the next day. Even her meager culinary experience contributed to the piquancy of the stews and soups—wild mint sprigs added to the rice and yogurt soup was greeted with oohs and aahs, but unfortunately didn't guarantee a second bowl. Her most remarkable efficiency was demonstrated by her housekeeping skills—never taught to the orphans before. Mastering them required extra time, testing Mannig's patience. Nevertheless, she tailed her sister everywhere.

The supervisor pulled Adrine's sleeve, stopping her from intervening in a quarrel between two girls. "Let them resolve it," she mouthed in a whisper—more audible than shouting above 200 voices prattling like geese. She waved a frayed leather-bound book at Adrine's face and added, "Let's sit and read."

Unlike other books, this one reminded Mannig of what Haji-doo had carried in Adapazar—and always clutched to her heart. Unlike her grandmother, the supervisor gave it to Adrine.

Mannig stopped sweeping the stairs and set the palm-frond broom against the wall properly, according to Adrine's instructions. She followed the two toward the brook.

Adrine thumbed through the frayed, yellowing pages. "I cannot read this," she said.

Why is Adrine lying? Mannig remembered her sister sitting at the edge of the divan in their parlor and reading without paying attention to the music, chatter, or the silliness occupying Mannig and her brother Setrak.

127

"You don't know how to read?" the supervisor's voice lifted an octave.

Will she reprimand me for assuring her that Adrine knew how to read?

"I know how to, but what language is it?"

"Armenian, of course. This is THE Bible," the supervisor said, retrieving it and placing her lips on it. "What other language could it be? I've heard it read to me all my life. I have memorized many verses. If you know how to read, then you can read this."

That's what I thought, too!

"The script is so elaborate, I can't decipher the alphabet," Adrine explained.

"If you've gone to school, then you can read." The supervisor told Adrine to squat beside her by the clump of myrtle and passed the Scriptures to her again.

Adrine turned to page one. "It may be in Armenian, but the characters are so ornate I can barely recognize the letters." She hesitated and flipped the pages past midway in the book. "M-a-t-t-e-o," she spelled aloud.

"Matteo!" the supervisor said jubilantly. "The book of Matthew— the first book in the New Testament. You DO know how to read!"

Phew! I am a truth-teller. Mannig relaxed about her own relationship with the supervisor. After all, the woman's allowing her to venture into Mosul in search of her sister depended upon Adrine's education.

Adrine read from the Bible—more or less. Never having examined it before, she stumbled over every word. She sounded each letter, often audibly, repeating each word then the whole line to adjust to the cadence of the sentence. At the end of each verse, she read from the beginning again—somewhat smoother. The verses memorized by the supervisor went fast, as the two assisted each other reading through chapter one of Matthew. Adrine questioned nothing, and no discussion followed. Afterwards she said, "Perhaps I ought to practice reading on my own, before we meet for these sessions."

The supervisor nodded.

The Biblical vernacular, indeed a language in itself, made no sense to Mannig even when she heard Adrine practicing a chapter several times in anticipation of the next meeting. Nevertheless, Mannig liked those sessions. She admired how Adrine put the individual letters together in her head and then sounded them out as a word. "Can you teach me how to read, too?" she asked.

"I am not a teacher," Adrine dismissed her sister, then concentrated on the next word.

Sitting by the myrtle doing nothing, just listening, was entertainment for Mannig. She often wondered if a cluster of orphans also liked hearing the text. Most just sat like her, focusing on Adrine's lips. But did they understand anything? They were lulled into doing nothing—except Lala, an older orphan. She brought her needlework. Day after day, her handiwork produced intricate doilies and collars for 'the future,' she asserted.

"Will you show us how to do what you do?" a few girls asked.

She instantly demonstrated the craft of crocheting and allowed each girl to replicate the finger maneuvers, inserting the hooked needle in and out of a complicated pattern of threads. "Very good," she commended one, and "You have perfect fingers," she said to another.

Why can't Adrine show me how to put letters together in the same way? Mannig dangled her legs above the gurgling brook. Her sister was smart, she thought, but not instructive.

A sudden pounding on the gate halted voices, chatter, and chores. The whole courtyard dropped into silence.

"Open the gate! It is me, Dikran. Open the gate!"

Dikran? Mannig's heart skipped a beat. How easily she forgot her hero of the rummaging days. They had become inseparable after he rescued her from the gang of scavengers fighting over dung. He had even collaborated with the supervisor to find Adrine and guide her to the orphanage. Yet Mannig, engrossed in her sister's presence, had stopped thinking about him. How unconscionable to completely forget him.

"Open the gate! I must speak with you!" Dikran's voice filled the courtyard.

Mannig leaped to her feet and darted to the gate, but the supervisor stood up, waving her arms to stop. "You are not welcome here, Dikran," she cupped her mouth, shouting. "Go back to wherever you came from."

"But I must speak with you," Dikran yelled.

"There is nothing you can say to me," the supervisor insisted.

"You don't understand. The priest sent me."

The supervisor held still, mouth open.

"I bear news from Baghdad," he continued. "I came to tell you about a new development. Please open the gate, so I can explain why I am here. It is getting late and I must return to Mosul before dark."

Mannig stood as motionless as the rest of the orphans, scrutinizing the supervisor's next move. Silence swallowed the courtyard babble.

"It is good news," Dikran implored. "Please open the gate."

His desperate voice triggered Mannig's resentment of the supervisor's ban. She remembered her love for Dikran and regretted having to put aside the shared memories of want and disappointment between them; ashamed how swiftly she had engrossed herself with Adrine, leaving scarcely a moment for thoughts of him. *I must help him.* Defiant, she sneaked around the supervisor's tunic to unlock the door.

"Tail your sister," she nudged Adrine. "Help her open the door."

Mannig barely restrained herself from hugging Dikran. Only his arched eyebrows remained familiar; otherwise, he appeared tall and muscular, hair swinging to his shoulders.

The supervisor studied him, head to khaki pants.

He darted toward her.

Mannig followed in the wake of his swooping steps. The sound of his clicking heels carried above the gurgling water and a sneeze from the back of the courtyard. His speedy and purposeful stride showed the urgency of his mission.

"Do not get near the children!" the supervisor commanded, acid tones edging her voice. "Stop where you are." She lifted the hem of her tunic and waddled toward him. "I don't want the children to hear anything you have to say. So what is your news? Speak to me."

"The news comes from Baghdad. It concerns everyone," he exclaimed. Pointing to the earthen jug, perched by the brook for cooling and filtering the drinking water, he asked, "May I have some?"

Mannig handed him her tin cup. "I am so glad you are here," she whispered, her words co-mingling with the water gurgling from the jug's spout.

He nodded and gulped the whole cupful. Wiping his chin with his sleeve, he faced the supervisor. "I have big news. Baghdad contacted the priest."

She sat down and gestured for him to do the same. Mannig, Adrine and others squatted nearby.

"We have received orders," Dikran began. "The priest is ... he has been told to assemble all the orphans to be moved to Ba'qubah."

"What is Ba'aaq...?" the supervisor stuttered.

"Ba'qubah is a town near Baghdad."

She glanced here and there, as though unashamed of her ignorance. She signaled for him to continue.

"We have been instructed to transport the orphans to Ba'qubah."

"And who is this we?" she sneered.

"The Armenians of Baghdad ... and Cairo and even Paris," Dikran explained, nodding respectfully as he related the details. "The world has finally heard of our plight. They know how the Turks killed us, massacred our families, stole our property. Boghos Nubar Pasha heard our cries and felt our pain. He spearheaded a movement to do something about our suffering ... and is doing everything possible."

The supervisor wiped her mouth and interrupted him. "And who may he be?"

"He is Armenian. He is known as the Patron of the Egyptian farmer. Apparently he came to prominence by improving the Egyptian peasants' lot. While the Ottomans still ruled, their Sultan bestowed upon him the title of 'Pasha' around 1900. They say the man's statue is located in the center of Alexandria with the inscription, 'Father of the Egyptian Farmers.' "

"After twenty years as a Pasha, he must be very rich," the supervisor said. "So, is he sending us money?"

"I don't know. But he collaborated with Armenian leaders of the world to collect the orphans from the desert, from the villages and from the city streets. And transport them to Ba'qubah."

"How far is Ba'qubah from here?" Lala asked, switching her focus from her crochet needle to Dikran.

"Long weeks of walking from here," he said. "We will either be going in a boat down the Tigris or taking the train. Either way, we will be transported in groups—maybe twenty or fifty at a time."

"Why to this Ba'aaq ...?" the supervisor stuttered again.

"There is a real orphanage in Ba'qubah."

A real orphanage? Mannig perked up. A real orphanage certainly meant schooling. No matter what language, finally she'd learn to read and write.

Ignoring Adrine's passive demeanor and the supervisor's colorless expression, she exclaimed, "When can we go?"

18—A Night at the Church

Images of a teacher, desks, and books in a real orphanage transported Mannig into ecstasy.

The joyful news overshadowed all her recent good fortune—reuniting with Adrine, enjoying the company of other orphans, developing pride in her heritage, finding shelter within the stone building, securing survival until adulthood. She looked forward to schooling, even at the expense of separation from what she had cherished up to now.

The supervisor assigned Adrine to lead the first group of a few boys and twenty girls to Mosul, each carrying a bundle and waiting in line. Mannig's heart beat quickly as the prospect of fulfilling her destiny. "Let us go! Let us go!" She stepped ahead of her sister.

The supervisor's tearful embrace of each orphan seemed never to end. Dikran said they'd meet again. Mannig pulled on Adrine's sleeve and sneaked a glance at the supervisor. "Why all this fuss? We'll see each other soon. Let's go."

The trek to Mosul along the scraggly palms and spotty streams seemed so much shorter than Mannig remembered. Once within the city, the complex intercrossing of one alley into the next seemed endless, especially when Adrine insisted on halting the foot-caravan to count every member of her *troupe*. Finally, the church appeared in the haze of dusk, veiled by smoke and bustling with hagglers.

"*Khoobooz!*" chanted one who held a large flat-bread. "*Mye-uh,*" enticed another, fanning the steaming, sweetened turnip.

Adrine hesitated by the wrought-iron gate and peaked. "Just as Dikran predicted," she said, raising her shoulders. "Indeed, the homeless Armenians have flocked here." She dropped her bundle by the brick-wall fence and stood on her toes, peering into the courtyard. "Does anyone see the priest? He's supposed to have instructions for us." She turned around and addressed the orphans, "I need to go in and find him. Wait for me here …"

"No, no," a few in the rear sighed, interrupting her.

"Don't leave us alone," echoed trembling voices.

"I'm not abandoning you," Adrine faced fretful eyes staring at her. "Listen to me. If we all go in now, we'll get lost amid the hordes of people, and we will lose sight of one another." She gazed above the heads of the pushers and shovers inside the courtyard and raised her voice above their cacophony. "If we ever become separated, God knows we will never find everyone. So do what I tell you. I promise I will come back. Stay here—in one cluster."

Masses and searching voices clashed in the courtyard.

Mannig heard nothing beyond the loudness of her heartbeat. Images of heaving crowds hurled her back into the deportation days. Similar commotion had preceded Sirarpi's suffocation in the boxcar … Haji-doo's fall off the donkey … the gendarme's barrage of bullets … "Don't leave me!" She tightened her grip on Adrine's wrist.

"Stop it. There are no gendarmes here," Adrine said, pulling her arm but unable to free it. "You are hurting me! I must find the priest …"

Mannig clung to her like a leach.

"The priest will tell us about the orphanage," Adrine yelled.

"The orphanage?" Mannig relaxed her grip.

"Of course," Adrine said, pulling herself free. "Now listen to me, all of you. Squat here, against the wall … don't wander … put down your bundles … don't get separated … I must find out what we must do next. I will return, I promise."

Mannig had barely scooted onto her knees when Adrine reappeared with a man. Might he be the teacher? She sprung up in due respect to authority. She dashed and grabbed her sister's hand while the others surrounded them.

He seemed rather thin and gaunt, with a long nose—more like a mini-eggplant than the typical Armenian dolma profile. He looked familiar. Where had she seen him before?

"You are fortunate, my children," he said, glancing at Adrine, "to be under the custody of this young maiden. She may be only slightly older than you, but she assumes responsibilities fit for an adult with remarkable dependability."

Adrine's fingers wiggled inside Mannig's grip; her limbs tensed on and off but her face remained placid, her gaze half-lowered. For the first time, Mannig thought her sister beautiful.

"I have good news," the man continued. "The Middle East Relief has established an orphanage. With God's power, you will be transported to Ba'qubah."

His velvety voice conveyed masculinity and his message authority.

He sounds like someone I've heard before. The Barone's friend? The one who had winked before registering her as a nameless and ageless starveling?

Mannig feared he might identify her as the one who had feigned destitution, who had failed to pass muster with the Barone. It behooved her to be prudent by keeping out of his way. She buried her chin in the fold of her arm and, falling behind Adrine, avoided eye contact.

"Many Armenians wish to protect the survivors of the Ottoman atrocities, especially the children," the gentleman continued, his words more like a speech than instructions about how to proceed. He scanned Adrine's group of twenty orphans, then addressed her, "Many great people from all over the world care about the welfare of the orphans. They assigned me to collect all of you in the Mosul area and plan your transport to Ba'qubah. I, too, will join you there, but not until I send the last orphan." Lowering his voice, he added, "I may even bring my little daughter with me."

How miraculous for a little girl to have a father.

Mannig peeked at him through a hole in the sleeve of her gingham tunic. She wanted to see what a father looked like. Clean shaven, he appeared gentle, as a father should. Unlike the refugees, this man wore a fitted suit and a tie with a silky sheen.

He wants to send his little girl to school with us …

"I am grateful to this young lady—your leader," the gentleman continued, putting his hand on Adrine's shoulder. "She protects you as she would her young siblings. What is your name, please?"

"Who, me?" Adrine seemed surprised. "I am Adi."

Her Arabic name? Mannig's jaw dropped. She must miss her life with the khatoon.

"Adi," he said. "Beautiful! Unusual Armenian name."

"I was christened Adrine," she said, "but *Moslawis* called me Adi."

"Adrine, *jahn*," the man said, adding the tag of endearment. "I need you to monitor these children from now on until Ba'qubah." He put his hand in his coat pocket and brought out a pencil and paper. "Now tell me," he hurried his speech as if to avoid Adrine's question or objection to such an awesome responsibility. "I need your family name, and the city of your deportation. Barone Mardiros needs this information to prepare for you and your children." He winked at her. "He has housed 600 orphans already. Where did you say your home was, Adrine-*jahn*?" he asked again.

Mannig guessed that the man talked a lot and quickly to prevent Adrine from interrupting. Why else would she open and shut her mouth, gaze at him, then at her feet? Mannig wanted to shout at him. Adrine said nothing, but noticing her sister's lips tightening and face turning pink, she exclaimed, "We are from Adapazar. We are sisters."

"God has blessed you greatly," he said, his eyes still focused on his paper. "The first miracle is your survival of the massacre; the second, that the two of you are together.

"A-d-a-p-a-z-a-r," he said aloud as he wrote the letters. "Good. Now, what did you say your family name is?"

Family name again!

"It's Dobajian," Adrine whispered.

"Adrine Dobajian of Adapazar," the man said, writing it down.

Dobajian. Dobajian. The name echoed in Mannig's head. If her sister is Adi, no, Adrine Dobajian, then, was she Mannig Dobajian? *Is Mannig my real name?* She was called many things: Maria by the baker trading the dung she collected for bread; *Y'abnayya* by the khatoon who had promised to take her under her wing, but who made her scratch the bottom of her feet; *Manyook* in lewd dialect. Hearing it from her sister's mouth relieved any anxiety about her identity. Adrine knows everything. Embarrassment wouldn't ever tie her tongue again as it had when the Barone registered her at the church.

"Well, Adrine Dobajian of Adapazar," the man said. "I am Sebouh Papazian of Baghdad. You may have heard of me—they call me, Sebouh *Effendi*."

Barone Mardiros and now Sebouh *Effendi*—more names to remember.

Haji-doo had instructed her grandchildren about the Armenian custom of calling men *Barone*, meaning mister. *Effendi*? When Baba dealt with Turkish businessmen, he addressed them, *Effendi*. Was Sebouh Effendi a Turk? *Nooooo! He speaks like us.* She relaxed, recalling how Armenians adapted by becoming bilingual—in their ethnic language and in the speech of their host country.

"I came to Mosul for the Armenian cause," Sebouh continued. "When we settle every displaced person, I shall return to my home in Baghdad." He explained that the train had departed with a full load of refugees already. "We can't wait for the train to transfer you; it won't get back for several weeks. So I made arrangements for your group to travel in boats down the Tigris River."

Sighs of anxiety rose sky-high.

"Not right now," he said hurriedly. "It's too late today. Everyone rests here until tomorrow." He gestured for them to follow him across the courtyard and then into the sanctuary. "Adrine, *Jahn*. See that you and your children sleep here tonight." He winked at her when stressing the word *children* and, before he departed, handed her a large sack filled with bread. "This is the only available food for tonight," he apologized. "When the other children arrive, they will also sleep here. Will you see that all get some to eat?"

Mannig waited for Adrine to find a spot on the stone floor of the church before she too dropped her bundle and leaned against it. The smell of emptiness surrounded the stark granite walls. Unlike the Adapazar church, the pulpit was glaringly drab—bare of icons, paintings, brocade-draped pedestals, or glowing candles. No aroma of burning incense, what Mannig loved best about church. A few haphazardly stacked benches barricaded the marble tub used for infant baptisms.

The narrow slits of windows in the dome of the cross-shaped structure allowed light to stream in from the fading sun's rays. The dank taste of shadows quenched the cool of the night while the novel tarragon leaves of the white bread channeled her thoughts to adventures-yet-to-come. She touched her sister's shoulder to ask a question or two—actually quite a few—but Adrine ignored her. She was waiting for the next batch of children.

When nearly 200 arrived, she handed them bread, returned and plopped by her bundle. Closed her eyes—without a word.

Mannig snuggled closer to her, scanning the innumerable orphans sprawled across the sanctuary. She ought to emulate her older sister and close her eyes …

What if Jesus came and there was no room in His house?

19—Down the Tigris

Sebouh *Effendi* led Adrine's group to the riverside early the next morning.

His leather shoes scraped against the pebbles of the sun-baked alley; he took fast steps, increasing Mannig's urgency need to board the boat. She hurried ahead of the orphans' strides but remained trailing Adrine, her flimsy sandals barely brushing the ground.

The ever-vigilant Adrine was swinging her head back and forth, checking on the children in her care, when Sebouh *Effendi* tapped her on the shoulder and insisted she relax. "Don't worry. The children will not wander." He waited for her to catch up and walk beside him.

Mannig grabbed her sister's hand, kept abreast with them, and relished this excellent opportunity to eavesdrop effortlessly on their conversation. Any impatience Mannig felt to sail down the river and promptly start school at the new orphanage evaporated. Adrine's responses to Sebouh *Effendi's* inquisitiveness about her life in Adapazar completely enthralled Mannig.

"What was your father's name?" he asked.

"Mama called Baba Bedros-*Jahn*," Adrine said with characteristic brevity.

"*Imshee!*" A vendor's warning came from behind; he carried herbs and seedlings on his back. He dashed by the caravan of children heading toward the entry of the *sooq*.

Adrine yielded to him, but her gaze focused on his load. "I remember," she said, looking at Sebouh, "my father's name was Bedros, and my mother designed a pansy flower bed in the shape of his name, in English."

"Where did she learn English?"

"She graduated from an American school ..." Adrine abruptly dropped her jaw, closed her eyes, and furrowed her eyebrows.

139

"Perhaps my questions upset you?" Sebouh apologized.

"No, no," Adrine shook her head, gaining composure. "I, I don't know why I forgot the name of her school ... I think it was a university."

"Aha! Was she a teacher then?"

"I don't think so. She devoted her life to raising us," Adrine whispered, tearfully.

Seeing Adrine's saddened expression, Mannig felt a lump in her throat.

Sebouh walked in silence, occasionally sped up and then slowed to allow the twenty orphans to catch up with them.

"My uncle's wife was a teacher," Mannig heard her sister say above the ruckus several boys were making, squabbling over a game of marbles. They held Mannig's attention momentarily—until she realized her sister had not finished answering. "Uncle Mihran's family lived in Boleess, and he managed the sale of flour that my father shipped to him from our Adapazar mills."

"*Vye!*" Sebouh Effendi sighed. "Your father ran a flour business? Such enterprises did very well before the Big War, and especially during the conflict."

"My father also was a partner in a pawn shop," a tinge of pride sounded in Adrine's voice, "but everything is gone now, I suppose."

"If only those butcher gendarmes had spared the Adapazaris," Sebouh moaned, shaking his head. "With your father's status and friends, he would surely have spearheaded the rescue of the orphans now, as we, the Baghdadi communities, are doing."

To Mannig's disappointment, silence ensued between the two. *Don't stop ... I want to hear more.* Family ties trumped any dreams she had of being educated. Moments earlier she couldn't wait to arrive at the real orphanage. Now, the two-hour walk to the dock seemed too short.

"My grandmother was a *Haji-doo*." Adrine's rhythmic phrases matched her steps.

"That's quite an honor," he said. "I don't know of anyone in Baghdad with a similar title."

"According to my father," Adrine continued, "she insisted on going to Jerusalem to fulfill her vow after surviving the Ottoman persecutions during the 1880s." Adrine's voice cracked, and the trapped tears glistened in her doe-like hazel eyes. "She carried the Bible all day long, and whenever she caught us being idle, she would make us go down on bended knee and pray to Jesus." Wiping her runny nose with her sleeve, she added, "She fell off the donkey during our deportation, and the gendarme shot her. What was the use of all that praying?"

"What makes you say such things?" His voice sounded disappointed but not chastising. "Look at you and your sister. You survived. Obviously, she prayed for your welfare. Did you know we did, too? We, the Baghdadis? We prayed for everyone during the persecution, ever since 1915, even though you were strangers to us."

Adrine cupped Mannig's hand, bringing both girls to tears.

"World relief organizations now estimate over two million Armenians perished in these lands," Sebouh said. "We prayed and entreated throughout the Big War persecutions. We prayed for all of you, for God to watch over you and deliver you to us. Praying was all we could do. The savage Turks, of course, intended to massacre us in Baghdad, too. Fortunately, the Allied forces advanced from Basra to Baghdad, defeating the Ottomans before they carried out their heinous plan to annihilate us. God protected us so that we could use our good fortune to relieve the misfortune of the orphans."

The trek across enclaves, bazaars, and residential quarters leading toward the river filled the gaps in Mannig's knowledge of her beloved family. So Baba called Mama *Heranoush-Jahn*, and she was the daughter of Reverend Baghdassarian, Protestant pastor in Izmid. "My mother wanted me to get an education similar to hers," Mannig heard her sister say. "So I was enrolled at the American Missionary School."

"What school did I go to?" Mannig asked, remembering that she and Setrak, her deceased brother, had gone to a different school just beyond their orchard.

"You went to the Apostolic Grammar School because ..." she hesitated.

Both Mannig and Sebouh *Effendi* looked puzzled by her pause, and together, they asked, "Because ...? Why ...?"

"It was a funny story," Adrine smiled, an expression Mannig had not seen in a long time. "To appease Haji-doo's devout apostolic roots, Baba enrolled you and Setrak at the Armenian school. To honor Mama's protestant ancestry, he consented to send me to an American school."

"We owe much to the Americans," Sebouh *Effendi* said. "Money from their people and Protestant Missionaries now enable us to rescue the orphans. Actually, the gendarmes spared the Protestants from deportation because of their missionary connections. Besides, I've heard that non-apostolic families have relocated in Europe now."

"Europe?" Adrine gazed at him. "Romania is in Europe, right? My mother's brother lives in Romania. She made me memorize his name and address just before she died in Deir Zor."

"Poor soul, your mother," Sebouh said, touching her shoulder. "Two hundred thousand refugees died in that town. Humanitarians these days call Deir Zor the world's largest Armenian cemetery." He looked back to check on the children. "Your mother must have been a very smart person. She trusted you and your memory to carry on your heritage."

In silence, he glanced at her, then back at the group trailing them.

"We probably can locate your uncle," he added, "with Barone Mardiros' help. When he returns from India, where he's raising funds for the orphanage. The directors of our organization in Baghdad plan to send him to Europe on a similar mission. We will speak with him about your uncle … and give him his address. After we get settled in Ba'qubah, of course."

Mannig's heart leaped with joy and pride for having a smart sister. How else could she memorize anything in the midst of homelessness, death, and heartbreak? Wherever Romania was, it promised family. She squeezed their clasped hands.

Barone Sebouh expelled a gigantic sneeze. "I always get a headache near large bodies of water," he said, taking short and controlled breaths through flaring nostrils. "This moist air signals the nearness of the river." He slowed his pace to blow his big nose into an embroidered white handkerchief and faced everyone behind him. "We'll see the boats soon. As I told you before, I cannot go with you today. I must complete my mission here first. I promise to see you in Ba'qubah very soon."

Past a grove of eucalyptus trees and grazing goats, Mannig halted, as did the rest of the orphans, at the bank of the Tigris River. Nervously, she gaped at Sebouh *Effendi's* "boats."

"Oooh."

"Nooo!"

Cries of "Impossible!" and "Never!" reverberated around the group.

20—The *Kalak*

Everyone gaped at the rafts hitched to inflated animal skins. Sebouh *Effendi* raised his arm and faced them, and the murmuring and tearful whimpers subsided.

"Don't worry about the *kalaks*," he said. "They look crude, but they've functioned on these rivers for centuries. They transport people, livestock, and merchandise daily." He grabbed Adrine's arm and signaled to the others to follow him down to the riverbank while he greeted the men reclining against the trunks of palms.

"I know the boatmen," he said, facing the children. "They are skillful and dependable. Over the past two months, they have delivered several groups to Ba'qubah safely and with perfect expertise. When you get hungry, they'll prepare food; if you have any trouble, they'll fix it. How many of you speak Arabic?" Almost all the children raised their index fingers as if in a classroom. "Good! If you see a problem or anything unusual, just tell any one of them."

Suddenly stirring, the reclining fellows jumped up and left their shady spots. A flock of grebes, bobbing along the shore, quacked into flight barely a yard above the water. The men wrapped their head-kerchiefs and rushed toward the *kalaks*. "*Eh-len wu seh-len*, Sebouh *Effendi!*" they greeted him in Arabic.

"*Salaam aleykum*, Mustafa," Sebouh addressed their leader. "*Inteh hadhur?*"

"Yes, *Effendi*, we are ready." Mustafa answered, pointing to the men and the three rafts. "My boatmen loaded the vessels with provisions, and they have rested long enough."

The sight of the vessels tethered to stumps along the muddy bank shriveled Mannig's expectations. She hid behind her sister and peered at the rafts of timber supported by inflated animal skins. A dozen ballooned goatskins encircled the boards of a *kalak*, holding it taut, steady, and afloat. The tied ends of the animal limbs piercing the air above the surface of the river reminded Mannig of the sloshing water in a similar animal skin tied to her sister's back on the deportation route. She had focused on those legs and avoided straying off into the hot and mirage-producing desert.

A good omen.

She relaxed her grip and followed Adrine to the edge of the river.

Her sister's grip tightened on her arm—soothing and reassuring. Without apprehension, she followed her lead.

Floating down the river might be exciting.

Mustafa pulled up the hem of his white robe and, swaddling his sinewy thighs, waded into the water with one foot; the other, on land, supported his weight. Gesturing to a passenger, he said, "*Ta'alee.* Come. I will lift you onto the *kalak.*"

Adrine nudged Mannig to go first. Before she could object, Mustafa picked her up and plopped her onto the raft. "*Ya-Allah,*" he said. "Go ... sit down." Within the minute, eight girls sat snuggly on their buttocks beside her, each cuddling her own bundle.

"*Allah wiyanneh!*" Chanting, 'God is with us,' Mustafa gestured to begin the voyage. Two boatmen pushed the raft into the flowing river by running along the bank before they hopped aboard. One man sat in front with a paddle, his back turned to the passengers; the other, Mustafa, at the rear of Mannig's *kalak.*

Mustafa framed his sun-baked face with his black and white checkered head kerchief, and yelled, "*Wahid. Ithnayn. Ya-allah.*" He repeated the numerical chant, "One. Two. In God's name," with each dip of the paddle. His contorted expression kept pace with his calls, and his fretful gaze veered back and forth between his passengers and the two other *kalaks.*

Sebouh *Effendi's* figure diminished on the shore and his hand stopped waving. The three rafts floated downstream with little maneuvering by the boatmen, even though they spoke with each other about the white caps, surging currents, or the occasional lazy stretch of water. Mostly, they discussed how to swerve around the water buffalo or steer clear of their floating dung.

The rafts drifted fast and free. The air cooled, chasing the sun's warmth. Touching the water made Mannig tingle, like a winter day transitioning into spring. She held her breath only once—heard no splash, no splatter, only the swishing of the current beneath the planks.

She wiggled her hips, moving her bundle aside to snuggle beside Adrine. A twinge in her belly made her abnormally weak. Her insides felt drained of energy—tummy contracting, thighs numbing. Just one look at her sister's composure reassured her about the voyage, while the cool air circulating above the water reminded her of being alive. *I'm imagining bad stuff.* She endured the cramping in her belly, refused to be affected by the sounds and sights along the eastern shore—as the bank grew nearer to the floating raft. Mangy reeds clung along the west bank of the wide Tigris, and a string of green eucalyptus trees zigzagged the horizon of the opposite bank.

The *kalak* flitted by giggling children playing in the water, chattering women rinsing clothes, and braying donkeys carrying water in earthen jugs. Grunting men, not far from the shore, pulled a similar raft upstream with taut ropes off their shoulders while sweaty boatmen rowed the raft. After drifting for over two hours, Mustafa hollered across the water to his partners in the other two *kalaks*, signaling them to row ashore. As soon as they tied the raft to a stump, Adrine disembarked. "Don't get lost!" she said to the orphans dashing hither and thither to relieve themselves. "I will wait for you by the boats," she yelled, her voice trailing the children running in search of a discreet spot to pull down their panties. Seeing the six boatmen rolling the hem of their white gowns up to their chests and wading waist-high to urinate in the current, Adrine instantly turned her back and scampered beyond the bank to relieve herself, Mannig in tow.

Out of nowhere, a female chant filled the air. "*L-a-b-a-n. L-a-b-a-n.* Fresh yoghurt anyone?"

Mannig stood mesmerized by the Bedou woman coming down the embankment. She balanced a stack of cylindrical drums—the load above her head as tall as her female frame. How many bowls? Mannig stood still, counting ... *Meg-Yergoo-Yerek* ... and to her surprise, she remembered the sequence just like her kindergarten days in Adapazar. "Nine," she yelled. "The woman has nine things on her head."

Wearing woven sandals and swaddled in a gown of knitted camel hair, the Bedou swayed her hips, in rhythm with her chant. "*L-a-b-a-n. L-a-b-a-n.* Fresh yoghurt anyone?"

Mustafa approached her. The two haggled in high pitched voices.

Finally, she consented to barter four bowls of her yoghurt for a basketful of his dates. Keeping her balance, she slowly bent her knees until they touched the ground. Resting her rump on her heels, she said, "Remove the top drum first."

Mustafa stood on tiptoe and stretched his hands up to reach the top of the stack. He handed one to each boatman and, holding the woman's free arm, helped her up to her feet again.

"Leave the empty drums on this stump, like you did last month," she said, setting the basket of dates beside a toppled tree amid a grove of date palms. "I will collect them after I sell the rest. *L-a-b-a-n!*" she chanted and, swaying her hips, disappeared beyond the embankment.

Mannig squatted on the ground with the others, surrounding the yoghurt container made of tightly woven palm fronds and sealed with tar. Her mouth watered at the few trapped bubbles on the taut surface of the creamy white yoghurt, glistening in the sun.

Mustafa took a loaf from a bag of bread. "Dunk the bread in the *laban*," he said, and slurped down a sample himself. "If any of you became nervous or nauseated on the raft, the laban will sooth you."

So, that's why my insides ached.

Mustafa set another basket by Adrine—date syrup oozing through its wicker fronds. "Wait a while for your stomach to rest with the yoghurt; after that, you should eat the dates." Before he headed to join his five partners a few yards away, he signaled to the Armenian boys. "You eat with us. Leave the women on their own." The male travelers segregated themselves from the nineteen girls.

Mannig dunked a chunk of the crispy flat bread and slurped the goat-milk yoghurt—the right food for her 'nervous' stomach. One bite sufficed. She liked the taste but felt full very quickly, while the unfamiliar 'nervousness' of her insides persisted. She snuggled next to Adrine, while the others gorged themselves with bread and yoghurt, topping each bite with a moist, sweet date.

Mustafa told everyone to relieve themselves again just before re-boarding for another two to three hours of gliding downstream.

Following Adrine's lead, Mannig pulled down her panties. Only a scraggly boulder stood between them. She saw crimson stains. After a second look at her panties, she screamed, "Adrine! Come here. Quick, Adrine!" she sobbed, tears trickling down and mouth frothing in fear, more to herself than loud enough to hear. "I am dying ... Jesus is punishing me," she whimpered, resting her head on her sister's shoulder. "I don't want to die. I have not done anything bad, or, or, or hurt anyone. I have not lived yet. I have not seen the world yet ..."

"Calm down. No one is dying," Adrine shushed her.

"Look at my panties ... See? Isn't this blood? I'm bleeding to death."

Adrine gave her panties a fleeting glance and smiled. "Stop the theatrics. No one dies from that!" she chuckled. "Surprise, surprise. You're becoming a woman, Mannig-*Jahn*. And at such an early age." She bent down, ripped a strip off the hem of her faded green gingham gown, and tore it lengthwise in half. She hung one half on her arm and, holding the other, she explained: "We fold this half twice or thrice for thickness. Now it is chunky enough to absorb the discharge. Take it. Line it inside your panties. Yes—just like that. Later, I'll look for a pin to fasten it to the panty, so it won't slip down your legs." She waited until Mannig pulled up her panty to hand her the second half of the strip. "When that gets soiled, you have to wash it and let it dry—in privacy, of course. Meanwhile, you can line your panties with the other strip."

"Am I not dying?" Mannig whispered. "Isn't this red blood?"

"It is blood, but you shall live," a sober Adrine said. "Your *amsagahn* has started—the monthly curse for every woman."

What curse? Mannig wanted to ask, but Mustafa was calling the stragglers. "*Y'allah*! Get on the *kalak*. We must cover a lot of distance yet. *Y'allah, Y'allah!* Hurry!"

Conscious of the bulge of cloth between her thighs, Mannig trailed behind Adrine onto the raft. Once snuggled next to her sister, she remained stiff and still. The troubles she had endured during the deportation hardly compared to the weakness in her lower back. *Might holding my breath help?* Struggling to do so for more than half a minute convinced her of the meaning of the 'curse.' She needed Adrine's expertise but refrained from asking. Instead, she listed her questions in her head, amid the noise of rushing waters or Mustafa's chanting back and forth with his oarsmen. Learning more about this curse must wait, Mannig convinced herself, as her eyelids weighted down. The bobbing of the *kalak* lolled her to sleep.

At dusk, the oarsmen moored the boats to boulders along the bank and erected two camel-hair tents—one for the females, the other for the males. The boatmen stewed eggplant with lentils in black iron caldrons, flavoring the meal with spices of cumin and cayenne, while Adrine watched attentively. She then helped them break the bread into wedges. Again the orphans dunked a chunk and lapped the stew.

At dawn, they sipped strong sweetened tea, broke camp, and floated downstream again, repeating the routine for the next four days. Mannig wished for yoghurt—but never tasted it again.

While floating by fishermen casting their circular nets off the round *guffa* boats, Mannig felt a tightening of her stomach muscles. The curse? Instead, images of a scary experience in a similar vessel engulfed her. It had happened crossing the Euphrates River on the deportation route. The gendarmes shoved and pushed the deportees—ten to twelve—into each *guffa*. A child had fallen off the edge of the packed boat and disappeared into the swift current. When nearing the opposite bank, Mannig, unable to hang on to the side of the boat, slipped off into the cold water. Someone from shore dashed in, seized her arm, and pulled her out. Touching the part of her arm where her unknown guardian had grabbed her sobered Mannig momentarily. Scooting closer to her sister in the *kalak* relaxed her.

Meanwhile, Mustafa was informing the *guffa* fishermen that he was taking the Armenian children to an orphanage.

The fishermen donated four fish for the "poor Armenys."

Within the hour, the *kalaks* pulled ashore, the nightly tents were erected, and Mustafa made his announcements. "We are preparing *masgouf* this evening," he said while the oarsmen gutted the fish and butterflied each flat, keeping the heads. "This is its brain," he added, pointing a branch from a palm frond at a cavity in the half-split head. "If it were bigger, the fish would not be caught in the net! But God made its brain tasty just as He did the eyeballs. After the fish has been roasted, we will allow the oarsmen to reward themselves with the fish heads."

Mannig's fascination continued as they skewered the fish—opened like a book—with branches from a palm tree. One oarsman held the butterflied fish upright—head, tail, spine, skin, and fins—while another dug the thick ends of the skewers into the ground until all four fish circled the fire with the flesh-side facing the flames.

Mannig's mouth watered at the aroma permeating the smoke. *Delicious ... did I ever eat fish in Adapazar?* While everyone sat around the fire, chatting and giggling, Mannig sensed she, too, must be getting used to the water-motion. She ignored her cramps; now her hunger struggled with the wait.

As soon as amber bubbles fizzed on the flesh, the boatmen freed the fish from the skewers and laid each one, skin side down, on the dying coals for a few more minutes. They sprinkled salt, curry, and turmeric on top and laid the sizzling meal on fronds.

One boatman dug his fingers into the soft tissue and ate,

encouraging the rest to follow his example—it did not matter how hot the morsel was, in the palm or the mouth.

The whitish meat tasted better than anything Mannig had ever eaten. She scraped the blubber hidden near the skin with each chunk and devoured bite after bite, unaware that the fish bones ought to be manipulated with the tongue and spit out.

Suddenly, she choked.

Her hacking cough spurred Mustafa to dash over. He grabbed her off her feet and gave her a big shake.

Mannig wheezed, face flushed and eyes flooded with tears.

Mustafa whacked her back again and again until she excreted the mouthful of fish and bones and gasped for breath.

Did I die? Then come back to life?

Mannig's coughing subsided only after Mustafa insisted she chew on some bread and swallow it. Right then and there the sight of fish repulsed her. For her, the feast was over.

She laid her head on her bundle and stared at the full moon rising in flaming orange and casting rainbow hues on the Tigris. The deep blue sky, crowded with stars, resembled an enchanting shawl embroidered with glitter. Unmoved, she gazed at this familiar scene of the past few nights. Even thoughts of the prospective orphanage evaporated from her head. The aching in her throat was in that moment the core of her life.

Upon hearing Mustafa's bedtime announcement, "We sail early in the morning," she rolled over and closed her eyes, only to sit up, eyes wide, as he continued, "Tomorrow, we will be in Ba'qubah."

Picture 1 - 23.8 Mannig Kouyoumdjian—portrait taken in
Baghdad, Iraq, circa 1936.

Picture 2 - 38.3   Mannig and Mardiros Kouyoumdjian
celebrating their marriage in Baghdad, Iraq, in 1922.

Picture 3 - 85.5 Orphanage in Nahr-el-Omar, Iraq, 1920.
Mannig is seated front row, first from left. The orphanage consisted
of several tents, each designated as a class for a special skill.
This tent was reserved for teaching crochet. Mannig was an expert.

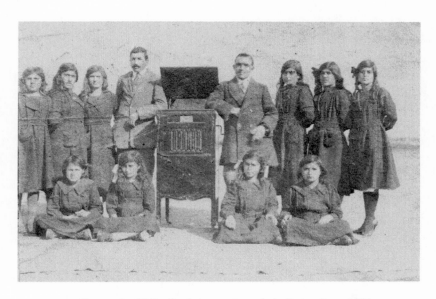

Picture 4 - 31.2 Orphanage grounds in Basra, Iraq, 1921.
Mardiros brought his personal gramophone and discs to teach
the orphans the foxtrot. From right to left: Mannig, unidentified girl,
Adrine, Mardiros, his right arm on His Masters Voice.
All others are unidentified.

Picture 5 - 90.5 His Excellency Hagop M. Kouyoumdjian,
born 1841, died 1913. (Photograph taken in Baghdad in 1913.)
Mardiros's father, decorated by the Ottoman Sultan for his
philanthropic contributions.

Picture 6 - 73 The five Kouyoumdjian brothers, photographed in
Baghdad in 1913. Seated, from left: Karnig Kouyoumdjian (the eldest),
Khosrof Kouyoumjian (five years younger). Standing, from left:
Toros Kouyoumdjian; Mardiros Kouyoumdjian (center);
Dikran Kouyoumdjian. Toros and Dikran were twins—ten years older
than Mardiros. Mardiros was the youngest in his family.

Picture 7 - 343.4   The Hagop Kouyoumdjian family in
Baghdad, 1913. The father and mother, Hagop Kouyoumdjian
and Managuile Kouyoumdjian, are seated in the center,
flanked by one daughter and three daughters-in-law.
The five sons are standing in the back, along with four
granddaughters and one grandson. Mardiros, age 23,
is the first from right, standing in the back row.
Seated on the floor are two grandsons and two granddaughters.

21—White City

A borderless field of white tents spread as far as the limits of the Ba'qubah horizon.

Where is the orphanage?

Mannig's gaze searched for a stone building. Off the *kalak* and standing on the river dike, not one structure fit her concept of a school—not beside, behind or beyond the peaks of the tents. Her hopes for a school fluttered away, mere figments of her imagination. *Will I ever see a school?* The setting sun reddened and the evening shadows lengthened, trailing Mustafa's wake. He guided his *kalak* passengers toward the so-called orphanage in Ba'qubah, a village 50 kilometers northeast of Baghdad, reputed for its innumerable hectares of citrus fruit groves.

"The Assyrians live in this section." Mustafa pointed left of Adrine, to a path defined by sturdy ropes securing rows of canvas tents. "The Chaldean refugees settled in the sector beyond them."

Mannig pulled on Adrine's sleeve. "Who is he talking about?"

"Homeless Christians, I think," Adrine said in a whisper. "These camps must be for people who survived the Turkish persecution, like you and me."

"And across them," Mustafa continued, "is the Armenian site— that's the largest camp. When the Big War ended, the *Englaizees* donated their army tents to the Middle East Relief and they, in turn, settled the refugees here. Now we have a tent city more expansive than Ba'qubah or its orange groves." He cleared his throat, spit a blob next to his foot, and lifted the heavy canvas flap of a vacant shelter. "This family must have moved on. Who knows? Perhaps they've settled in Persia ... Oh, Iran ... they're calling that country Iran now. Rumor is that people can find work just across the border. Jobs in our Arab lands are scarce, especially here. I hear that this territory will be called

Al-Iraq. A new name for an old country hasn't made our businesses more prosperous."

Names of countries flitted beyond Mannig's comprehension. She wanted to ask Adrine, but her sister's vacant look reflected similar ignorance about the immediate geography, least of all knowledge of national boundaries established following the Big War.

When I'm in class, I'll ask my teacher—teachers know everything.

As if to clarify the facts for himself, Mustafa sought Adrine's attention. "Settling the refugees here has been good for the people of Ba'qubah … unexpected trading and bartering is always good. The locals would really benefit if there were site constructions. I think everybody suspects tent settlements are migratory." He stepped outside the narrow path of one campsite's margin and into another. "Now we are in the Armenian camp … very big," he said. "Maybe four hundred families live here."

The squalor of the surrounding tents jarred Mannig's memory of her own enclave in Adapazar. Instead of an enticing profusion of steaming yeast from bakeries, the air was weighted with dung smoke. Packed mud paths loomed ahead in place of cobblestone lanes. *This can't be Armenian.* The voices, on the other hand, contradicted her first impression; they seemed genuine. Wistfully, she listened to a woman's sing-song call, *"Aram! Hosse yegoor!"* commanding a boy to come hither; then another, "Despina? *Oor ess aghcheeg?*" seeking her daughter's whereabouts.

I wish Mama summoned me.

Mannig swallowed a painful lump, remembering how her mother had died. It was during the horrible influenza epidemic while they were held hostage by the Ottoman gendarmes in Deir Zor.

"Some children found their relatives or older siblings," Mustafa continued, guiding his group across the campsite. "So they left the orphan-city and reunited with their families. Now they live here."

Depressed by the impoverishment of the refugees, Mannig hoped she and Adrine would never be sent here. Discreetly, she released her grip from her sister's and trailed at a distance. With a fearful heart, she prayed for the sight of the orphanage. After they were registered and settled, she could resume a relationship with her sibling in secret.

"How far before we reach our destination?" Adrine asked Mustafa.

"As soon as we cut across this part and get close to the river again, we'll see the orphan-city. It, too, stretches across a wide territory. There are more than six hundred starvelings ..."

"*Eh-len wu seh-len*, Say-yid Mustafa," a woman's guttural voice greeted him in an Arabic, heavily laced with an Armenian accent. In spite of her slightly hunched stature, the woman's attire and demeanor set her instantly apart from the refugees. The wide collar of her white blouse broadened her shoulders beyond its normal size, slenderizing the appearance of her otherwise wide hips inside a long black skirt.

"*Wu salaam aleykum, khatoon Perouz*," Mustafa returned her greetings. Facing his children, he added, "She is your mistress. You better behave for her."

Diggin Perouz smiled broadly, accentuating a sliver of separation between her two front teeth. "We have been waiting for you since yesterday. I'm glad you got here safely. *Selamat*, thank God. I brought oranges to welcome you. How many children do you have this time, Mustafa?" As the two exchanged information, she handed a beautiful thin-skin orange to each child with a few left over in her bag.

The spherical and velvety touch of the fruit in her palm satisfied Mannig's expectations; perhaps life at the orphanage would be perfect. Comforted by its feel, she even recalled its taste after so many years. While she debated whether to save it for later or gobble it right then, all attention was drawn to a girl gagging and spitting skin and pulp.

Diggin Perouz dashed to her side. "Poor child," she said, bringing out another orange from her bag. "You must only eat the inside of this fruit. Peel the skin like this, and see these wedges? You eat them, not the skin." After her demonstration, she headed toward a large tent containing #10 cans of gee, gunny-sacks of grains, and stacks of military utensils and metal dishes.

Following a set routine, the Diggin handed a tin mug to each orphan, while Mustafa passed out bowls. She talked with him continuously, leading the group toward a tent where the air was permeated with smoke and spices.

Two women holding ladles waited by a caldron dangling above a smoldering hearth.

"Children," the Diggin instructed. "Fall into line."

When pushing and shoving ensued, she sized up Adrine from head to foot and compared her with the other children, saying, "You're a tall one ... and look older than the rest. We need order here. How about letting the youngest child go to the front? We always feed the little ones first."

At the sight of food, Mannig's aloofness from her sister was quickly forgotten. She nudged Adrine to be the first in line, but was prodded aside and positioned behind four smaller orphans. Her hurt feelings lasted only a moment. What if, instead, she had been reprimanded by name and their relationship had been revealed? Surely, the two sisters would be denied admittance to the orphanage and sent to live at the Armenian camp.

Being anonymous and number four in line is very good.

Demurely, she extended her metal bowl to be served. The cook's heavy ladle clicked against the rim of her bowl. Garlic smell wafted from the thick soup of barley, wheat, and rice embellished with onions and tomatoes. She slid her finger up the spilled broth streaming outside her bowl and licked it, preparing to move on.

"Wait." One of the serving women grabbed her sleeve. "Your dry bones need this," and she dribbled a layer of melted gee on the soup.

Clarified butter tastes better than it looks floating atop the soup.

Joining the rest, Mannig squatted and lapped it up, perfectly satisfied. *My dry bones needed that.*

"We have prepared this special meal for you, as newcomers," Diggin Perouz said, addressing Adrine. "We can feed the children with an extra meal like this only occasionally. But they will always have their fill at regular eating times." She pulled out a gray head kerchief from her pocket and wrapped it around her plump cheeks. "When everyone is full, I will take you to your shelters."

She filled a bowl and handed it to Mustafa. "Sit down and rest. Your tent has been kept vacant for you and your partners, and there are enough mattresses for all. Come to my abode later for a snack."

"*Laa, W'allah.*" Mustafa slurped a few mouthfuls and thanked her with regret. "My men are in Ba'qubah already. I must join them and load the *kalaks* with supplies. Sebouh *Effendi* wanted oranges for the children in Mosul. He is waiting anxiously. So we'll rest in the village before we head upstream."

"*Allah wiyaak,*" Diggin Perouz said, bidding God's watchful eye on him. She reached inside her skirt pocket and brought out an envelope. "Since I will not see you before you leave, will you give this to my brother-in-law?"

"Sebouh *Effendi* suspected you probably had a message for him," Mustafa said, and, folding the envelope into thirds, he slid it inside his *dizhdasheh*, resting it above his belted robe.

"God willing, I will see you on your next assignment—*Inshaa-Allah*," Diggin Perouz bid him farewell. She then faced the orphans. "I'll show you your tents. There is a mattress for every two of you. Although they are laid on the tent floor, they are kept dry and comfortable. You must be very tired. Yes?"

Who cares about being tired?

Unable to contain her impatience any longer, Mannig burst out in defiance, "We want to go to the orphanage."

"Aha!" Diggin Perouz voiced surprise. "We have someone with a tongue. What is your name, child?"

Equally surprised, Mannig cowered and remained silent.

"She is my sister," Adrine said politely. "Her name is Mannig, and I am Adrine. She has been very excited about Ba'qubah."

Oh, no! Why did I say anything? And Adrine blurted out our relationship! Oh, dear God. Don't let her banish us out to the Armenian camp before we even enter the orphanage.

"Well, Mannig," Diggin Perouz said. "You ARE in the orphanage. All these white tents make up our home. You ate soup at the orphanage kitchen. Its wafting smells will beckon you every morning, noon, and evening. You will sleep in one of those tents, five to eight girls in each. Girls! So you need to regroup yourselves for the night. If you fail to make a good match, don't worry. Tomorrow, we may rearrange again. You, boys, how many of you are there? One, two … Oh, there are just four of you. You will sleep in one tent."

Mannig lugged her bundle and followed Adrine, right behind Diggin Perouz. She did not know whether to like this woman or not. According to Mustafa, she was the mistress; might she be the teacher, too? *Oh, why did I even open my mouth?*

"See those sheds?" Diggin Perouz pointed at a few small structures made of palm fronds lined at the edge of the river dike. "They are in Turkey."

Perplexed gazes riveted from her to the sheds. What's in Turkey?

"That's where you go when you need to relieve yourselves," she said sternly, but winking at Adrine, "Turkey deserves nothing but our latrines."

Mannig detected both Adrine and the Diggin snickering.

"We hang a lantern on that special post to guide your way at night," she continued orienting the new arrivals. "But if some of you must go to Turkey now, we'll wait for you."

Adrine held Mannig's hand and led the way toward a shed, going in first. "I can't say this is civilization," she said upon exiting, holding the wobbly door ajar for Mannig.

With trepidation, Mannig stepped into putrid odors. Smells fuming toward the open roof assaulted her. Buzzing flies popping up clung to the mat-walls made of wicker palm fronds. A long-necked pottery pitcher filled with water sat on the floor-planks within reach for washing both the self and the hands. A narrow slit between two boards formed a hole, deeper than Mannig cared to know. Hearing lapping waves and feeling an upward draft, she guessed the waste somehow flowed into the river. What if she fell through the opening? Scared, she dashed out and decided never to go there at night, posted light or not.

"We have a system here," Diggin Perouz was saying when Mannig regrouped back on the path. "After you pay your respects to Turkey in the mornings, you must run upstream and wash your hands and faces in the river. After that, you can come to the kitchen for tea—hot and sweetened tea."

She led them to a mid-sized tent. "This is the Infirmary," she said. "See the flag above it?" She pointed to a fluttering Red Crescent on a white cloth rising from its peak. "You must tell me if you are sick so we can take you to this tent. We have medicine, too. Dr. Papazian, my husband, sent a few emergency items in case we need any. Luckily, no one is sick now." She stopped to catch her breath. "We must keep clean at all times. That's the law. The river is near us so we can wash ourselves and our clothes. And once a week, we will heat water to bathe you until you are seriously clean."

Next she stopped by a standard-sized tent. "Which six girls want to stay in this one?" she asked, addressing Adrine. "You probably should not settle down until all your children are sheltered first."

She led the depleted group from one tent past several others until all were housed except four. She put her hand on Adrine's shoulder and whispered, "Adrine, *Jahn*. This is a good place for you and the rest. Two Vanetsi sisters live here. But I'm sure they're already asleep. They get tired from all the dancing and singing they do throughout the day."

Dancing? Singing?

Mannig gazed at Diggin Perouz. The woman was full of surprises. As if naming the toilets 'Turkey' were not enough! How about her instructions that one had to, 'run to the river,' 'splash the face with cold water,' and 'before the morning tea?' *What else do they do?*

They dance.

Her already confused image of a school melted into a vision of herself twirling in her yellow ruffled dress. Would it be called dancing if she gyrated and wailed in a sack cloth as she had in Mosul? Or between the lines of these tents? She fell behind Adrine to hop across a few stakes in her path.

Diggin Perouz lifted the entrance flap of the tent. "There are two extra mattresses for the four of you. I am certain you will sleep like gazelles tonight. Adrine-*Jahn*! You are still a very young maiden, yet you have done the job of a grown woman. I assume Sebouh enlisted you to escort these children from Mosul to Ba'qubah."

Adrine nodded.

"An awesome responsibility. And you have done it well. You deserve a good night's sleep. Sleep peacefully. Well," she chuckled. "I can guarantee you a restful night, but tomorrow, it will be different. I will need your assistance. We must see that all the orphans are settled, clean, and ready before Barone Mardiros arrives. We must make a good impression. He is bringing bolts of cloth for winter dresses and shoes for everyone."

Shoes?

Mannig had forgotten what shoes felt like. She had worn her last pair three or four years ago. Triggered by the memory, her toes curled within the straps of her sandals. She had discarded her shoes in the middle of the desert because they weighed her down and slowed her pace in keeping abreast with the deportees. She remembered the instant relief of bare-footedness. But more so, she recalled that the reprieve had been fleeting. The desert thorns had their heyday and, by that evening, her soles had turned into a bristly hide of slivers.

How would my feet feel in shoes, after all this time?

22—Tête-à-Tête

Trailing Diggin Perouz, Mardiros stopped at the entrance of the large tent reserved for visiting dignitaries. He slapped the dust off his khaki britches and kicked one boot against the other before stepping inside. Then, he removed his Topy, the British military hat used in the desert. "You are a marvel, Diggin Perouz," he said, while she lit the lantern. "In spite of my late arrival, you accomplished much today."

She hung the lamp from a hook dangling from the central peak of the tent. "Work goes fast when the children are happy," she said, facing him in the yellow haze flooding the interior. "You saw how their eyes shone—as radiantly as the sheen of the shoes each hugged as a prize." She watched him wipe his brow above the tan line left by the brim of his hat and wave off a moth. She returned to the entrance and dropped the flap, impeding the surge of mosquitoes, veiling the moonless sky, and muffling nocturnal murmurs. She gazed at Mardiros, whose expression mirrored the excitement of the orphans. "Who did you say donated the shoes?"

"Orozdi Bak, the department store," he said, assisting her with unfolding an army cot. "Not all of the shoes, of course. We spent a nominal amount in the *sook* for another hundred or so. We wondered about sizes, so we selected a bunch of *babooj*-type loafers as well. We didn't want any child to be without shoes."

"The children will remember this day forever," Diggin Perouz said, airing a sheet above the cot. "Regrettably, this is all we can offer for your comfort," she apologized. "Wasn't unloading all those bolts of cloth a joyous sight, too? I will devise a fair plan to allot ample yardage to each child—so no orphan shall be without a new dress."

And no one shall learn the hazardous risk of the delivery, Mardiros thought to himself.

159

The long horseback ride from Baghdad had demanded great alertness. He had escorted the mule-drawn carts, pyramided with supplies, for three days. Along with the six drivers, all wearing gun belts, he had trekked during the day and pretended to rest the two nights they had spent under the velvety dome of the sky, spangled with flickering stars.

He shuddered, remembering how one night his consignment had almost been looted, and that the lives of the hired-hands—and his—might have ended.

The yells and growls of hyenas had kept them alert. They built a fire for tea and augmented their waking hours with stories going back to the Babylonian empires about the wildlife in these ancient lands. "At least the ancient lions aren't roaming these parts anymore," the lead driver said, blowing at a chunk of charcoal flaming in the brazier.

"The Assyrian Emperor was a great hunter," another said, stretching his legs on the bedding—a quilt arranged on a straw mat. "He used wildlife for sport."

"But didn't stoop below his royal status to aim his arrows at those vicious scavengers who pester at night."

"Hyenas are not only the desert 'cleanup-crew' of carcasses left behind," one driver said, rolling a cigarette. "My nephew got attached to a hyena pup, so his father let him keep it as a pet. The two were inseparable. Cute gray striped creature … made us laugh. It had a zigzag trot that made it look like it was climbing uphill. The beast was harmless until it was about two years old. Then one day, it used its strong jaws on a baby-goat and ate the poor creature alive."

All eyes riveted on him, radiant and restless as the eyes of the hyenas glimmering from the hillside along the Eastern border of Iraq.

Mardiros added a few more coals into the brazier. "We had better keep this ablaze until the sun comes up." He urged the men to rest with one eye always open and both ears pricked for unusual sounds.

He had hardly reclined on his mat when a shotgun rattled the quiet of the open sky.

They were surrounded by marauders of the desert.

The fire had served its purpose—it had deterred the hyenas from approaching their prey. But it had beckoned the robbers to their target.

Confronted by the leader of the gang approaching on horseback, Mardiros, presupposing leadership, initiated a tactic for negotiation. "We carry no ammunition and no valuables," he said, opening his cloak to show that there were no weapons in his belt. "Our cargo is shoes ... we're taking shoes to the orphans in Ba'qubah ..."

The chief raider fired a shot in the air and shouted to his cronies. "Wait!" He approached Mardiros for a better look. "*Salamet*," their leader apologized, lowering his shotgun. "We didn't know it was you, *Say-yid* Metrolose."

A collective gasp preceded a hush among the robbers.

"*Say-yid Metrolose* is the son of Hagop Bey of Felloujah," he continued. "My father and his were the best neighborly landowners before the Big War." He wheeled his horse about, wrapped his mouth with his red-and-white checkered *kaffieh*, and fired another shot in the air. "Tonight is not ours." He led his gang galloping into the darkness of the western wasteland.

"What was that about?"

"Since when do you befriend pilferers?"

"Why did he call you, *Metrolose*?"

"Wait a minute," Mardiros protested. "I need to catch my breath, too."

Only after taking several lengthy puffs of his cigarette did he try to explain.

"That scoundrel and I grew up not too far apart from the Kouyoumdjian lands of Felloujah. He and I played war together. He could never pronounce Mardiros without stuttering. So he devised a nickname, *Metrolose*."

"That's a good one," the head driver said. "You do spew your words out fast like a machine gun." He laughed, invoking the others into a nervous laughter.

Their cackling resurfaced in his memory and he found it hard to repress his yearning to tell about escaping the harrowing incident to Diggin Perouz. He could not fully shake off the anxiety, which overwhelmed him even two days after the confrontation. He hoped his drivers would also be discreet; he had instructed them not to recount their experiences while under his employ, but wait until their return to their own families. News about marauding raiders could stop the flow of donations earmarked for the orphans.

Watching Diggin Perouz unroll a mattress on the cot comforted him. The sanctuary of the camp restored his sense of accomplishment, although bearing news that might disrupt the orphanage disheartened him. He waited until Diggin Perouz aired a muslin covered quilt and set it at one end of the mattress before he spoke. "You are a great organizer," he said, opening two folding canvas chairs. "Your cheerfulness and coordinating ability are hailed all over Baghdad." He gestured for her to sit on one, while he sat in the other and crossed his legs. "I wish we could secure a few more volunteers like you."

She smiled. "Shall I make some tea?"

'No, no," he said, glad to delay divulging the new plans about the orphanage. "I have a better suggestion." He darted over to his brown valise, the smallest of his three ochre leather bags. He unbuckled the two straps and lifted the engraved flap with his initials M.H.K— Mardiros Hagop Kouyoumdjian. He fumbled through the starched white shirts and monogrammed handkerchiefs that his valet in Baghdad had packed and finally retrieved a tear-shaped, clear bottle of cognac. "This is for you."

"Well, what took you so long? Let us sample it together." She gestured for him to remove the wax seal of the crystal stopper. She reached inside the wicker cabinet, pulled out a shawl clinking with dishes, and set it on his cot. After untying its ends, she selected two glass teacups. "Not exactly snifters, but like Arabic tea, we can savor its rich caramel color as well."

He cradled the tiny two-ounce glass cup in his palm for a few moments to warm his cognac while she inhaled the bouquet of hers. They sipped with eyelids half-closed.

"I had hoped your entourage included a few new helpers," Diggin Perouz said.

"It is useless," Mardiros shook his head. "I'm disappointed in my Baghdadi community. They shun work themselves because their money talks. There is no one like you, Diggin Perouz—generous with money, self, and time."

"There's you," she interrupted, raising her drink to him.

"Unlike you, I am a bachelor and have no responsibilities," he said. "In fact, I have a good excuse to avoid that stuffy, decadent society of ours. I go to the parties because their money supports these orphans. In spite of the grumbling I get from my mother and the Kouyoumdjian females about my bachelorhood, I refuse to dally with snobbish society mothers, who flaunt their unmarried daughters at every social event."

"I would do the same if my daughter wasn't already married," Diggin Perouz said, and sipped her drink to the last drop. "These glasses are tiny."

He refilled hers, but refrained from quenching his palate. *I brought the cognac for her consumption, after all.* Instead, he took out his golden cigarette case and coyly held it open for her—unsure how free she felt to smoke in his presence. "My brother recently returned from London and brought these factory-rolled cigarettes with him."

She winked. "Who outside this tent would gossip about my smoking?" She reached for one and studied its perfect roll from tip to base, then repeated an old saying: "God save the dumb from the wicked."

Mardiros laughed. He lit her cigarette and a second one for himself. In silence, he watched puffs of smoke fill the tent as he debated the best time to inform her about the future of the orphanage. Remembering the letter from her husband, Dr. Papazian, he relished another excuse to delay revealing the plans to move the orphanage. He reached inside the pocket of his tweed jacket and handed her a sealed letter. "Your husband is anxious to see you back at home, I think."

"Only after someone replaces me," she said, putting the letter in her skirt pocket without reading it. She poured another ounce of cognac into her glass. "I really don't want to return to Baghdad. I am useful here—I feel wanted and I know I am filling a need. Seeing the orphans' faces every morning is an affirmation I've missed in my life. You know of my teaching training. After all these years, I'm grateful to finally put it to good use. I enjoyed mingling with our friends in Baghdad while the children were growing up. After they were on their own, my existence seemed frivolous. Patients occupy my husband's days, and the servants take care of everything. I felt useless and worthless. When I heard you at one of those society receptions, your plea for assistance moved me. I understood the need and knew I could fill it."

"I remember that very well," Mardiros said. "You delighted us all with pertinent questions about AGBU's origin and whether its board members had ulterior motives."

"You convinced me when you said the Armenian General Benevolent Union was Nubar Pasha's brain child. I knew he disdained political organizations that are disguised as philanthropy. Like the Baghdadi Armenians, I had ignored the desperate needs of the surviving orphans until that evening in your presence."

"Obviously, your husband recognized those needs, also."

"Because he offered his medical services?" she asked.

"Yes—and because he donated medicine for emergencies," Mardiros said, un-strapping a second suitcase. "This time, he donated liquid quinine for malaria, and serum for bilharzias. He promised to ride here immediately, if life and death situations arose, such as an epidemic, God forbid. He also volunteered your ability to use a syringe, if necessary."

"He has faith in me." She shook her head, looking at the long glass tube with a needle at its end. "He knows I'm skillful with an enema!"

They both laughed as he clicked the lock of the bag shut.

"When you tour the orphanage tomorrow," she said, "we will put these supplies in the Infirmary Tent, which, luckily, has no occupants yet."

"You will show me around?" he asked.

"Of course! We have been planning for your arrival for a week. The children are anxious to meet their Dear Father of the Orphans."

Mardiros let out a guffaw. "Father? You have made me a parent even before I am married." He was as delighted with his title and her creative labeling as he was with the company of this unassuming lady. Noting her desire to talk about her thoughts, he further delayed his announcement. He offered her another cigarette.

"One is enough," she said. "You know, Barone Mardiros, other than Eghishe Vartanian, the teacher, and his wife, there are no adults here who can assume the responsibility of managing the orphanage. Many women from the Armenian camp help in spite of being needy themselves. But we can't always expect them to give up their own burdens to help us. Luckily, several older orphans are eager to work. You will meet the girls from Moush who are our creative cooks; the ones from Bitlis are strong as well as handy; and the Vanetsi girls, with their dances and songs, cheer everyone. All the orphans contribute to the day-to-day chores. But my advice, guidance, and presence are in great demand, since none is as old as twenty. And then, there is the orienting of new arrivals such as the twenty-four orphans from Mosul a week ago."

"Why only twenty-four?" Mardiros asked, knowing he had enrolled 200 or more orphans in Mosul before his mission to India to raise funds.

"Due to the capacity of the rafts," she said. "According to Sebouh's note, my brother-in-law says they're having problems with the train's engine and no one knows when it will be operational. So he hired *kalaks* to take them down the Tigris River. Their arrival surprised me. No one fell off or drowned. God must have floated with them."

"I must change some plans, then," Mardiros said, more to himself than to be heard. "I hope there is a telegraph office in Ba'qubah to notify Sebouh. He must stop sending the rest of the orphans to Ba'qubah."

"Should we all expect a change in plans?"

"Yes—a big change. When the details are finalized, the officials in Baghdad will send a telegram about the go-ahead. We'll have to wait for specifics."

Diggin Perouz put the stopper in the cognac bottle and pushed it deep. "I'm listening."

"AGBU decided to regroup all the orphanages throughout Iraq in Basra."

"Basra?" Her voice rose several notes. "What can Basra offer that we cannot?"

"Indeed, we own an outstanding organizational compound here," he said. "Barone Gharibian, the AGBU representative from Basra, and the World Relief committee, decided Basra would provide the orphans a permanent solution."

"I'm not surprised the Basrawi Armenians are outshining the Baghdadi ones," she snickered, standing up to leave.

He also rose and accompanied her outside the tent. "The British barracks there will become a school. Teachers from Basra can commute daily. I tell you, Diggin Perouz, the problem of access to teachers is much on the minds of the benefactors. How do you manage here with almost 600 children?"

"As you know, Eghishe Vartanian is the only teacher," she sighed, and flung a black crocheted shawl over the wide collar of her white blouse. "I have appointed the older girls to teach the younger ones whatever they know of reading and writing. You will meet the pretend-teachers tomorrow. Oh," she looked at him, delight emanating from her voice. "One of those girls just arrived from Mosul. She must have received an excellent education in Adapazar before deportation. In one week, she has assisted me in classifying students according to their grades." Stepping outside the tent, she looked at the glittering canopy of the deep dark sky. "That girl is my star! We will talk more tomorrow. Good night."

He waited until she walked past one tent and entered hers before he went in and pulled off his boots. Even if his thirty-year-old body could ignore its exhaustion, he knew he would function better after a good night's sleep. Before touring the camp or meeting the pseudo-faculty, he must ride to Ba'qubah and send a telegram to Sebouh ... the Mosul orphans must be transported directly to Basra ... not in *kalaks*, for heaven's sake! By train and only after the line was running again.

He lit his bedtime cigarette and stretched his aching legs on the wobbly cot. Inhaling while resting his head doubled his fatigue. Mosul orphans? Only a few months ago he had finished registering them. Adapazar? It reminded him of the little imp conniving her way into the orphanage. She was from Adapazar.

Could she be Diggin Perouz's prize?

23—Father of the Orphans

Confident in Diggin Perouz's ability to allot the yardage of fabric to the orphans and distribute the shoes, Mardiros deprived himself of his essential daybreak drink, Turkish coffee, and bid her adieu. For nearly an hour, he cantered non-stop to Ba'qubah.

Chasing and babbling children slowed him down along with farmers bearing produce and vendors hauling their carts toward the village *sook*. Pedestrians ogled his British Topy and khaki britches. He laughed at their remarks: "He is Lawrence's twin," and "The *Englaizees* are coming," only to surprise them with his native Arabic.

"My clothes are like an Englishman's," he said, "but I am Armeny. I am with the Armenian orphans." He dismounted and approached a huddle of young men. "Where is your telegraph station?"

They pointed in his horse's direction. "Go. It's not far."

He hoped the 'not far' was literal, and not just the men's customary way of trying to impress a stranger with their knowledge.

Seeing black graffiti on a rolled-down tin door that spelled *teleghraff* in Arabic, he straightened his shoulders and relaxed—no need to travel to Baghdad just to send a message. He dismounted. Padlocked? Of course! A pastoral community would be unlikely to depend upon modern technology.

"*Ehlen*," an elderly man said, leaning on his cane. With his free hand, he pulled on the corner of his white cotton *Kaffieh* scarf, flipped it over his *Aggaal* and tucked it under the shiny jet-black coil that secured his head gear. Approaching the bay gelding, he touched the horse's cheek with his palm and murmured words of endearment into its ear.

Mardiros greeted the perceptive man and, pointing to the sagging wires from the telegraph shed made of sun-dried bricks, asked, "Who can send a telegram for me?"

"Hamid," the sage said, his gnarled fingers brushing the horse's silky mane.

"Can you find Hamid for me?"

"Can't," the man replied, sliding his palm along the horse's neck.

Mardiros assumed the information required a price. He dismounted, patted dust off the loins of his horse, and facing the man, offered him a cigarette.

"La, la!" the man refused.

Mardiros put a cigarette between his own lips and held the case open, allowing the informant to change his mind.

"La, la! I am a *narghille* fellow," he said, pointing to a brass-based water pipe sitting on the ledge of the *kebab* stand across the station.

Mardiros lit his own cigarette and tried again. "Take a few anyway."

The man took a couple, carefully sliding them into the side pocket of his tawny tunic. "*Turkee?*"

"La, *Englaizee*," Mardiros labeled the cigarettes being English, not Turkish.

"*Moomtahz!*" the man uttered. "Excellent!"

Confident of having established a rapport, Mardiros asked, "Do you know where I can find Hamid?"

"Across the river."

Mardiros quickly mounted his horse. "Where is the bridge?"

"Burned down!"

Mardiros agonized. He knew very well how the Ottoman military burned the bridges upon their retreat from the British forces at the end of the war. None had been replaced. Two years earlier, the Falloujah Bridge had met a similar fate. From the balcony of the Kouyoumdjian Qasr, his family's summer mansion on the west side of the Euphrates River, he had watched it sink into flames. The infrastructure of the post-war Iraqi government proceeded as nonchalantly as a scorpion, even in Falloujah—the strategic juncture between Baghdad and Jordan.

Insignificant Ba'qubah couldn't have a new bridge yet. He shook his head. *Ahkh!* The Tigris was too wide to cross on horseback.

College texts describing the rivers of the Middle East in his irrigation engineering classes graded the Tigris as one of the world's greatest rivers. At the Ba'qubah site, it ran deep and fast until it met its sister, the Euphrates, at Shat-El-Arab, due north of Basra at the southern tip of Iraq.

The task of finding a telegraph operator was as daunting as locating orphans on these lands in the aftermath of war. Like a yo-yo, he dismounted again. "Where are the *bellems*?" He asked about a boat.

The fellow whispered into the stallion's ear and released the bridle. After tethering the horse to a large rock beside his kebab stand, he gestured to Mardiros to head west. Instead of uttering his customary one-or-two word answers, he ululated and one of the congregated boys approached. "Mahmood," he said, putting his hand on the boy's shoulder and positioning him to lead Mardiros to the river.

Completely trusting the Arab with his stallion, Mardiros followed Mahmood while a jabbering pack of boys trailed behind them.

Mahmood, swaying his hand-woven cloak striped in ecru browns and mustard yellows, hopped and jogged ahead of Mardiros toward the river, seemingly happy to guide a man in Western attire.

Mardiros marched, erect and determined, leading with his broad shoulders—developed as a star athlete of track and gymnastics at Roberts College in Constantinople. In Mahmood's wake, Mardiros's stride set their pace until they reached the riverbank.

Mahmood kept his palm outstretched like a beggar's while the children ogled the *bakhsheesh*.

Mardiros jingled several 5-Fils pieces into Mahmood's hand, and the boy immediately fisted the coins and dashed out of sight, the children yelling at his heals for a piece of his luck.

Knowing Hamid's whereabouts, the first boatman, sitting idly at the stern of his bellem, agreed to row Mardiros across the Tigris for 50 Fils. "Worth two loaves," he grumbled, his hands sizing the circumference of the Arabic flat bread. He then ran up the bank and yelled, "Anyone want to go across?" "I can take three more passengers …" and lastly, "This is the one and only crossing for today." He waited a while and then repeated his call. Indignantly, he waved his left arm and scampered back to the boat. Holding its stern, he pushed it off the land and waved his *salaams* to the other boatmen.

Mardiros hopped into the boat without rocking it too much then swiftly scooted to the bow. He faced the boatman in silence for half-an-hour while the man struggled with the current.

"Hamid works with the *fellahin* these days," the boatman said, pointing to the wheat fields and pocketing the fare. "When you're ready to return to the village, meet me several yards up stream. That will be 100 *Fils* each way."

Rascal! He ups the fare because he knows I have to get back.

Within three hours, Mardiros found Hamid. The two stepped into the *bellem*, and plop! His legs demanded relief. Age catching up? Passing the age of thirty fell short of the magic people claimed. Might the wonder be in pursuing new passions? Memories of his impetuous teen days or the thrill-seeking of his twenties waned in comparison to the exhilaration he felt at the orphanage. He shrugged his shoulders as though to toss out youthful joys and lit a cigarette. Inhaling smoke guided him into darker thoughts of isolation and helped him retreat from the trivia of life. For a moment, his eyes glazed, his neck drooped, and his back hunched. *Why am I here? Who am I?*

A fresh gust from the surface of the river reawakened him.

Noticing Hamid and the boatman ogle his cigarette, he held his case open. "Hamid, take ... one for yourself and light another for the boatman."

The boat glided quickly and the boatman's cigarette, half smoked, was still between his lips when they arrived.

Mardiros handed him two 100 *Fils*, and having forgotten the man's demand for the increased fare, added a bonus by habit.

The boatman was so excited that he reached to kiss his hand.

Mardiros determinedly snapped his hand away. "*Shukran*," he said in thanks and bid him farewell.

Quietly, he followed the operator through the *sook*. The crowd was at its peak, with fresh deliveries atop donkeys jingling their way beside pedestrians and merchants.

The tranquil scene at the kebab stand made him smile. His stallion nibbled on barley in a burlap nosebag draped from his head and the old man, fingering his *subha*, prayer beads, reclined on a mat woven of palm fronds—saddle and satchel resting beside him. Without disturbing the old man he stood behind Hamid, anxiously waiting for the unlocking of the station's padlock. Hamid rolled open the screeching tin door, and Madiros followed him into the shed.

The man pulled wires, wound exposed ends together, and sparked connections. He split another pair and joined others. "Works," he said. He blew dust off the telegraph bench and rubbed his sleeve on the key until the copper lever shone in the dim shed. "Has not been used in two years." He tapped the lever. No reaction. He withdrew his dagger from his waistband and tightened a screw. He flipped a switch on and off, shook wires back and forth, and for a few minutes listened keenly to the metallic gurgling of the system.

Mardiros held his breath.

Hamid's lips parted and his thick mustache barely exposed a smile.

Mardiros took the breath of relief for a *fait accompli*. Innovation did what technology promised.

Hamid tapped the key pulsating fast and slow and transmitted the message to Sebouh in Arabic:

Change original plans STOP
Communiqué from Baghdad forthcoming STOP
Halt transport orphans to Ba'qubah STOP
Signed—Your friend, Mardiros

Mardiros pressed his shoulders together and then, with a sigh, tightened them further. *I pray no child will be lost in the shuffle.* He was not a religious person, but he was dedicated to Armenianness—where deep-rooted Christianity defined its heritage. He pleaded for the sake of the orphans.

Even if a few children were already floating down the Tigris— stupid idea—they ought to arrive at Ba'qubah before the commencement of the final transport to Basra. *In a few days, I'll send a more comprehensive telegram from Baghdad, demanding the children be transferred by train and only by train … directly … and directly to Basra.*

He let his tense shoulders collapse and handed the telegrapher one Dinar—equivalent to 1000 *Fils*—trying to gauge if his reaction to the amount was contentment or disdain.

"*In-shah-Allah*, your message is in Mosul now," Hamid exclaimed, his trust in God's willingness for the deed. "Perhaps the delivery boy will hand it over to your man tonight." He then counted the ten 100-*Fils* coins, and dropped them in his pocket. "*Shukran*," he said in thanks.

Mardiros stepped outside and saw his gelding saddled, satchel attached to one side and prepared for his return. His eyes scanned the horizon above the flat-roofed buildings—still two hours until dusk. The smell of smoke from the kebab stand beckoned to a growling stomach. He had neither eaten breakfast nor sipped tea all day. He smiled. *My fatigue is not due to old age but to hunger, after all.*

"Come," he said to the operator, offering him a bite. "*Essufra da'eema*—a spread, always."

"*La, Wa-Allah*," the man excused himself, padlocked the station, and departed in a hurry.

Mardiros approached the sage. "Your coal is hot," he said, unsuccessfully shooing flies off the bowl of ground meat. "Smelling your *tikke* is not enough. Let us taste it." He kicked off his boots. Even without them, his steps creaked on the yellow palm-frond mat. He reclined with a grunt and crossed his legs. He reached for a string of prayer beads in a basket for customers. *"Shakku makku?"* He asked about world events.

"Allah Kareem—God is merciful," the sage replied, raising his gaze heavenward in thankfulness, and squeezed a palm full of lean ground lamb onto a flat metal skewer. He dipped his hand in a cup of water frequently as his gnarled but nimble fingers pressed up and down the skewer, pressing the meat tightly together—all the while blowing away the relentless flies. With a second naked skewer, he spread the pyramid of burning coal across the brazier. The minute he placed the kebab to be grilled, the tantalizing rosemary smell mushroomed. He fanned the coals with a palm-frond fan, its blackened, burned rim barely escaping the shooting sparks. In minutes, the *tikke kebab* sizzled while the round Arabic bread beside it turned ochre toasty. The bread in one hand, he slid the foot-long sputtering-kebab onto the bubbly side of the bread. He sprinkled salt generously and added a few grains of coarsely pounded peppercorns. He topped the meat with thinly sliced onions marinated in crushed *sumac*. He folded the wrap in threes and handed it to Mardiros.

Mardiros bit into it. "May Allah keep your hands delicious, forever," he said, savoring the tasty combinations of the spices. He relished this leisure, convincing himself that delaying his return to Baghdad a day or more would cause no particular hardship. Inspecting the orphanage with Diggin Perouz would take up one day and writing his report to the World Relief Organization (WRO) another—giving him as much time to write a comprehensive a report as he had ever had. He prided in his evaluation of the "lost" Armenian children located by his scouts among the Arabs; likewise, the report about his fund raising efforts in India, Java, and Singapore. The 395,000 rupees collected from Armenians in the Asian regions had amazed the committee and provided WRO support for thousands of orphans. The Ba'qubah orphanage report must emphasize children's educational needs. Definitely. The higher-up personnel trusted his judgment.

While he was a celebrated personality among the directors of AGBU and WRO at home and abroad, he preferred the straightforwardness of field work. He experienced total fulfillment with the orphans and envisioned a long-range involvement in this philanthropy even after the children's settlement in Basra.

In his head he mapped out grandiose plans for them, but regrettably, a kebab like the one in his hand for each orphan must wait for a while.

However, he decided to treat Diggin Perouz with one of these delicious local snacks. He let out a big belch in the traditional Arab appreciation for the food and, seeing that the sage lacked additional business, he said, "Make me two more wraps to take with me."

The vendor offered coffee. Mardiros preferred sweetened Turkish coffee, but he accepted the strong and bitter Arabic variety the man served in a small conical porcelain cup. A few sips sufficed. He paid the man with newly minted Iraqi coins.

The vendor shifted the variety of denominations in his palm. "I've never seen 100 *Fils*." He dropped it in his tunic pocket. "For my son."

Mardiros handed him another coin. "I bet this 500 *Fils* is also new. Give it, too, to your son." He dropped the highest of the coin denominations into the vendor's palm.

The sage held back, but quickly accepted it when Mardiros insisted the taste of his *tikke* was heavenly. The man, swishing inside his pocket, brought out a handful of colorful candy-balls and dropped them into Mardiros' hand.

Mardiros gazed at the sweet and sour candy in yellow, pink, and green. Wouldn't such candy thrill the orphans? But superfluous items remained beyond the budget.

I could spend my own money.

For the first time, he regarded his family wealth as a blessing. He realized he was privileged to aid the orphans not just with time, but with expenses, too. "Where can I buy more of these?" he asked.

The sage smiled and, seeing a boy dawdling nearby, handed him a few candy drops and pointed his shoulders toward, "Hakim's."

Mardiros stuffed the kebab snacks for Diggin Perouz into a pocket of his satchel, bid his *salaams* to the sage and, leading his stallion, tailed the lad to the mouth of the *sook*. He eyed a pyramid of the mini-marble sized balls. The pastel-colored candy glistened translucently in the rays of the setting sun and radiated a rosewater fragrance. "How many balls in a kilo?" he asked.

"A kilo?" Hakim said, his jaw dropping with disbelief. "No one has bought as much as a kilo from me. A quarter of a kilo, yes, but let me see ...” He grabbed a handful and let the balls cascade back onto the pyramid, “maybe 200 pieces in a kilo.”

Mardiros figured one or two pieces for each of the orphans. “Let me see what one kilo looks like,” he said, jingling coins in his pocket.

Hakim scooped up the sweets with two hands onto one of two metal plates of a makeshift scale. He held a polished stone and said, “Most people buy one stone’s worth ... one quarter of a kilo.” He placed it and three others into the second plate. He picked up the leveling stick at its center and carefully raised it, lifting the two metal plates hanging on three equidistant strings. They almost balanced. With his free hand, he added a few more balls. “That is one kilo, *effendi*,” he said.

“Give me five kilos, then,” Mardiros said, and opened his satchel for the first batch.

“La, la, *effendi*,” Mahmood rejected the satchel and handed him a gunny sack. “You deserve a bag.”

“Won’t you need it?” Mardiros objected.

“You bring it back next time you ride to our village,” Hakim said, dismissing the argument.

“Well, in that case, we’ll leave the haggling to other customers. How much do you want for the candy?”

“For you, *effendi?* Whatever you want to pay.”

Mardiros felt as generous as the salesman and wanted to treat the children before they went to sleep. He handed over 500 *Fils* and waited for the vendor’s reaction. When the man praised Allah, Mardiros slung the bag of candy across the saddle and mounted his horse. “*Inshah Allah*, God shall bring me back.”

He cantered south toward the orphanage.

Within the hour, Mardiros heard the children’s voices wafting from the orphanage. Singing?

A group of children crouched between the tent lines facing Diggin Perouz, intoning vespers.

He tethered his horse by the guest tent and, careful not to disrupt them, quietly blended in behind a group of girls.

The melisma in the youthful voices soothed his psyche, transcending any body aches accumulated throughout the day. The chanting filled an emptiness deep, deep within him. The endless void he experienced in Baghdad society must have taken up residence inside another person—it vanished in this primitive environment. He felt complete, whole, and no longer sensing a chunk missing from his soul. Had he arrived at the true meaning and purpose of his life?

The children hummed or just sang la-la-la in tune. Only a few of them uttered the lyrics. As with him, the melancholy Gregorian chant remained melodically rooted in their memories, but not the ancient Biblical vernacular. Immersed like them, he hummed along until the concluding Lord's Prayer—the portion he liked best in the entire Armenian liturgy, notwithstanding the high notes in the finale. Having memorized the last phrase, he sang loudly, oblivious as to how his husky tenor overpowered the children's voices. His passion was compelling, and all eyes were riveted on him.

"Barone Mardiros has returned," Diggin Perouz said. "Everyone stand up!"

"No, no, no!" Mardiros objected in vain, even as she approached him and the children applauded.

"I should have stayed in the tent," he whispered to Diggin Perouz, loosening his tie.

"No, no, no," she said. "You are part of us and very important to everyone."

He showed her the sack with the treats. "Since the children have congregated around you, should we give them the candy now?"

"You are the Father of the Orphans." She responded to his whisper with a nod.

❧

Mannig stood among the last in line, not questioning the purpose of the queue. She assumed all activities had a purpose and all were designed to prepare the children for the future. Without jockeying ahead as she normally would, she followed at the heels of the sisters from Van in silence, focusing on her new shoes. They hugged her feet in beautiful leather with a black buttoned strap. She adored their shine even in the darkness of the night.

As soon as Diggin Perouz had fitted them earlier that morning, Mannig knew she and the shoes had become one—they were as inseparable as her arms. Melded into them, her feet were a model of decorum. She was proud of owning this pair and promised herself never again to discard them. Never again would she free her feet from the weight of shoes. Maybe removing her shoes had helped her escape the gendarme's whips during the deportation, but she couldn't forget how the scorching desert engulfed her and how thorns and thistles had pierced her shoeless feet.

Besides, these shoes were different; their newness inspired her to imagine stepping into exciting paths and seeing fanciful sights. She wiggled her toes. But being confined, they could not dance. She yearned for their animation. Step in, step out ... she emulated the sisters, visualizing a replication of the dance steps they had proposed to teach in the morning. *Ah! I can hop and jig wearing real shoes, just like in Adapazar.*

Mannig kept her place behind the sisters more by sensing their forms than observing the actual activity of the pale shadows ahead. The lantern on the pole beside the latrine failed to illuminate anything but its immediate location and the suicidal moths fluttering in its beams. Too distant to see or hear the procedure at the head of the line, she guessed the orphans shook the Barone's hand or maybe kissed it as one would a bishop.

Closer to the front, she finally heard Diggin Perouz prompt the Van sister, "Say thank you to the Father of the Orphans."

Mannig's turn came quickly after that. She curtsied, as in concluding a dance. "Thank you. Oops! Father of the Orphans," she said, and passed on.

Barone Mardiros touched her shoulder. "Don't you like candy?"

Candy?

She looked at him, bewildered. The word was not part of her vocabulary. Yet its taste lingered in her memory. He put three mini-marble-size balls in her palm and sent her on.

She kept her fingers locked, cuddling the candy until she entered her tent.

The sisters from Van were already sucking theirs, purring, their eyelids half-shut.

Mannig relaxed her fingers. Her gaze froze at the pearlescent yellow, pink and green orbs. *Sweet and sour?* She remembered being bribed with similar sweets ... to scratch the khatoon's feet. No. That can't be. Even if that were the case, there were many girls ahead of her who could fill that obligation.

Upon deeper reflection, they reminded her of her own father, on a train ride from Adapazar to Constantinople to visit her cousins. She had been scampering between the isles, among the passengers, chasing her brother, being chased by her little sister, squealing, giggling, when Mama had forced her to sit. She complied when Baba brought out a paper bag from his valise and placed several pieces of the sweet and sour candy balls in her palm. They emitted rainbow sparks of yellow, pink and green—exactly like the candy in the tent.

Who really gave these to me?

She dashed outside.

A beam from the lantern shone on his face, the Barone. He was still standing there, the bag of candy in his hand.

24—Not All Good Deeds
Meet All Needs

Melodic echoes and rhythmic thumps from the camp diverted Mardiros's attention as he dipped his pen into the inkwell. *I can finish my report later.* He blotted the last paragraph and lifted the entry flap of his tent. The glimpse from the sidelines of the city of white canvas enticed him to put on his boots and step out.

A long serpentine line of orphans, without a beginning or end, swayed in-and-out of his sight. Children sang and clapped with a pulsating tune; others danced and bobbed between the tent cables. Small fingers linked each child to the next, all melding together in a circle dance. Their steps followed a predictable pattern set by a leader, peek-a-booing into view. The ensemble replicated her moves and if a dancer modified a step—clumsily or independently—the rest resisted the change until uniformity ensued.

The lead dancer waved a tattered floral handkerchief. Taking two steps forward and one step back, short and fast first then long and slow, she undulated toward the inner circle, the chain of dancers in step with her. She bowed her head and, arching her neck heavenward, flaunted a flirtatious glance behind her. Retracting her steps backward to the outer circle, she smiled at the dancers in tow.

The girls' zest and the gleeful tempo overwhelmed Mardiros. He marveled at the mutual yet elusive charm of teamwork. Every dancer blended with her neighbors. He moved forward for an uncompromised view and enjoyed the triune of rhythmic movement, sweet young voices, and his cigarette. He recognized some melodies and wished he could contribute, perhaps accompanying them with his flute. *I'll pack it on my next ride from Baghdad.*

The orphans plunged into an unfamiliar folk song. He suspected the forceful beat and the weighty guttural lyrics represented the style of mountain people. A song of Van? Only a native of the eastern region of Anatolia could improvise in the traditional manner. He was vastly relieved. Someone from there had survived the carnage, after all.

While lighting another cigarette, he spotted a child outside the swaying dancers, sitting on the ground, hugging her knees. She peeked at the circling girls, lowered her dewy eyes to her feet, then looked again at the frolicking group before looking back down at her shoes.

Why isn't she dancing?

"Mannig!" he heard a girl from the circle call. "Come ye and dance with us."

The little girl shook her head while casting her glistening eyes back down to her feet. With the hem of her khaki skirt, she dusted a speck off the toe of her black leather shoes, and then slid her finger atop the strap to the button before she cupped the stumpy flat heel.

Happiness is new shoes. He could foresee much more joy after she slipped on a new dress made out of the colorful bolts of cloth piled up in Diggin Perouz's tent.

Her stance prompted him to approach her. "What kind of a dance is this?"

Upon seeing him, she rose slinkily to her feet—unlike an energetic youngster—and curtsied. "The dance of Van, Father of the Orphans."

"You don't have to call me 'Father,' " he said, "or stand up. We are not in a classroom now." He gestured to her to go back to her sitting position. "Are you from Van?"

The girl pointed to the lead dancers in the circle. "They are—the Vanetsi sisters. I am from Adapazar."

"Adapazar—a nice town. When I was in Robert's College, one day I traveled to …" He stopped mid-sentence, wondering if he was repeating himself. *Who was I speaking with about the town near Boleess?* Someone from Adapazar, and recently. Maybe in Singapore. Which society lady?

He eyed the little girl. "Why aren't you dancing?"

She raised her shoulders, feigning indifference.

Her resignation reeked of sadness. He scooted down, crouching beside her, looking at the dancers' feet. "Those are complicated steps, aren't they?"

"I can do them," she mumbled wiping a shoe with her sleeve.

"But you don't want to dance?"

"I can't," she whispered.

He leaned toward her. "You confuse me, young lady. You say you can do the steps, and then you say you can't. Now which one is it?"

A shadow crept over her face. She hung her head between her knees.

Puffing on his cigarette, he glanced at her. *She loves her shoes.*

One of the lead dancers broke her link in the circle and, hopping into a two-step gait, sing-songed, "Mannig, Mannig. Why art thou denying thyself the fun of dancing?"

Amused by her regionalized vernacular, Mardiros listened in. He'd heard about the archaic use of pronouns by the people of Van, but had never known anyone who spoke with this peculiar accent.

Focused on her dialect, he remained oblivious to Mannig's demeanor, when suddenly the Vanetsi came down to her knees. "Why art thou crying, Mannig-*jahn?*" she said, wiping the girl's tears with her sleeve.

Mannig spluttered a troubled sound, squeezing her knees close to her chest.

"Thou wert so happy and excited this morning when I showeth thee this dance," the Vanetsi said. "Thou learned the intricate steps fast and wanted to go on and on. Thou continued even when we stopped. Where hast thou hid thy liveliness and passion? Might ye not like to dance anymore?"

"Vanouhi, I like to dance," Mannig sniffled between words. "I want to dance. I know the steps. I am eager. Everything is the same."

"Why art thou not dancing, then?"

Mannig coughed tear-filled words. "The shoes hurt my feet."

Mardiros held his breath—ashamed of his lack of awareness. How callous to have misinterpreted the little girl's agony as pleasure in owning a new pair of shoes! She had stared at them all evening, grunted while rising to pay her respects then crouching again with relief. He had not noticed any of the signs.

Mannig's tears trickled down, her eyes guarding the shoes.

How could her pain escape me? Had he been by himself, he would have bombarded himself with profanities and vociferously reprimanded himself for focusing on his own self-aggrandizing image. How dare he project his own thoughts, feelings, and behavior onto this child?

"Let me remove them for thee." Vanouhi reached to pull the shoes off.

"Nooooooooo!" Mannig screamed, tucking her feet further under her seat. "They're mine. I want them. I will never take them off."

Mardiros's heart ached. How dense of him to believe the children accepted his generosity with complete contentment. This suffering child had refused to show ingratitude to the Father of the Orphans and tolerated discomfort for the sake of her heart's desire. She preferred to endure pain in order to own a pair of shoes.

"They are thine and thou may keep them, forever," Vanouhi said. "But let me take them off for thee, now." She cupped Mannig's face in her palms and cajoled with looks and voice. She unbuttoned the strap and, bit by bit, wiggled the shoe off.

A swollen foot, splattered with ruptured blisters, hung at the end of Mannig's leg.

Dumbfounded, Mardiros stared, his eyeballs nearly bursting from his head. "*Amahn, Amahn!*" His gasp and Vanouhi's coincided.

"Thy foot hath forgotten how to be caged," Vanouhi said, dismissing the painful sight.

That the children lived without footwear was not one of Mardiros's concerns. Barefoot, they had rambled in deserts, alleys or mud-paths, for three, four, or many more years. Naturally, their feet would retaliate when disciplined by brand-new shoes. He cringed as if someone had sprinkled salt onto his wounded soul.

"It shan't be long," Vanouhi said, while attentively relieving Mannig's other foot from its shoe. "The twain shall become accustomed to each other very soon—thy feet as well as thy shoes. Ye shalt wear them again and ye shalt dance in them every day."

Mannig released an adult-like sigh of relief.

Mardiros pulled a starched monogrammed handkerchief from his pocket and handed it to Vanouhi. "Wrap her foot with this while I get bandages from the infirmary."

"Thank ye, Father of the Orphans." Vanouhi rejected the hanky. "Mannig-*Jahn* need not tread on her feet. Mine sister and I wilt carry her to bed." She stood up, facing the circle of dancers and, at the top of her voice, yelled, "Takouhi! I need thy help."

Her sister broke her link in the circle and dashed toward Vanouhi. She flinched at the sight of Mannig's feet but, without comment, linked arms with her sister, devising a seat with interlocking limbs. The two urged Mannig to scoot her buttocks onto the portable seat.

Mardiros lifted Mannig up and onto the girls' arms. She was as light as a scarf and compliant, the shoes cuddled to her chest.

"I shall wash thy feet," Vanouhi said, moving in step with Takouhi.

"I shall salve them for thee," Takouhi chimed in staccato, matching her sister's stride. In everything, they mirrored each other, and every time, one echoed the sentiments of the other.

"Tomorrow, thou shalt not walk," Vanouhi said.

"Neither shalt thou work," Takouhi completed the plan, doting over Mannig.

Mardiros's gaze followed the departing threesome—Mannig, seated on a pedestal formed of human limbs, holding her head high and bobbing taller than anyone. Her legs dangled freely as she wrapped her left arm around Vanouhi's neck and clutched her shoes with the other. They moved away from him, beyond the dancers and across the cables, until the female make-shift pyramid veered behind a row of tents.

He hoped the pampering she received would lessen her pain. He despaired at his inability to sooth the blisters caused by his generosity. His shoulders slumped, and his thoughts shriveled.

Mannig moved out of his sight, but her blisters remained engraved in his vision. He despised himself for being so deeply engrossed in his own good deeds. Why else had he projected gratitude into the feelings, thoughts, and behavior of that child? Those shoes fell far short of the manna from heaven he had presumed. He had witnessed the suffering of one child but suspected there were many more. His arrogance ripped at his heart. Not all good deeds meet all needs.

Empathizing with the pain he caused Mannig, he kicked off his boots as soon as he entered his tent. He lit the lantern, pulled off his socks, and checked his feet. No blisters. But the girl's traumatic experience had gotten under his skin. He shuddered. The sting in his brain surpassed the chill of his loneliness. The silence of his solitude compromised the quietness of the tent city at night. He lit a cigarette. Paced the floor. Smoked puff by puff and paced inch by inch ...

Suddenly he stared at the entry flap of his shelter.

He was not alone, after all.

His shadow, large and distinct, flickered at him.

Am I really the Father of the Orphans, or just the shadow of one? An honest assessment emerged, drowning in the pits of his beliefs. There wouldn't be a remedy until his silhouette and self became one.

He flipped the pages of his dossier to a blank sheet. He sat at his table, dipped his pen into the inkwell and, with the beautifully trained penmanship of an engineer, wrote at the top:

Urgent Needs at the Orphanage in Ba'qubah.

Below the title, he marked a vertical line and titled the left column, 'Achievable,' the second, 'Elusive.'

Without further thought, he wrote in the 'Achievable' column: "400 pairs of socks" They'd pad and protect the children's feet in new shoes, he assumed. And keep their tiny feet warm, before the onslaught of chilly evenings of autumn.

Pen in hand, he placed his wrist in the adjacent column, labeled "Elusive" ...

No words flowed through the ink of his pen. He scanned the walls of the tent ... stared at the lantern ... closed his eyes. He had no idea.

What were the children's heartfelt needs?

25—Childlike

Mardiros corked the inkwell and closed his ledger.

If he included all the orphans' needs, he would produce a tome. Notebooks and pencils topped his list, but permanent items such as chalkboards remained off the chart. The school in Basra provided everything. But he needed to return to Baghdad for these basic needs immediately.

He packed his smelly shirts and socks to prepare for an early start home. He craved a real cleansing at the bathhouse. A week's accumulation of dried sweat had beaded his armpit hair. He refused to speculate the condition of the growth on his back. Girlish squealing and giggles wafting from the riverbank tempted him to bathe as they did, but he lacked the courage to immerse himself in the cold river. He had emphatically forbidden any orphan to serve him by heating water in a caldron and lugging it to his tent. The alternative was what he assumed Diggin Perouz did—having to resort to wiping himself with a soaked towel, dripping the cold water down his torso and legs and messing the tent floor. Unaccustomed to cleaning up after himself, he hoped no one discovered the puddle until after his departure.

The first place I go in Baghdad will be the bathhouse. Then ask Ya'qoub, the Kouyoumdjian household valet, how to manage in the primitive surroundings of the orphanage.

"Barone Mardiros?" Diggin Perouz called outside his tent. "May I speak with you?"

"One moment." He grabbed his burnoose, wrapped it around himself, and lifted the entry flap to face her. "Is there a problem?"

"No, on the contrary," she said. "The orphans want to make a presentation on your last night with us."

"But I'll be back before they realize I've gone."

"I know," she whispered. "But the children don't count on their

185

tomorrows. Their hopes and expectations evaporated in the heat of the desert along with their loved ones. They've learned to live life one day at a time. They want to show their appreciation to you tonight."

A lump blocked his speech as he suppressed his sorrow. Sadness was easier felt than spoken. "Give me a moment," he said, and pulled up his trousers. He stepped out, slipping on his khaki jacket and following her to the clearing beside the kitchen tent.

He greeted Barone Eghishe, the teacher, seated on a bench along with the few older students who assisted with his daily instructions.

They jumped to their feet in deference to authority and pointed to one of the two folding chairs reserved for them.

"No, no!" Mardiros gestured to them to relax and helped Diggin Perouz to her seat.

"Do you hear giggling?" Diggin Perouz giggled herself. "They are hiding behind the kitchen tent."

"This is all their idea," Barone Eghishe cupped his mouth and leaned toward Mardiros. "The orphans rearranged the benches to make it look like a stage. I am very anxious to see their performance myself."

A whistle startled Mardiros.

A line of the older girls flanking the kitchen tent approached him, held up their tattered skirts, bashfully curtsied, and then hopped to the periphery of the makeshift stage. They formed a human arc as a backdrop. Joy emanated from their sparkling eyes; radiant faces reflected their exuberance.

Mardiros marveled at their high spirits. Who would guess they had suffered so much?

"Next time, they will be wearing their new uniforms," Diggin Perouz whispered, while a band of small girls clad in rags filled the stage barely two yards from the spectators' seats. "I see something interesting," she continued. "The lead girls in the back row are the Van sisters, and the ones in the front are their tent mates. They must be the inspiration behind this production."

A shaky soprano in the back row led the entertainers into a song. Some voices rose with confidence, others faded with apprehension. They stood in place—stiff as mummies—wide eyes fixed on Mardiros, lips barely moving and bolstering their courage to sing *Mare Hyereneek*, the Armenian National anthem.

Mardiros' eyes beaded with tears. He couldn't remember the last time he had heard the Fatherland melody or reflected on its lyrics. The orphanage emerged as a single kaleidoscopic humanity bound with invisible strings he failed to define. He wondered about his own Armenianness. Who could have foretold, even a year ago, that he would be sitting practically in the middle of the desert and appreciating the ethnic culture of his ancestors? The Kouyoumdjians had long accustomed themselves to the European lifestyle of the wealthy Middle Easterners. They valued German opera, played Chopin and Debussy on musical instruments, and decorated their homes with Renaissance art. They preferred to speak English or French when hobnobbing with the highbrow intelligentsia.

Mardiros easily recalled the evolution of his involvement with the orphans. Scene after scene replayed in his mind—his initial encounter with the philanthropic delegation of AGBU at an afternoon tea party, the day he had impulsively volunteered, his first contact with an Armenian starveling and consequent registering of strange family names from remote enclaves of Asia Minor. Momentous or trivial, incidents flowed in and out of his stream of consciousness. He had discovered his identity wrapped up in a folding chair in the open air of Ba'qubah, and he knew his life would be empty without the orphans.

He drifted off for a time before he realized the singers were now dancing. They jigged in one spot, then another; bopped around, then twirled, intertwining their hands and clapping. Their faces radiated ecstasy, their footsteps, exuberance. Their joyfulness lifted him up. What luck to experience this!

His heart throbbed as it never had at the Agoomp, the Armenian Club in Singapore. There, surrounded by beautiful society ladies gowned in the latest European finery, the entertainment included opera singers and professional can-can dancers. There, he had cajoled the wealthy patrons to reach into their pockets for large contributions. In Ba'qubah, his heart needed nothing in return. His head was stimulated by life in Singapore, but here at the orphanage, it was his heart that was fulfilled.

The orphans linked their pinky fingers and, while stomping in a circle dance, burst into a robust song. Free of inhibitions, children big and small, on stage and backstage, hopped and swayed, seemingly more for themselves than to please the Father of the Orphans.

After several rounds of the dance, Diggin Perouz stood up and coaxed the adult spectators to join in. "The steps are simple. Everyone can do them. Come, let's share in the children's enjoyment." She clasped Mardiros' hand in her left and Barone Eghishe's in her right and pulled them into the circle, cutting into the pinky-to-pinky links of the dancers.

Unaccustomed to Armenian traditional folk dances, Mardiros was less than confident. He kept his sight glued to the feet of his partners to copy their rhythm, to follow their pace, but alas! He remained embarrassingly clumsy. If his family saw him doing a circle dance they would never again call him 'maestro' or 'debonair' as they had when he waltzed or fox-trotted with the society ladies. Even doing the tango in Singapore for the first time had soon become second nature. Folk dancing? That required a knack he lacked.

At first, he fell behind the beat and bungled the foot patterns. When he managed to catch up, the circle enlarged its perimeter to link in new dancers. Two of them found his little fingers. Vanouhi, the dance teacher from Van, held his left hand. He smiled and squirmed. He depended on her lead yet felt intimidated by her expertise. The face of the petite girl to his right remained hidden behind thick chestnut hair. He felt her vigor streaming from her little finger to his, helping him to master the pre-patterned movements. Her vitality propelled him to go on and on, wishing the night would have no end.

"Mannig! Mannig!" a few dancers chanted, standing in place and clapping in rhythm. "Mannig! Do your Adapazar jig!"

Others echoed the call. "Yes! Do the Adapazar jig!"

Mardiros' left pinky lost its link, and his arm hung limp and awkward. Not knowing what to do, he slipped his unused hand into his pocket and stood motionless in the circle.

The little girl with the thick chestnut hair moved to the center of the circle, dancing to her own music—not in step or unison but twirling round in loops, jigging in place, then skipping in and out—a simple dance imbued with complex feeling. She hopped and bopped on bare feet, her movement portraying a life of past anguish and present joy.

Mardiros recognized her. The girl with the sore feet. They called her Mannig. *Did I hear Adapazar?* He kept his focus on her as best he could, while her twirling became faster and bouncier and the chanting of the orphans grew louder and faster.

In a flash, he remembered Mannig of Adapazar. The same little girl in Mosul who had tried to fool him into admitting her into the orphanage, even after the other officials had shooed her away. Why had they refused to register her? 'She is self-sufficient and not as needy as the others,' they explained. For reasons Mardiros himself couldn't explain, he had overridden the others' decision and registered her. He breathed in a sigh of relief. *I'm glad this waif is in Ba'qubah.*

Mannig danced as if she would never stop. Giggles and laughter accompanied her twirls. Finally dizzy, she fell. Everyone gasped. But she got up and continued to twirl, peppier than before. Her energy was boundless.

Concerned, Mardiros reached out and caught her arm. "Stop!"

"Why?" she chuckled. Freeing her arm, she twirled away.

Why? Mardiros fell silent. Why, indeed? No one should interfere with joy. The girl lived in her own world of unforgettable moments. She was one of a kind, and no one was going to deflate her grand image of herself. No one could know what memories and experiences ran like hot lava through her mind. She was building her own museum of extraordinary sights and sounds. Who was he to limit her treasures? And what for? Because she was dizzy? Here was a little girl at last enjoying life.

Who was he to interfere?

Normally, his life consisted of one task after another, leaving him constantly preoccupied with his own agenda. Tonight, he had no obligations—no errands to complete, no reports to write.

Under the azure sky of the Ba'qubah night, he came face to face with life. Joy had invited him in, and he had almost let it pass by.

The children's vitality flowed into him. His spirit soared free and fierce. He held Vanouhi's arm, linked his little finger with hers, and sidled in with the dancers. He linked his other pinky with Mannig's. He liked being squeezed between Mannig and Vanouhi. He concentrated on his partners' feet, trying to follow their lead—two steps, right; one step, left. The repetitiveness helped his confidence. He ignored his body's need for rest but went on and on—just like Mannig.

Mannig looked at him and then at his reluctant feet. Scanning the dancers' faces and their confident movements, she smiled and squeezed his pinky in hers. "You are almost good."

26—The Ladder of Joy

On December 31, 1920, a deep cloudless sky accompanied near-freezing weather, but Mannig's canvas tent kept the warmth from escaping.

She was huddled with her beloved tent mates around a brazier, her cheeks rosy with the heat from the burning coals. The company and conversation of her friends lifted her spirits. A quilt on her shoulders, and a bowl in her hands, she sipped the three-grain soup and reveled in the novel sensation of chewing chunks of meat.

"An extraordinary meal for a special day," Vanouhi said, indicating how much the meat enhanced the soup.

"A treat to end the Old Year and welcome New Year's Day," Takouhi added.

Mannig loved her tent mates—all seven of them, the two sisters from Van topping her list. They were her dancing mentors, and the seamstresses who were designing her uniform with special stitches. The word 'design' was perhaps an exaggeration, but to Mannig, the two panels of navy colored cloth dangling off her bony shoulders transcended style. While the sisters measured her arms to fit the sleeves, they argued about the length of the hem.

Mannig impetuously kissed each one of them on their cheeks.

"Long sleeves keepeth thy arms warm," Vanouhi said, stitching a square cloth into the armhole.

"It addeth flair to thy dancing," Takouhi added.

Her bare skin tingled at the touch of the bristly wool fiber. The garment was not unlike the yellow organdy dress in Adapazar without the silk chemise. *Chemise!* Mannig snickered at the futility of visualizing her genteel lifestyle of old. She wore her new dress with love, scratchy as it was. She knew it wouldn't ever wear out, even though it wore out her skin. But whenever she twirled, whirled and swayed at the camp, in her mind's eye, she was dancing in her Adapazar dress. She put one foot forward, lifted the hem of her rectangular dress and curtsied to the applause coming not from her parents but from the sisters from Van.

Mannig often brushed kisses on their cheeks. She wanted to love her sister, Adrine, also, but was rebuffed. Mannig assumed the rejection was not personal, but Adrine's way to protect herself from horrible memories of her rape. Adrine would touch Mannig, but she never allowed anyone to touch her in return. Mannig's skin tingled and she felt comforted when her sister ruffled her hair before she braided it for the night. She likened her sister's soft touch to Mama's. Adrine's nearness helped sooth her when the sky thundered or when dinner occasionally consisted of just sweetened tea and bread. She relished sharing the tent with family.

She relentlessly dipped into her sister's reservoir of knowledge about anything and everything. As much as she loved dancing, she loved knowledge more. After the two slipped under their quilts for the night, they whispered about facts and figures instead of giggling as most children did. She revered her sister's scholarship. When Mr. Eghishe observed Mannig's aptitude and declared, "You can advance to an upper class," Mannig wanted to smother Adrine with kisses and shout, *I owe my knowledge to my smart sister.* But Adrine recoiled from being hugged, although she smiled at Mannig's words, "I owe my progress to our bedtime talks."

Mannig proudly entered the brown bannered tent of the advanced students. She paid close attention to the history lesson until her attention was diverted. Recitations wafted in from the green bannered tent where the beginners were memorizing their multiplication tables. She mouthed the words *chors-ankam-ootu* before her former classmates' childish voices repeated, four-times-eight ....

An hour later, she became fascinated by the geography lesson about Iraq, Iran and Syria. "These are the new names of our ancient lands," Mr. Eghishe explained. "They butchered our ancient lands to appease the political demands of the victorious British and French ...."

Again Mannig's focus shifted to the wafting childish voices, chiming, "*Aip-pen-kim-ta,*" the Armenian alphabet. She missed her peers—the giggling, the whispering and delighting in uncomplicated matters. More so because four of her tent mates, all older than she, were segregated in the beginners' class.

"They, too, will advance soon," Adrine promised. "You ought to become their mentor and tutor them."

Mannig cherished her sister's confidence in her and whatever Adrine said, happened. At seventeen—a senior adult at the camp—Adrine coordinated their tent routine with few words, concise directions and authority.

Adrine's restlessness on this very cold night piqued Mannig's curiosity. More talkative than usual, she was jabbering while performing a routine chore. "Here is more coal," she said, replenishing the brazier several times. "We will burn the lamp deep into the night." She giggled as she refilled the kerosene lamp, a task she normally assigned one of the tent mates in the mornings. She always insisted that they study by daylight to save fuel. Her excessive blinking and frequent gazing at the tent entry flap made Mannig suspect that something was imminent.

A sudden thump outside hushed all sounds in the tent except the crackling of coals. While everyone held their breaths, Adrine dashed to the entryway. She put a finger to her pouting lips and shrugged her shoulders to feign ignorance. She stared into Mannig's petrified countenance, then at each girl.

Adrine's impish look, exaggerated body movements and high pitched voice foretold a treat.

"What's that?" Adrine squealed, lifting the entry flap then dropping it shut. She tiptoed to the edge of the flap. Hesitantly, she peeked through the gap and singsonged, "Who is out there?"

The sisters from Van dashed to her side.

"Go away!" Vanouhi shouted unconvincingly.

"Don't bother us!" Takouhi echoed.

Adrine held them at bay and opened the entry wide. "Who comes visiting us at midnight on New Year's Eve?"

The sisters stared into the outside darkness. "Someone has cometh and gone," Vanouhi said.

"He left his mark with a thump," Takouhi added.

"Aha!" Adrine exclaimed. She went outside then came back in clutching a bag of oranges. She went from girl to girl, handing one to each, keeping the last one for herself.

"They fell from the sky," Vanouhi said, rubbing her hands all over the piece of fruit.

"From the basket of Gaghant-Baba," Takouhi named the gift-giving Patron of the New Year.

"Gaghant-Baba watches children all year long," Adrine said. "He gives gifts to the good children on New Year's Eve."

Dazzled by the glistening fruit in her palm, Mannig held the orange as if she had caught a star. She shook it near her ear, hearing only the whisper made by the tips of her fingers brushing against her hair. She whiffed its tanginess, rolled the cool skin against her cheek and, imitating Adrine, dug her fingernails to score the peel. A splattering zest sprayed into her eyes with a bitter sting. Nevertheless, like everyone else, she cast the peels into the brazier and was dizzied by the fragrance. Finally, she popped a wedge into her mouth and let it swirl between her teeth. Squishing it slowly, she relished the sweet juice showering her mouth. She popped in a second wedge.

A desperate cry, "Mine is bad!" focused all eyes on a little girl kneeling on her mattress. She held up the rotten wedges as tears rolled down her cheeks.

Mannig froze mid-bite. Silence blazed in the tent. The girl's tears rolled down in a deluge.

As pained as the girl, Mannig darted over to her to share one of her own plump, juicy wedges. A moment later another girl dashed over with a wedge of her own.

The remaining bites of Mannig's orange tasted the sweetest of them all.

27—Happiness is …

On New Year's Day Mannig settled into her usual routine. Like a horsewoman, she dashed to 'Turkey' to relieve herself. She squatted as a mourner might; then strutted away from the latrine like a queen. The frigid water she dabbed on her cheeks from the Tigris felt like a wet kiss. She slurped a cup of sweetened hot tea from the bubbling caldron by the kitchen tent. To increase her satisfaction, she took longer gnawing on a chunk of bread. Belly full, she still hungered, only now it was knowledge in Mr. Eghishe's class.

Ignoring her chattering classmates, she sat on the floor in the front row, a cushion for a seat. She pulled on the hem of her new uniform to cover her knees and, as usual, erased one of the pages of her notebook in preparation for the day's lesson. A shortage of supplies made Mannig memorize every word she wrote down. She would then erase the page completely to make room for Mr. Eghishe's latest lesson.

He was very informative. He uttered every word with gusto, often spraying his words at the pupils in the front row. On such occasions, Mannig tucked in her chin and shut her eyes. "Come Monday, it shall be January sixth," Mr. Eghishe began the lesson. "That day is called Epiphany, the holiest of days for Armenians." Because of a shortage of blackboard and chalk, he spelled out E-p-i-p-h-a-n-y and allowed time for the pupils to write it down. Using her knee as a desk, Mannig entered the new vocabulary word on the erased page of her notebook. Next to the word, *Epiphany*, she drew the 'equal' sign, anxious to jot down its meaning.

"On Epiphany, we celebrate Christmas," he continued. "The Bishop of Baghdad shall be here to enlighten us about the divine nature of Christ."

Mannig remembered Haji-doo, her grandmother, mention Christ, and consequently insisting the Dobajian children kneel beside her. *Will the bishop make me pray?*

"In AD 300, Armenia became the first nation to adopt Christianity as its state religion," Mr. Eghishe continued, over and above Mannig's wandering thoughts.

Will we pray on bended knee like Haji-doo?

"Christ empowered our kings to lead a great nation. The people's prayers have guided our warriors to defeat the fire-worshiping Persians, and ..."

What good did Haji-doo's prayers do?

"We have survived as Armenians for so many centuries because Christ protected us ..."

Why didn't Christ protect my family from the whips of the gendarmes?

"... neither a nation nor a king anymore," Mr. Eghishe continued. "Only Christ keeps our history, language, and faith intact." His voice was lost in the shadows of Mannig's grief for her lost family.

The taste of the orange given by the Patron Saint of the New Year soured in her memory. Too disheartened to continue, she flipped her notebook closed and let her mind wander for the rest of his lecture until she sensed her classmates standing up in deference to Diggin Perouz who had inconspicuously entered the tent-classroom.

"Diggin Perouz will continue now," Mr. Eghishe said, departing for his next lecture at the boys' tent. Unlike previous days, Mannig wasn't sad to see him go, even though she wondered as usual whether he taught the boys the same subjects or difficult lessons because they were smarter. *I'm certain Christ is the subject of all his lectures today.*

"We have much to do," Diggin Perouz began, gesturing to the pupils to sit down. "I want to add to what Mr. Eghishe has already told you ..."

Mannig's spirit sank into her roots. *Not more about Christ!*

"We must prepare for January 6th," Diggin Perouz said. "Important dignitaries are coming. When they visit your tent-classroom, you must all be present, in clean uniforms and with groomed hair. They will probably ask academic questions—about every subject that you have been studying with Mr. Eghishe and me."

Mannig agonized over her inattentiveness to Mr. Eghishe's lesson on religion—he may have called it *history* since he scrambled Armenia's history with Christianity. Might Vanouhi's notes explain the missing links in her understanding?

"I know you are all very studious girls," Diggin Perouz said. "Like gold in the mud, I am confident you will shine." She raised her voice with enthusiasm. "You could also impress the visitors culturally by organizing a show in their honor."

Mannig's ears perked up.

"You can sing patriotic songs," she continued. "Some of you can recite poetry and others can narrate ancient stories."

Enthralled, Mannig raised her hand and waved it. "Can we dance, too?"

Diggin Perouz smiled. "Actually, Mannig, I have something else in mind for you," she said, scrabbling through layers of her skirt until she retrieved a piece of paper from her pocket. "I have composed a message of gratitude. It expresses our thankfulness for everything the philanthropists have done for our camp. I want you to read it." She handed the paper to Mannig. "Can you do that?"

Although disappointed about the dancing, Mannig delighted in the assignment. *Diggin Perouz equates me to the taller and older girls in my class.*

"When you read about our appreciation to our guests," Diggin Perouz said, "I want you to address it to the head of the philanthropic delegation—Barone Mardiros. Do you remember him? The Father of the Orphans?"

Who could forget him? Mannig nodded.

Mannig was thrilled to have such an adult responsibility bestowed upon her. She practiced reading the message so many times she knew it by heart. It became her passion. It occupied every waking moment, becoming the central focus of her existence. She mouthed it on her way to 'Turkey' and later on while in bed, referring to the paper for accuracy. By January 6th, she could recite it backward and forward.

Like all the girls, Mannig took extra care with her appearance on January 6th. The freshly washed navy uniform clung neatly to her body and her soft, braided hair hung gracefully to her shoulders. She joined the long line of orphans applauding the arrival of Bishop Moushegh of Baghdad and the dignitaries who trailed in his wake.

She craned her neck, looking for Barone Mardiros. Was he tall enough to stand out amid the procession? She wanted a glimpse of him before showering him with gratitude.

The Bishop's miter swayed above the procession. Behind him, four balding heads bobbed above the columns of orphans.

Mannig stood on her toes and focused on the fifth man, flaunting a thick head of hair. *Is that the Barone?* She hopped up for a second glance and caught a glint of his hazel eyes. *Ah, yes! That was he.* Her anxiety decreased and she felt a surge of confidence. Above all, she wanted to make Diggin Perouz proud. She waited patiently to give the performance of her life.

Mannig was slated to appear at the finale of the show. She lined up with the group of performers on the makeshift stage in the kitchen area. Facing the dignitaries seated on the benches intimidated her.

The Bishop sat in the center with the miter in his lap, waiting. The dignitaries flanking him were also waiting. Diggin Perouz was at the end of the row.

Mannig scanned the audience for Barone Mardiros. He sat stage left. *I must remember his location when my turn comes.*

Mannig's temples throbbed, and beads of sweat dotted her forehead. She wiped her sleeve across her face just as the chorus lurched into song. Her dry throat kept her from singing with the chorus—she just mouthed the lyrics of the patriotic song. The audience's applause encouraged her. She glanced at the guests of honor again and caught Diggin Perouz staring at her. *I must please her.* From then on, Mannig heard her own voice amid the sopranos.

Adrine stood center stage and read two full pages about Armenia's early history. Vanouhi read a fable and Takouhi recited parts of an ancient ballad.

Following the enthusiastic applause, Mannig broke ranks with the others and stepped forward, only a yard from the audience. She turned sideways and faced Barone Mardiros. Clasping her hands behind her, she began: "Dear Father of the Orphanage." She smiled, vaguely aware of having said something unscripted. Instead of getting embarrassed and stammering through the rest of her speech, she felt overwhelmed with passion for the camp. Instead of reciting the message exactly as written, she concentrated on its meaning. She loved the ground where she stood, and this love gave her a huge surge of energy. Her heart and soul went into her expression of thankfulness for the orphanage. She sensed her place in the universe. *I am who I am*, she thought, *the one doing the right thing at the right time in the right way with the right spirit*. With vibrant face and mellow voice, she eloquently related her admiration for the benefactors. Her fervor was greeted by loud applause when she bowed at the end.

The Bishop rose to his feet, applauding; the dignitaries, too, gave her a standing ovation; and to Mannig's surprise, the other orphans clapped their hands red. She felt a strong sense of connectedness with everyone. She hugged them and received cuddling squeezes in return; the praise raised her spirits and the success excited her. She had agreed to recite the message in order to please the Diggin and impress Barone Mardiros. The adulation and praise from her camp mates was a wonderful surprise.

Immediately after the ceremony, Mannig felt a tug on her sleeve.

Diggin Perouz stood at her side. "Follow me," she said.

28—Where is America?

Diggin Perouz did not compliment Mannig on her performance. Although baffled at the silence, Mannig trailed her respectfully. *Thank goodness, she is walking normally, not like an angry person.* Perhaps she would not reprimand her for adlibbing the text.

The orphanage supervisor stopped by a large tent reserved for guests. Mannig was perplexed to be standing at the edge of the pavilion with its sky-piercing peak. Light streaming from its mosquito-screened windows raised her curiosity.

Casting a faint smile at Mannig, Diggin Perouz rapped at the entry flap. "May we enter?"

Barone Mardiros appeared, lifting the flap. "We've been waiting for you. Won't you come in?"

The day-like illumination of the interior dazzled Mannig. Accustomed to a single lantern in her tent that faintly lighted the path to her mattress, she was amazed by the brilliance that emanated from several lanterns hanging along the periphery. *I'm in a palace.* She looked sideways and then lowered her gaze to avoid the penetrating beams. She stepped in. The plush carpeting hugged her feet.

"Remove your sandals," Diggin Perouz murmured, removing her own. "Let's not muddy anything."

Enjoying the warm fuzz on her bare feet, Mannig wanted to comb her fingers through the fringes; she was reminded of her work in the Carding Cave. *I could separate the orange from the brown and the black.* Or was that at the Weavers' Web or perhaps the Teaser Gazebo? How Garina's labels for those stations at the Mosul khan had amused her! Garina ... the Sup had expelled her for having sex with Dikran. Good riddance! But she missed Dikran. How could she forget him?

"Wait here." Diggin Perouz's voice jolted Mannig back to the present. While she still relished the wondrous sensation on her feet, she watched how the orphanage supervisor's ankle-length striped skirt swayed as she approached the man seated in a chair. A silver cross on a long chain shimmered on his black robe. He looked familiar, but not the two gentlemen in brown suits and ties flanking him.

"You have managed to create an amazing orphanage," the man in black said, letting Diggin Perouz kiss his hand. She knelt at his feet. "I'm so grateful to have come from Baghdad to witness the accomplishments of your beautiful children. Beautiful children."

Aha! He is the Bishop—minus his brocade cape and miter.

He urged her to rise. "It was a very impressive program, Diggin Perouz."

"Their performance in your honor, Your Most Holiness, has also made them very happy," she said. After fixing the ruffled collar of her white blouse, she shook hands with the two gentlemen and again with Barone Mardiros.

The choreography of who sat where intrigued Mannig. The two gentlemen, one stockier than the other, deliberated back and forth before they occupied a divan across from the Bishop. In the meantime, Barone Mardiros pulled up a folding chair for himself. He straightened the creases of his khaki trousers, sat down and crossed his legs.

Mannig tensed. Her knees were locked, rooting her at the edge of the carpet, the knots of the fringe teasing her toes. *Why am I summoned to this scene?* Her eyes blazed when Barone Mardiros struck a match to light his cigarette. His wide forehead glistened in the flickering flame, and a plume of smoke veiled his elongated hazel eyes. His whole demeanor gave an impression of gentleness. *A handsome man.* She thought of him as a benefactor—someone who brought needed amenities to the orphanage—uniforms and shoes. Perhaps the oranges were his gift, too. A kind man. Might he even be the Patron Saint of the New Year?

She liked the way he looked at her. Quickly, she lowered her gaze, partly for the sake of decorum, partly from wonder. She snuck a glimpse at him again—he was still staring at her. She looked at the other gentlemen and disliked the way they scrutinized her.

Each ogled her, whispered to his partner and nodded. They squinted at her hair, snuck a glimpse at her waist, and focused on her feet on the carpet. Their inspection lingered too long for comfort.

Mannig clamped her jaw shut and felt her toes cramp and knees stiffen.

"Come here, my child," Bishop Moushegh said, extending his arm.

Diggin Perouz gestured that she should kiss his hand.

Reluctant but obedient, Mannig stepped forward. The small step she took toward him made her fearful; he intimidated her more as a man than he did as a bishop. She wished she could relax but she couldn't ignore everyone's scrutiny. *No matter what, I must not disappoint Diggin Perouz or Barone Mardiros.*

She closed her eyes, stepped forward, and reached out to kiss the hand.

The warmth of his nearness dizzied her. She craned her neck and squeezed her eyelids shut. She felt as if she were floundering until a hand raised her chin.

"Not *my* hand," Barone Mardiros was whispering. "Kiss the Bishop's."

Embarrassed, Mannig felt blood surge into her cheeks. *I wish a dust-devil would yank me out ... bury me in a desert fissure.* Disoriented, she let Barone Mardiros direct her toward the Bishop.

"God has watched over you and continues to do so even as we speak, my child," the Bishop said, extending the back of his hand to her.

Mannig dropped to her knees more in relief than out of respect for tradition. She kissed his hand and remained stooped, a pretence to shield herself from the curious adults. She focused on the paisley swirls of the floor covering.

"You may rise, my child," she heard the Bishop say.

"Mannig, come and sit by me," said Diggin Perouz.

"Maybe I should help her up." It was Barone Mardiros' voice.

Everyone inside this grand pavilion was a dignitary. *Why am I here at all?* Mannig obeyed the voices prompting her, wishing to escape anywhere, even where exits did not exist. She felt the Barone's hand on her shoulder guiding her toward Diggin Perouz. *Why is Diggin Perouz honoring me to share the divan with her?*

"Sit down, Mannig," Diggin Perouz said, tapping on the space beside her. "These gentlemen want to speak with you."

The Bishop spoke first. "We are grateful to our Lord Jesus Christ for saving you from the great massacre." He stood up and gestured with the silver cross on his neck chain for all to do the same. "Thank you, Lord. Thou hast answered our prayers of yesteryear and our prayers on this day. Our lives are the confirmation of thy great love for us. Amen." He sat down. The rest followed suit.

Mannig copied Diggin Perouz in everything, even making the sign of the cross.

"Mannig—that's your name, right?" the Bishop continued. "Mannig-*jahn*. Our Lord has spared your life for a purpose. He spared you from perishing in the wastelands of the Mesopotamian desert. Our hearts suffer for your precious family, whose bodies lie in the biggest Armenian cemetery on earth, but their souls serve our Lord in heaven. Mannig-*jahn*. Let us pray in particular for their spirits that hovered between the two rivers, fluting out east and west throughout the Turkish plateau."

Mannig swallowed a lump and dammed up her tears. In deference to the important people surrounding her, she refused to display her grief.

When all were seated again, Diggin Perouz touched Mannig's arm and said, "These two gentlemen are from America. Do you know where America is?"

Mannig knew nothing, of course. The place was as far away as her uncle's country, according to Adrine. "Is it in Romania?"

"No!" and "No!" filled the gaps between bouts of laughter.

"America is very far from Romania," the Bishop explained. "It is even beyond the Atlantic Ocean, my child. It is so far away that it is called The New World."

"Our guests from America want to say something very special to you," Diggin Perouz said.

Mannig lowered her chin and, from beneath her dark eyebrows, gazed at them. The two gestured, debating as to who ought to speak first.

"We want to take you to America with us," the stocky gentleman said.

"In a big ship across the great ocean," his partner continued.

"We liked your speech."

"You articulated your feelings very impressively," the partner agreed.

The stocky gentleman sat at the edge of the divan and with a penetrating gaze addressed Mannig: "On behalf of an Armenian family in Brooklyn, we have come to select an orphan for adoption."

"We believe you are the ideal child for them," his partner added.

"And we have chosen you."

"You will live in a very nice house."

"With a very nice family."

"In Brooklyn."

"Brooklyn is in America," the Bishop interrupted the gentlemen's dialogue.

The Bishop might as well have said Brooklyn was on the moon, the sun, or a star. It meant nothing to Mannig.

"In a year or two, you will marry a wonderful American," the stocky man said.

"An American-Armenian," the other nodded.

The men spoke slowly and deliberately so that Mannig heard everything they said; however, the words whirred around in her head, their meaning incomprehensible. Their penetrating stares oppressed her. She snuggled closer to Diggin Perouz and tucked her feet under the divan.

They described a glorious future with a good family in a grand house in a faraway place—even farther away than her uncle's country. But why so far from here? She loved the orphanage. Why leave a place where she was so happy? Or leave a classroom where she excelled? Or be separated from classmates she adored? And most of all, why bid adieu to the teachers who encouraged her? Why, indeed?

She pictured the people in Brooklyn caring for her as the Bedouin of the desert. They had rescued her from the scorching desert, nurtured her, and treated her as one of their own. She cared for them, too, and was grateful for everything, but she remained a stranger. She felt like an alien among the natives—an *odaar*—and never bonded with anyone. In America, she'd live in an Armenian home, but her heart would remain in Ba'qubah. If she went with these men, everything she loved would end.

"Is my sister going to the New World, too?" she asked.

"No. We can only take you with us," the stocky person said.

"You are the lucky girl," his associate said. "The luckiest person in the world."

"So what do you say?"

"We must depart Ba'qubah tomorrow."

"Can you pack your things for an early departure?" the stocky one said, standing up.

Mannig leaned back into the divan and folded her arms. A life without Adrine? Life without her sister would be empty.

Adrine was the one and only link to her family. She confirmed her identity. They shared childhood memories. She had opened the avenues to learning more about her perished parents. She cherished her time with her one and only surviving sister.

For a long time Mannig focused on the carpet, spread flat under her feet. She wiggled her toes in the fuzz. She closed her eyes and reminisced about all the warm moments spent with Adrine. Filled with love for her sister, she heard her heart beat faster. Overwhelmed, she murmured, "I cannot be separated from my sister. Adrine is the only family I have. I want to stay with her."

Barone Mardiros jumped up like a champion at the end of an athletic competition. "Nothing further needs to be said," he said with finality. "Come, Mannig. Let's go ... you may go." He strode toward the entry and held the flap open.

Diggin Perouz stood up to leave, too, but lingered on and on in the customary Armenian way. She clarified a few details with the two from America and then kissed the Bishop's hand. She gestured to Mannig to follow her out of the tent.

Barone Mardiros stepped out behind them and touched Mannig's shoulder. "You are a very special person," he said. "They were urging you to make a decision that is difficult even for adults to make. They should not have expected you to choose family over comfort in these times of hardship." He reached out and shook her hand. "You were outstanding—both in the Bishop's presence and," he cleared his throat, "your speech ... you aroused everyone's passion. I congratulate you on your performance." He winked at her, reached inside his trouser pocket, and handed her candy. "This is the last of the sweet and sour candy. I was touched deeply by your words about this place. But you really delighted me when you addressed me as the Father of the Orphanage and not the Father of the Orphans."

৵৽৻

What a strange experience! Mannig rushed back to her tent in a daze and was welcomed back to normalcy by familiar faces and doting voices.

The sisters from Van hovered over her.

"What wanteth the Bishop?"

"Why wert thou in the big tent so long?"

"How is the pavilion furnished?"

Mannig plopped on her mattress. "They wanted to take me to America."

"Really?" Vanoohi said in a high pitched voice that she immediately hushed to mid-range, surprised at her own exuberance.

"How lucky art thou," Takouhi whispered with sparkling eyes.

"When might ye be leaving us?" Vanouhi asked.

"Thou shalt be missed, dearly," Takouhi sighed.

"I'm not going anywhere," Mannig said nonchalantly. She glanced around to see if her own sister wished to question her, but Adrine lay on the mattress, eyes tightly shut and body bundled up in her quilt.

Mannig guessed that Adrine might not really be asleep.

"I'm staying right here," she said to the sisters. "At the orphanage. In Ba'qubah. The best place in the whole world ... in the whole New World or in ... this old one."

"Art thou crazy?" Vanoohi said. "Going to America and getting married is the ultimate fate for anyone. Every girl giveth her life for marriage."

"Remember Sona?" Takouhi said. "She married by correspondence. She knew not a wit about the man, his age, work, or his family—not even what country he liveth in. She grabbeth the proposal and left us. Most girls can't even dream about America. Thou, on the other hand, let the prize bird escapeth from thy hand!"

"Thou canst not mean to tell us thou actually refuseth such an offer," Vanouhi said.

Mannig nodded. "I don't want to leave the orphanage. I don't want to live somewhere else. I like our life. I'm as free as the wind. I sing and dance when I want to. I love our wonderful teachers—I learn and discover so much from them. Why leave?"

"And thou canst not do all that in America?" Vanouhi snickered.

"I don't know," Mannig whispered. "I'm happy here. I would miss this wonderful place, and I couldn't bear losing all of you. Even the thought of separation put a terrible ache in my heart. Why would I want to go anywhere else?"

Mannig wanted to hear immediate affirmation from her sister. There was no movement on the mattress—not a toss or a turn from Adrine, no shushing or yanking the quilt.

Mannig resignedly slipped inside her own quilt, next to her sister, still seeking approval for her decision. She relished the nearness and warmth of her sister's company on the same mattress. *Sleeping side by side is worth more than going to America.*

"Good night, Mannig-*Jahn*," Vanouhi whispered as she covered the brazier with a screen for the night, secured the exit flap, and blew out the lantern. "We love thee, too, Mannig. Thou maketh us happy, too."

The things that Mannig understood about the sisters from Van only made her more conscious about her own sister. They cared for her continuously, braided her hair, sewed her uniform, and taught her dances. Adrine, on the other hand, remained aloof—a sister in name, only.

Typically, Adrine remained silent much of the time, creating a gulf between her and the tent mates. She kept to herself, always apart from others. Her body language spoke of her separateness—she walked at a distance from the others and spoke only when they posed a direct question. She came in and went out without greetings or smiles. She studied her notes and slid beneath her quilt without a sound. Mannig seldom heard approvals or complaints from her sister.

At eighteen and older than her tent mates, Adrine had retained much of the formal education received prior to the deportation. Assigned to teach, she organized the orphans' routines with few missteps or complaints and rarely spoke outside of the classroom or showed emotion. Mannig wondered if her sister's peculiarity was the result of the awkward role assigned to her—to live in a tent housing mere students. Was she a teacher or a sister? Couldn't she be both? Either way, she was still an orphan among orphans. She seldom smiled and if she did, the smile had a stern edge. When Adrine holed herself up in an oasis of silence amid mountains of chattering tent mates, Mannig often suspected the memories of the rape must be haunting her sister.

From her side of the mattress, Mannig studied her sister's face in the flickering beams coming from the dying coals in the brazier. Adrine's long lashes brushed against her pale cheek bones and her shallow breathing barely fluttered her nostrils.

If Adrine had eavesdropped, would she rejoice over Mannig's decision to stay or, like the sisters from Van, think she had missed the opportunity of a lifetime? Except for a sliver of a forced edge to her sister's thin lips, Mannig failed to detect sorrow or joy on her face.

Adrine is asleep, after all. Mannig planned to retell the whole sequence with the bishop and the gentlemen from America in the morning.

She might have relaxed and fallen asleep but for one serious question needling her. Why did Barone Mardiros prefer being called the Father of the Orphanage instead of the Father of the Orphans? Only Adrine could clarify it for her—she understood hidden meanings, solved puzzles instantly, and understood why people acted in certain ways. She relied on her intellect, and she was endowed with a lively one.

Mannig hesitated confiding in the sisters from Van about Barone Mardiros. No one ranked as high as her own sister, despite her elusiveness. What luck that they shared a mattress! It would have been cozier if they shared the same quilt, but everyone knew it was a privilege to own a personal quilt.

Mannig rolled over, turning her back to her sister, and gazed at the brazier. Her body melded with the mattress, her eyelids grew heavy. She fell half asleep but remained conscious of her own breathing. Thoughts about absolutely nothing echoed through her brain, her chest, her limbs ... For how long? Ten seconds? A whole minute?

Then, gradually, she sensed Adrine's arm snaking inside her own quilt, scaling up her neck and gently resting on her shoulder. A warm and moist breath against the nape of her neck followed the firm cleaving onto her thin arm. With their bodies pressed together and arms intertwined, Mannig felt a warm gladness swell inside her.

Her longing to find a place in her sister's heart had been satisfied in the still of the night.

Adrine approves my decision.

She smiled.

29—To Basra

A crowd of orphans scampered with the tumbling thistles in the desert wind, scurrying toward the train tracks in the outskirts of Ba'qubah. Some lugged pillowcases filled with belongings, others carried large kerchiefs holding goods. The young ones latched onto their taller companions—speculating about the imminent train ride to Basra. They all had high hopes for the new orphanage in the big port city of southern Iraq. They longed for a taste of life beyond the familiar tent world. Might they locate lost relatives when joined with the others?

In spite of the excitement in the air, Mannig's spirit remained unmoved. She lingered among them, yet apart. Unlike her tent mates, she had taken her time packing her possessions. With no sense of urgency, she repeatedly folded and straightened her pretty floral dress, visualizing the way it clung to her body like skin.

Barone Mardiros had brought a handful of cotton dresses in different powdery shades of green. "These are for the younger girls," he declared. Although Mannig disliked being labeled, 'young,' she was proud to own the beautifully feminine garment. Not since Adapazar had anything so refined covered her body. The supple feel of the fabric revived images of twirling in her yellow organdy dress in their cozy parlor while Mama played the violin. She shed a tear for those happy days gone forever. Perhaps she would also find joy in this graceful outfit. Warm, colorful, and happy times awaited her—no more the drab days in shades of gray. The orphans were told to travel in their newest outfits, so she donned her navy uniform and tightened its belt to show off her waist. Then she rolled her pretty dress into her tent-cloth uniform before wrapping her ration of bread and dates and putting it all into one big bundle.

The square kerchief of belongings hanging off one shoulder and her school notebook tightly grasped in her hand, she tagged Adrine, who was assisting with the evacuation. Heavy-hearted, Mannig didn't wish to admit that their happy life at the Ba'qubah orphanage was over. She kept her eyes fixed on her sister who, with cupped hands, called out to the orphans to head out toward the train tracks or dashed about from tent to tent making sure everyone had departed.

The two joined Diggin Perouz and Barone Mardiros in escorting flocks of orphans toward the makeshift train station—smack in the middle of nowhere—far beyond the edge of the campsite and near the solitary and glistening train tracks that ran north and south.

"You are an amazing person," Diggin Perouz was saying to Barone Mardiros. "How did you persuade the conductor to make an unscheduled stop here just for us?"

"It was his idea," the Barone said, switching hands with his suitcase and valise. "Boarding so many orphans in the middle of the wasteland was more practical than trying to do it at the tiny station in town. You know Sebouh Effendi's orphans from Mosul are on this train already. The conductor warned me of overcrowded cars."

Overcrowded cars? Mannig held her breath.

The ominous phrase awakened terrible memories. Would this be a repetition of the dreadful train ride? Forced into a cattle car packed with shoulder-to-shoulder deportees? The stench? Humidity? Death from suffocation?

"If Sebouh Effendi gets off in Baghdad, as I am planning to do," Diggin Perouz continued, "there will be two fewer passengers to Basra."

"No, no," Barone Mardiros said. "We need him in Basra. We need you, too, of course. But it is understandable that Dr. Papazian wants you to return home."

"My husband has been anxious over my lengthy absence," she said. "I think he feels I have neglected him too long. I will continue with our special Relief work from Baghdad, of course, and if there is really a great need in Basra, I will join you sometime later."

"Sebouh Effendi and I will manage for a while, I'm sure," he said. "The Basrawis are assisting, of course. Do you realize this train will transport nearly 700 orphans? That's a lot of children. We will be packed in."

We will be packed in? Packed? Pack ...? Mannig held her breath again, but only for a minute. A screeching train whistle diverted her attention. While the orphans yelled in jubilation, she held her breath. Her pulse quickened with the shrieking train sounds; sweat rolled down her spine. The cacophony overwhelmed her. She clung to her sister's skirt and hid behind her, attempting to block out ghastly memories of overcrowded cars. *The train will be packed …*

A flashback hurled Mannig into the onset of the deportation. Sirarpi, her beautiful little sister, and she, separated from the rest of her family, were hurled into a cattle car packed with deportees. Crammed full of bodies. Compressed for breath. Crowded to suffocation. Mannig had slithered, clawed the car floor, crawled between the people's feet and stuck her nose into a hole in the wall of the car to breathe the fresh air of life.

Could I get smothered to death like Sirarpi?

Covering her ears and saying a prayer, she blocked the resurgence of the dreadful past.

The smell of black smoke swirling around the approaching engine startled her. Her bundle slipped from her shoulder and plopped onto the soil. The hissing steam raised a riot of dust and gave her the jitters, causing her to let go of her notebook. It, too, fell to the ground.

The onrush of orphans flooded the gates of the cars.

I won't board this train.

Mannig's arms swept around and clung onto her sister's waistband. Panicked, her fingernails fiercely dug into her sister's legs. She rooted herself into the ground, resisting movement toward the train.

"Adrine-*jahn*," Diggin Perouz called from the open window of the passenger car. "What are you waiting for? Hurry and climb up!"

"I can't," Adrine called back, trying to free herself from Mannig's grip. "What is the matter with you?" she yelled at Mannig. "Let me go! Are you crazy? The train will go without us."

Mannig shook and shuddered, digging her heels into the ground and refusing to be dragged a centimeter to the left or to the right.

Her staccato screams halted Adrine's advance. "What is scaring you?"

Mannig opened her mouth to explain, but her throat dried up. Panic had put her in a daze, and the surrounding noises diminished like echoes inside a clay barrel. Fear boomed in her heart. She felt suspended in a nightmarish silence.

Then a voice stirred her. "Everything will be all right."

Eyes still closed, she wanted to hear the same voice again and again.

"There is nothing to fear," the voice continued. "Give me your hand, and let us walk together."

His words restored her breathing; his tone, a normalcy to her pulse.

Those words were meant for her; every phrase, directed at her; the tone, purely personal. She understood the sentences—all were tailored for her. Each pause filled with hope and the syllables accented with the flavor of love suggested all was well.

Tears stung behind her lids, and Mannig opened her eyes.

Hands stretched out to her, and Barone Mardiros stood at her side like an angel, looking at her with his dewy hazel eyes.

He leaned forward, holding her left shoulder, then the right. All at once, he gazed at her eyes, fixed on her face. He didn't sneer as if she were an impudent girl, nor did he look away in indifference. They stared at each other for a long moment—melting down all of Mannig's fear in the restless atmosphere of boarding the train.

She surrendered to him.

Reaching for his hand, she glued hers in his. Without holding back, she followed him.

Suddenly he stopped and looked back. "Your bundle, Mannig," he said, and dashed back to pick it up, dragging her along.

He climbed into the nearest car, fully packed with over-excited orphans. Some stacked belongings on racks above; others squeezed them under the wooden seats. Barone Mardiros stopped just inside the door, unable to proceed down the aisle.

Over and above the heads, Diggin Perouz indicated a vacant seat beside her. He stepped forward, but Mannig's grip held him back. He looked at her once, up at Diggin Perouz, and then raised two fingers, meaning he needed two seats, to which Diggin Perouz shook her head.

Mannig dared to glance at him, thinking he must be the most selfless person alive. She believed he sacrificed much more than a seat for her. She felt his presence could alleviate any unforeseen discomfort. Partly by accident and partly on purpose, she let her arm brush against his khaki shirt. She felt blood rushing to her cheeks, forcing her to cast her eyes downward.

"Please, Barone Mardiros," Adrine called, tiptoeing through the bundles in the aisle. "Here's a seat for two—I can stand."

Mannig in tow, he moved ahead, tripping over bundles and losing his balance once or twice. "Thanks," he said to Adrine and, shaking his clasped hand in the air, he winked. "You and I can take turns standing—if Mannig ever releases me!"

"Your bag, Barone Mardiros!" Adrine said, pointing out the window. "I'll get it," and she dashed out.

Mannig's gaze followed her sister down the steps, out the car, and toward the solitary suitcase. She grabbed it and, in spite of its weight, lifted it. She hobbled on a few steps before balancing the weight. Finally, she dragged it the last few yards from the car.

The train whistled.

Mannig felt a lump of fear in her throat. Would her sister be left behind? But a flash of white ten yards from the tracks shifted her gaze. The pages of a notebook flipped in the desert wind. She checked her bundle in her lap. Her cherished notebook was not there. Her notebook contained all her precious notes from Mr. Eghishe's classes about geography and history. She read and re-read them like Haji-doo read her Bible. The notebook was her only possession of value. She couldn't survive without it.

Without further thought, freeing her hand, she jumped to her feet and pushed her way to the window. With both fists pounding on it, she yelled, "My book! Adrine! Get my book!"

30—Modern Man

A n hour from Ba'qubah, the orphans piled against Mannig's side of the train, eyeing the group of dignitaries at the Baghdad station.

Vanouhi jiggled the wood frame of the window and squeaked it down until it was stuck halfway open. The jabbering of the girls induced Mannig to peek. She craned her neck above and then below the wood-window-frame and settled after a quick glance. She preferred to concentrate on her immediate past and recall the thrill of sitting next to Barone Mardiros, feeling the warmth of his presence while the train wheels clanged. As soon as the train hissed to a stop, he had disembarked.

Her eyes followed him as he escorted Diggin Perouz off the train. Once on the platform, he clutched his khaki Topy in his armpit and shook hands with the gentlemen wearing top hats and black suits. Then he approached three elegantly dressed ladies in wide brimmed hats.

"That Barone Mardiros is a ladies' man," Vanouhi said. "How he hobnobbeth from lady to lady."

"... And chit-chatteth endearments!" Takouhi added.

"Maybe they commeth to the station to be flattered by him," Vanouhi snickered.

"One of those ladies is not a lady." Adrine's voice hushed everyone.

Her sister's words surprised Mannig. Having dropped her usual aloof composure, Adrine, too, kept her focus on the dignitaries. Might she becoming sociable? Mannig relished this change in her sister.

"Do you see the two children getting out of the motorcar?" Adrine asked, pointing to a boy of ten and a younger girl dashing to hug Diggin Perouz on the platform. "She is their mother."

"The girl's dress is beautiful!" Takouhi said. "I never owneth anything so fluffy and modern."

I have. Mannig thought of her yellow dress, but quickly refocused on the intense affection displayed by Diggin Perouz, kissing her children. Everyone in the train was silent —no whisper, no breath. All eyes gazed at this mother who could still love her own children, feel them and hear their longing voices.

"The woman with those children is their nursemaid," Adrine said, breaking the deep silence. "She attends to them day and night. She is like their second mother."

"Those children have two mothers?" Vanouhi gasped.

"That canst not be!" Takouhi wailed. "No one amongst us has even one mother."

A hush ensued as if everyone were grieving. Could it be that all her friends' mothers died in the death city of Deir Zor, like Mannig's mama? A lump formed in her throat. She remembered how her beautiful and talented mother had sacrificed so much to keep her family together. Alas, only Adrine and she had survived. *At least I have my sister.* Mannig grabbed Adrine's hand, sealing their togetherness.

Adrine squeezed it back.

"Those children will have a new sister for a while," she commented again. "Sebouh Effendi's little daughter will be living with Diggin Perouz while he goes with us to the Basra orphanage."

"Which mighteth Sebouh Effendi be?" Vanouhi asked.

"That very thin gentleman," said Adrine. "He got off the train with Barone Mardiros. Don't you remember how he supervised the Mosul orphanage? The Moslawi orphans on this train are his responsibility. I was surprised when he recognized me and asked me to assist him with his work in Basra. He told me that since his wife's death in childbirth, his daughter accompanies him everywhere. But in Basra, he needs to be free at the orphanage. Diggin Perouz, who is his sister-in-law, offered to take care of his little girl in Baghdad while he devotes his time to us. He is a very nice person."

"First time mine eyes see-eth such noble clothing." Takouhi said, pointing to a lady in a long dress made of brown lace, a straw hat spanning across her shoulders.

Like Mama's dress. She had donned a fashionable European garment and a hat when she had gone to the mayor of Adapazar to plead for her family. She had convinced the Turk that, as Protestants— like Turkey's German allies—her family should be exempted from deportation. The Mayor agreed to grant her and her children the request, but denied the same privilege to her husband, who was not a Protestant, but a follower of the Armenian Apostolic church. Naturally, her mama had refused such a separation, and the fate of the whole family of nine had been sealed.

Mannig tightened her grip on Adrine's hand, the one remaining link to her family.

"Those people reeketh of money," Vanouhi said.

"I am sure they are wealthy," Adrine replied. "By virtue of geography, Baghdadi Armenians escaped the massacre. Baghdad is very far from the Ottoman government seat in Constantinople. Spared deportation, many in these territories profited from the war. Some did business first with the Turkish military and later continued commerce with the British troops."

"I thinketh Barone Mardiros can tend to the business of the orphans," Takouhi said, "because his family is wealthy and he needeth not work for his living."

Hearing his name thrilled Mannig. She was glad Barone Mardiros was rich enough to devote his time to the orphans. *He'll be with us again.* She suppressed her smile. She'd prove herself as an outstanding student and coordinate students' shows for the dignitaries. *He'll notice me.*

She scanned the welcoming delegation on the platform. They were elegant, European, and eminent. She scowled. She wished the Barone would stop flirting on and on with the ladies. She wanted the train to keep going and yearned for him to climb back into the train. She even fancied him looking for his seat beside her. *Ah! Might his khaki trousers rub against my bare calves again?*

She shoved the girls off her bench in preparation for his return.

⤝⤞

Barone Mardiros had not reappeared on the train. Mannig concentrated on the clatter of the train wheels. It soothed the sting of his absence but not the wound in her heart. Was he still hobnobbing with the "ladies" on the platform or perhaps sitting next to one of those elegant ladies who might have boarded the car with him? How could she find him on this long train, transporting 600 orphans? Maybe he was hobnobbing with the orphans in another car. *Hobnob,*

hobnob ... she disliked the new word. She wasn't sure of its meaning, but she refused to ask anyone.

Her ears perked up only when the orphans praised the Barone*'s* dedication to the Armenian cause—his determination to see the orphans settled properly, his contributions to their welfare.

I know all that. But where is he?

The slightest jerk of the train induced her to swivel her head from side to side in search of him. She repressed her desire to ask about his whereabouts, lest her tone reveal her infatuation. It hurt to feel so much for him. Matters of the heart were kept secret in Armenian culture. Seeking a confidante to vent her pain would have been taboo.

Concealing her interest in the Barone in deference to decorum was proving difficult. Her cheeks burned in fear, lest her friends suspect her obsession. She feared someone might have noticed how attentive he had been. Above all, she worried that someone had noticed how she exchanged glances with him and allowed her knees and elbows to touch his throughout the train ride.

Mannig cast her focus inward and concentrated on her longing. Hope stirred her heart and desire made her cling to the belief that he would eventually return. She refused to give him up. She tucked his image into a deep spot in her head and wrapped her heart with fantasies.

In time, she relinquished the seat beside her to Adrine and reconciled herself to the security of her sister's proximity. She scooted closer and leaned her head on her sister's shoulder. *Vye! Vye!* Her thoughts echoed an older woman's gasp. She had almost lost her one and only family member when Adrine had stopped to pick up her notebook. As it was, Adrine had glanced at the flipping pages of Mannig's notebook, hesitated, but seeing the train jerk to a start, grabbed the upright bar. She flung Barone Mardiros' suitcase for an orphan to clutch. As the train gathered speed, Adrine barely was able to drag herself up onto the metal step.

Mannig sighed over losing this concrete souvenir from her stay at Ba'qubah. But her sister's presence was far more important. Besides, Adrine reminded her repeatedly that Basra promised great educational opportunities.

At sunset, the train stopped.

"Basra! Basra!" A surge of excited voices rose among the orphans.

Mannig perked up slightly, hoping to see Barone Mardiros among the few men in European suits assembled on the platform. His British-style khaki uniform ought to make him stand out among them. But he did not surface. She regretted being transported to Basra. She missed him. She longed to return to her life in Ba'qubah—dancing, reciting and entertaining ... and the Barone. She wondered if she'd ever perform again and if he'd ever again be seated in the front row with a glitter in his hazel eyes, watching the show.

"Why did we leave Ba'qubah, anyway?" she asked Adrine.

"This is a better place for us," her sister replied. "Sebouh Effendi worked very hard to improve our lives. They, he and Barone Mardiros, began their mission in Mosul ... and you remember the Mosul orphanage? Nothing but a collection site. In Ba'qubah, we got some education. In Basra, everything will be better."

Will it?

Sputtering British army trucks, as many as ten, spewed fumes along the platform until they lined up and stopped their motors. Arab drivers, heads wrapped in red-checkered kerchiefs, rushed to drop the tailgates of the flat-bedded trucks. "*Ya-allah! Ya-allah!* Get on the lorry," they urged the orphans. "Hurry. Everybody. Nightfall is at hand."

Mannig held onto Adrine's sleeve. The uniform felt as coarse as the rough ride the lorry promised. Holding her sack of belongings, she scurried to climb up. Traveling in a truck promised novelty, but being loaded onto a motorized vehicle jogged memories from the deportation. She feared becoming overwhelmed as on the train ride from Eski-sehir. She glanced at her sister, whose demeanor stayed calm and gaze reflected confidence. *Well, Adrine must know something.* After all, at eighteen—four years older than she—the remnants of her Adapazar education had proved to be a great asset to the local philanthropists. Most of their future plans for the orphans would require Adrine's assistance. If her sister feared nothing, then clinging to her would be the right thing to do. Mannig stayed close to her, wondering at the novelty of traveling standing up.

Together with thirty girls, Mannig squeezed herself between Adrine and the railing of the flat-bed truck. Soon she discovered that facing forward put her at a disadvantage. The similarly crammed truck leading the convoy spewed desert dust. Granules mixed with fine soil, and twigs twirled behind the wheels and pricked her face. She struggled to rotate her whole body until she faced the rear.

Squalls rising from the sides and back of her own lorry also assaulted her every time the vehicle hit ruts and potholes. Noticing how the others used rags to shield their eyes and heads, she reached for her bundle, but was too hampered by bodies to rummage around for a wrap. Instead, she ducked her head and closed her eyes. The rumble of the wheels and the erratic motion as they negotiated the rocky terrain added to her discomfort. Amid the occasional choking cough, she thought fleetingly of Barone Mardiros.

She wondered why he hadn't returned to his seat in her car. It saddened her to think that his wants and desires differed from hers. After all, he was an aristocrat. Modern. Rich. The automobile at the Baghdad station might have belonged to him. He could have traveled in it instead of enduring that stifling journey.

He'll be coming to Basra, she assured herself.

Wherever this lorry stops, he and his *Topy* will be there.

31—New Place, New Awareness

The Basra orphanage at Nahr-el-Omar housed 900 orphans in a British military barracks in the center of a boundless field of white Army tents—just like Ba'qubah. And like Ba'qubah, at sunrise Mannig ran to the latrine section dubbed "Turkey" to relieve herself and then splashed her face in the cold river water.

"Phew!" She exclaimed at the murky water. Is this supposed to be better than Ba'qubah?

"This is not the Tigris by itself," Vanouhi said, wiping a twig off Mannig's face, "but conjoineth with its twin sister, the Euphrates."

"They call it Shatt-el-Arab," Adrine said in her teacher's voice, "meaning the Arab River."

"It looketh like a vast sea even before it falleth into the Persian Gulf," Vanouhi said, scanning a body of water without shores.

Mannig gazed at the seafaring ships that were visible from the camp. *So what?* Such novelty was an interesting diversion, but it caused no thrill. Although surrounded by joyous tent mates, she remained lethargic, meandering aimlessly through her routine. Day after day, longing for her life in Ba'qubah hovered in the back of her thoughts, against the backdrop of conjuring up excuses for Barone Mardiros' absence.

"What a breakfast!" Vanouhi exclaimed. "Canst thou remember tasting cheese as velvety as we eateth this morning?"

"It's the Basra water," Takouhi said. "Even the bread tasteth divine."

"The best kind of wheat is grown in this southern region," Adrine interjected.

"And aplenty," Vanouhi said, dunking the crusty Arabic bread into her sweetened tea and sucking it unabashedly. The tent mates often squatted on palm-frond mats and chatted, sipping tea brewed in a metal tea pot in their own private tent.

Mannig mostly listened. Naïve desire for Barone Mardiros fed her loneliness, and all its pain left room for little else. She hid her feelings behind empty smiles, in memories and mostly in the back of her mind—she barely understood her own thoughts. She existed in a passive state, while remaining attentive to her tent mates, who fumed at criticisms, lost heart at rejections, smiled at praises, and reveled in successes. Through all this, Mannig remained aloof.

"Art we fortunate that Mr. Eghishe is our teacher," Vanouhi said, drooling over the fact that he graduated from the Varjabedanotz College of Van. "He is a master of history and geography."

"He is so good, one can even ignore his Van dialect," Adrine teased the sisters, who themselves were from Van. "His fluency is commendable."

"I can never remember everything he sayeth," Takouhi sighed.

"Mannig seems to," Vanouhi said. "She repeats his lessons without having to memorize them."

"Yes, yes," Takouhi said. "We may seeketh her help any time."

On previous occasions Mannig would have prized their assessment. Now she remained unmoved. Her performance in class earlier that day had been her dream come true—her dream of raising her hand to answer the teacher's question correctly … although the tent was her classroom, a hassock, her seat, and her knee, the desk. When called up to the slate blackboard—propped up on a makeshift easel, crudely constructed by the older boys at the camp—she was handed the chalk Mr. Eghishe kept in his pocket. She sketched and labeled the boundaries of Iraq on the blackboard. She zigzagged two feathery lines from the north to the south to show the sister rivers. Somewhere on the banks of the Tigris she marked a star for Baghdad.

"Excellent! Excellent!" Mr. Eghishe Vartanian said, taking the chalk and putting it in his pocket. "You didn't once peek at the big map against the tent for reference. I want all of you to memorize the shape of our new country the way Mannig has done. In the coming days, you must locate all the major cities of our Iraq and recite its history."

Everyone adored Mr. Eghishe—Mannig, too. Unimpressed by her own performance, she sat in the front row, gobbling up the words coming out of his mouth. Those sessions kept Mannig truly immersed in the moment. He pronounced some concepts with such vigor that his mouth watered and occasionally sprayed them—even so, she preferred to sit in the front. She remained focused, interested and involved until he departed to teach the boys' highest class in an adjoining tent. On such occasions, she wanted to be in the neighboring tent, but as it was, only her imagination followed him. The boys, of course, occupied separate quarters and separate classrooms, so Mannig often wondered if Mr. Eghishe taught them differently.

Yes, she excelled at reciting Iraq's history backward and forward—from the Babylonian Empires and the Islamic invasion to the current occupation by the Western countries. Her tent mates benefited greatly, but her heart dwelt elsewhere. Pulling her pink muslin-covered quilt over her shoulders, she rolled onto her cot.

"Imagine! We each owneth our own cot and only four of us liveth in a tent!" Vanouhi exclaimed, glancing around the room, well-lit after Takouhi had pumped the Primus lantern. "Who expecteth such luxury?"

A singing spree wafting from the boys' tent interrupted the girls' evening chitchat. Mannig hoped the hush would allow her thoughts to wander back to Barone Mardiros. She valued silence, which gave her space to imagine him nearby.

"Or expecteth so many boys at our camp?" Takouhi said, picking up her spindle. She never sat idle and the spindle seldom left her hands. "I hope to marry someday, have children … see my grandchildren …." Her forlorn voice spun out in much the same way as her spindle twirled in the air, spinning fine thread for her trousseau.

"I hopeth as well," Vanouhi sighed, as she crocheted a doily. "These boys are too young for us. I pray that the Basra community arrangeth worthy husbands who can stand shoulder to shoulder with us, suiting our age and heritage."

Mannig widened her eyes. Talk about boys spiced up her thoughts.

Am I growing up?

The boys and girls were all growing up—together and individually, perhaps as unaware as Mannig was. Mannig's group, now fourteen years old and still labeled "little orphans," were the youngest at the Basra camp. This had been the case in Mosul and Ba'qubah for the past three years. "Little" described neither their growth nor their behavior. They kept their pampered status because no child younger than they had survived the deportation.

Mannig knew nothing of the clues, causes and consequences of adolescence. To her, menstruation—called "the curse"—was an aberration caused by her ordeal and her sensitive breasts, misshapen anomalies. She disliked her pubic hair and suspected that it was tied to the "curse." Why else would the hair dry into clots, requiring warm water and dexterous fingers to cleanse? Such a nuisance, such embarrassment! She died a thousand deaths while washing the soiled rags in full view by the river. As painful as was her confusion about her monthly flow, she learned how to contend with it by invading someone else's privacy. She spied on the older girls, who washed their menstrual cloths and let them dry in unobtrusive areas. She learned by osmosis—no questions asked, no explanations given. When something confounded her, she tossed the ensuing sensations and emotional turmoil under her cot.

Vanouhi and her sister, among the groups of "big ones" in their late teens, worried about dying as spinsters. Their anxiety over the absence of traditional matchmaking between parents and relatives loomed large. Mannig vaguely understood their desperation to find suitable mates. They often wept for so-and-so in Van, probably intended for them, and damned the gendarmes for confiscating their precious trousseaux. "*Vye, vye, vye!*" Takouhi often moaned.

"Without youth, without beauty, what haveth we?" mourned Vanouhi.

"What wits haveth we to find a husband?" Takouhi murmured.

Getting married remained far from Mannig's thoughts. Lately, however, her own nervousness in the presence of boys puzzled her—especially during the evening recreational sessions. When among the girls, vivaciousness seasoned her dancing, her playing "jack" with stones collected from the riverside. As soon as the boys stomped into their masculine dance, Mannig's stance stiffened and gaze dropped. Her pulse thumped in her temples as she watched a string of boys, locked together in a circle shoulder-to-shoulder, stomping a folk dance.

She panted in tempo to their earthy rhythm.

Her eyes followed one special boy.

Taller than the others, he danced in a controlled fashion—like an experienced adult. Unlike the rest, chin lined up with his right shoulder, he thumped his steps in sync with the dancers, never glancing at his footwork. His style mesmerized her. *I could do the same with the girls.* She focused on his face. *Nice.* His pointed nose separated his long dark eyebrows and a fine mustache hugged his upper lip. *Dazzling.*

She shook her head to cast out sad memories and returned her attention to the good-looking boy. *Intelligent.* She wanted to speak with him, but for a dry lump rising in her throat. After all, boys and girls were segregated in all aspects of the orphanage life. They studied in separate classes, slept in secluded tents, huddled with their own gender on the other side of the nightly bonfire and lined up only with one another to perform the masculine folk dances.

Mingle with him. She hesitated. *Learn his dance steps.* Not while others watched. As much as Mannig's instincts urged her to act, she resisted. Be it from shyness or decorum, Mannig refrained from asking about him. Since traditionally Armenian boys received special treatment, Mannig inferred that one should talk with them only if absolutely necessary. Imposing silence upon her own self became normal. It sufficed to observe that he was handsome. Her heart chimed for him, but her mind prevented her from revealing her curiosity. Her entire being wondered at the crossfire between her head and her heart. She dared not express emotions, even if she could name such feelings.

Resting on her cot that night, she veiled her longing. Aware of emotions both indefinable and unfamiliar, she felt alone, and the loneliness pained her. She needed a confidante, a listener, a mother. *I want you, Mama.* Tears rolled sideways onto her pillow—her smothered heavy breathing accompanying their silent sting.

She wondered if a mother spoke the language of the heart. Deprived of parental guidance, she also lacked experience with adults. She could learn nothing about sensitive issues from her tent mates— they were inexperienced adults, only a few years older than she. She dared not confide in Adrine lest she trigger the trauma of her rape in the desert. She had no background to help her make intelligent guesses about the opposite gender. She could only depend upon her intuition.

She pulled her quilt up to her neck and drew her knees to her chin. Visualizing the tall boy's posture, she mused about his mustache. How did he manage to eat without the bristles stealing their share? What a nuisance. Her father wore a mustache. How did he manage in Adapazar? Glimpses of long ago ... she was so little ... memories faded ... the gendarmes killed him. She wondered if Mama had been as attracted to him at a dance as she was to this boy now at the Basra orphanage. She liked being this young man's secret admirer. There was no harm done if it lasted only a few days. Her infatuation shifted from boy to boy as predictably as evenings followed days.

One late night, when singing and dancing ended and all withdrew to sleep, an extraordinary music breezed inside the walls of Mannig's tent. The vocalist's phrasing and accent soared above the rich and profound melody. The rich orchestration of woodwinds, brass and percussion, though unfamiliar, melodiously vanished into the deep, cool and moonless night. A team of stringed instruments in the background reminded her of her mother's violin in Adapazar. She focused on them. The vibrations fell hauntingly upon Mannig's ears.

Music? Not in the desert.

32—The Foxtrot

Mardiros removed the *"Plaisir d'Amour"* song from his gramophone, wiped the disc with a velvet dust-glove and slid it into its slot in the accordion storage.

The midnight calm slowed his fingers' search for a foxtrot. Might the music be audible outside his tent? He had requested a tent at the edge of the orphanage, preferring an inconspicuous location. His lodging was an army tent among a hundred others, and his bed was a cot, like all the orphans'. The similarities ended there.

He lowered the volume while considering which disc he should introduce to the children. Sometime tomorrow, he ought to play an aria by Enrico Caruso or Dame Nellie Melba. He wanted the orphans to experience a sampling of the fine arts—to replenish some of the deprivation in their lives. A good beginning might be one or two of the latest European dances. Granted, the music was hardly necessary for the welfare of the orphans. He could teach them the foxtrot. That would bring novelty to the camp. *And hold Mannig in my arms?* A sheepish smile spanned to his ears.

He had just arrived from Baghdad. The train ride, delayed several times and lasting longer than usual, had tired him. He sniffed the remainder of his brandy, brought from Moscow by Khosrov, his oldest brother, on his pre-war emissarial stint. The overpowering aroma lacked the subtlety of French cognac. He swished it gently in the tea glass and gulped it. He pulled up his silk pajamas, purchased in Sumatra during his mission raising funds for the Armenian orphans. Treading barefoot on the Persian carpet, he lit one final cigarette and reclined on his padded cot.

He almost saw his mother's smile in the rings of his cigarette smoke—Belgian cigarette smoke. Beaming internally, he reflected how she had kept her silence throughout the emotional outburst on the balcony of their *Qasr* in Baghdad—only the night before.

All four brothers and their families had assembled on the balcony, an extension of the parlor cantilevered over the Tigris River. The sprawling ceramic tile floor had provided the setting for many soirées prior to the war, but since then, it had become the family's communal gathering place after supper.

By 1921 and in the Kouyoumdjian tradition, the family had resumed the interrupted ritual in full style again. The servants walked in and out, back and forth, several times carrying trays of iced plum-juice and tartlets. The men received permission from their mother— Managuile Hanum, the widowed matriarch of the Kouyoumdjians—to take off their jackets, and the ladies fanned themselves, shooing away flies. A dozen cousins, ages six to late teens, mingled near the gramophone cabinet inside the louvered doors of the parlor while the adults lounged on divans along the balcony rails for the cool breeze. They made disclosures and confessions and aired squabbles within the hearing of the matriarch.

Mardiros, having been absent for a while, became the center of attention, especially after announcing his plan to return to the orphanage in the morning.

"Not again?" Khosrov, the oldest brother, reprimanded him with a wagging finger. "You forget quickly. All four of us brothers sat on the very same divan, in the exact same place, and agreed to band together after the war and indulge in new ventures at the Felloujah farms."

"Why did I bother to go all the way to the World Agronomy Exposition in Belgium?" Dikran, his other brother, blazed with anger while puffing on cigarettes he had brought back with him. "We planned to combine my newly acquired knowledge with your engineering skills."

Mardiros refrained from belittling them for their selfishness and insensitivity to the life and death matters of the orphans. He knew not to alienate any Kouyoumdjian. They remained extremely generous with monetary contributions to save the Armenian children, even though only he gave of himself to the cause.

"At 32, you are still a vagabond," Diggin Rose—the widow of Karnig who had died in the Turkish prison in 1917—rebuked him in her usual turned-up nose manner. "No wife, no family, no bow to decorum."

"When are you going to settle down?" Diggin Hermine, his other sister-in-law, continued. "Listen to your brothers. They are all older, wiser and more practical than you. Besides, we want a wedding from you."

Mardiros disdained any matchmaking attempts, but Diggin Hermine was his favorite sister-in-law, so he tolerated her interference. For the sake of family harmony, he camouflaged his boredom over their plans to find him a suitable bride. Certainly, he did not disclose his attraction to a special orphan—especially since orphans, like step-children and non-lineage maidens, were shunned from the matrimonial ladder. *Phew!* His lips were sealed. He knew his heart, and he knew who occupied it. His overheated state prompted him to stand and lean across the balcony railing for cool air.

A few passenger *bellems* glided from shore to shore, disrupting the mellow beams of a near full moon reflected downstream. He wished he could share the picturesque scene with Mannig. He had grown up with all the material comforts, but now he longed for something beyond riches. He knew Mannig's capacity to overcome the stigma of orphan-hood. He hoped his family would come to admire her as he did.

He knew he must leave.

He loosened his tie and went back to justifying his quest to see the orphans properly settled. He refrained from lecturing about their needs, simply predicting that they would soon be permanently taken care of. "The Patriarchate of Jerusalem is about to declare its grand plan for them," he said to explain why he was neglecting his family and business affairs. "I will return to normal life very soon."

A glance at his mother convinced him he had satisfied her expectations. The amber prayer beads with their black tassel still coiled in her hand rested in the lap of her gray satin skirt. Her eyes narrowed at him and a twitch raised the edges of her upper lip. He wanted affirmation and he found it in her contented expression. "That's settled," he said and kissed her hand.

He veered toward the circle of children mouthing the lyrics of a French song. He put on another disc and cranked up the gramophone. "Now, who will foxtrot with me before I pack away 'His Master's Voice' and retreat to my quarters?" He took the hand of Isgouhi, his oldest niece, before giving the others a chance. "Out on the balcony," he said, quick-stepping into the open air. He held her close and led as smoothly as a professional dancer. While he visualized holding Mannig

231

in his arms, he caught a glimpse of delight in the watchful eyes of his family, especially his mother.

Early next morning, he awakened feeling determined and doubly encouraged.

Very unlike a matriarch, Managuile Hanum stealthily stopped Mardiros' valet at the door of her quarters. "Hamid, after you load his luggage in the motorcar, come back here," she instructed. "I want Barone Mardiros to have a few personal things at the camp."

Upon her insistence, Hamid managed to fit a rolled up Persian carpet and two leather-covered hassocks into the trunk, necessitating the wrapping of His Master's Voice in a quilt and holding it in his lap in the passenger's seat, next to Mardiros.

"The drive from here to the train station is close," she said to appease Hamid. Leaning over to Mardiros, she gave him a bundled embroidered shawl. "Don't tell your brothers I gave those to you. Now, go! God be with you ... send me a telegram as soon as you arrive in Basra."

Mardiros smiled when he saw the contents of the bundle—a carton of Belgian cigarettes and a bottle of Russian brandy—gifts his brothers had given her from their travels in foreign lands. He always wondered whether she favored him for being her youngest child or whether she actually admired his compassion for the orphans. He hoped for the latter.

Now Mardiros lay on his cot, looking at the tent ceiling beyond the glow of his Belgian cigarette. He understood why the Kouyoumdjians preferred comfort, luxury and society, to a life in the 'camp,' as they referred to the orphanage, denigrating the status of its inhabitants. But he felt compelled to finish his job. Seeing the orphan's permanently settled would be his biggest and final task.

He crushed out the butt of his cigarette and rolled over to one side. Content with his decision, he needed to rest tonight; tomorrow he'd let the fire in his belly glow.

The wake-up bells chimed with the sun's appearance along the horizon. The ringing invited Mardiros out to catch the jutting rays vying with the rising mist along Shatt el-Arab. Dewdrops glistened on the tent's lines. The fresh breeze recharged his resolve. He watched the delicate rays suffuse the atmosphere.

"Welcome within our midst, again!" Sebouh called, approaching. "You slept well, I pray?"

"The best," Mardiros said, stretching his arms. "Those cots are a match for any four-poster mahogany bed."

The two men—both gentlemen, benefactors, and teammates—patted each other's shoulders and proceeded toward the smoke, the ringing bell and the chatter of the breakfast crew.

Sebouh enumerated the improvements made at the orphanage during Mardiros' absence. He had secured blankets for the approaching winter, replaced the volunteer girls with real cooks and installed drainer-pipes for the latrines. "The girls are really happy that we have raised a big tent for large gatherings," he concluded his oral report.

"It looks the Basra community has come to our aid," Mardiros said.

"Now it is your turn," Sebouh said, retrieving a silver cigarette case from the pocket of his tweed jacket. "You must go to Basra, hire teachers and promise them decent pay. Let's hope some will be willing to trek out of Basra daily."

"The distance is an easy ride," Mardiros said while he scanned the area—beyond the tents and the improved pathways. He glanced from orphan to orphan, head to head, face to face, near and far. The tall communal tent, dotting the sky, towered over the smaller tents in its shade. Which small tent might be Mannig's? He hoped her abode might be en route to his tent.

"The Basrawi Armenians and I cannot see eye-to-eye on many issues," Sebouh said. "You are a better negotiator. I'm certain they will lend an ear to you." He offered Mardiros a cigarette before putting one between his thin lips.

Mardiros scrutinized Sebouh, thankful for the credit he gave him, which was due to his coup in securing funds from the Singapore Armenians. He lit a match and, reaching to light Sebouh's, noticed a carefully groomed moustache—a radical change in his customarily clean shaven appearance. After lighting his cigarette, he inhaled a long stream of smoke, his gaze fanning the area in search of Mannig.

"Sebouh Effendi, Sebouh Effendi!" The call caused the two men to turn and take notice.

Adrine stood at their heels. "You probably need to spend time with Barone Mardiros today," she said. "Would you like me to take your class?"

Mardiros relished being recognized, especially since she had approached them from behind. He glanced at Sebouh and noticed a complete change in his expression. His eyes mellowed and his breathing grew more rapid, disturbing his black moustache. Furthermore, he flaunted a generous smile, a challenge to gentlemanly manners. Could Sebouh be attracted to this girl? He looked at her again. A pretty girl. A slender Greek nose accentuated her hazel eyes. Although she flinched at times while addressing Sebouh, she remained composed. She held herself erect and, with great self-assurance, listed the topics that needed reviewing in class.

"Yes, very good ... very good ..." Sebouh stammered. "Your insight amazes me." He touched Mardiros's elbow and introduced him. "This is Adrine. She has helped with our curricular program. And what an assistant she has been! Invaluable. She is from Adapazar."

Adapazar?

Mardiros almost interjected, *Oh, I know Adapazar. I visited Adapazar when I attended Robert's College* ... Somehow, he had uttered those same words very recently. Where? To whom? He looked at Adrine. *No.* He couldn't recall seeing her before. "Noble Armenians come from Adapazar," he said, resuming his search for Mannig.

"Let's plan the lesson together," Sebouh said to her in a controlled staccato. "Sit with us." He waited for her to slide onto a bench before he scooted next to her. "How much sugar do you like in your tea?" he asked, pouring bubbling claret tea into a glass cup.

Mardiros remained standing, glancing hither and thither. Then he noticed the chestnut braid of an orphan a few rows away. It swung on her back as she slid onto a bench. Then she swung her head into full view as if searching for someone in his direction.

Mannig!

His heart raced. His gaze kissed hers. For a moment, he existed for her alone. He lost himself in the music that emanated from her eyes. He stared for a few seconds longer until he felt embarrassed without knowing why. Certainly, looking was not rude, especially while attending to Sebouh's chatter. Might seeing her have stirred concealed emotions? Perhaps her proximity caused his palpitating heart. He looked at her again; her face glowed with grace and harmony. She smiled. Her deep brown eyes lit up like lanterns, rays of affection shining at him. *So beautiful.* Her whole being was more radiant than the sun. Unaffected by her surroundings, her poise and demeanor set her apart from the orphans. *Obviously, she belongs to the aristocracy.* She would fit perfectly into his life—promenading in the Kouyoumdjian marble halls, sipping tea with his sisters-in-law and entertaining dignitaries. She had conquered his heart. Would she win his family's affection? The female entourage of his relatives would dress her like one of them—in a high neckline, her chignon complemented by a wide-brimmed hat.

Never!

Mannig was a young girl, not a fuddy-duddy stiff! Actually, younger than some of his nieces. She ought to wear styles for teenagers—let her hair down, with ribbons and bows. He visualized her looking gorgeous in one of the pretty dresses donated to the orphans by Orozdi-Bak, the Swiss department store in Baghdad. He had brought about fifty floral and linen outfits, still packed in his luggage. Fifty, total? How might he control their distribution to ensure Mannig receives one? He must avoid the appearance of favoring one orphan over the others. How, how? He really wanted to see her wear a dress that was not a uniform. He knew she would be transformed into a work of art in motion.

"… will hire teachers with expertise," Sebouh was saying, "and you, Adrine, will be able to study advanced subjects."

"Who will hire the experts?" Mardiros asked as he dunked a chunk of rye bread into a bowl of date-syrup. With closed eyes, he sucked the aromatic condiment before taking a bite.

"You, of course!" Sebouh said, nudging him. "You, the great motivator. The great negotiator, the wizard. I wanted to talk to you about real education. The children's needs are overwhelming. Some students are very intelligent, always wanting more … some even want to learn foreign languages."

Mardiros sipped tea while contemplating Sebouh's words. "I could go to Basra … see what I can do. But today, I must distribute a few items I brought along, including a pouch of letters."

"You have brought letters?" Adrine cried, eyes sparkling.

"She wrote a letter to her uncle in Bulgaria," Sebouh explained. "She has been waiting to hear from him." He lowered his voice to play down his excitement over the mail. "I suppose we ought to see those letters."

Within a few minutes, Mardiros emptied the pouch on the carpet his mother convinced him he'd appreciate at 'the camp.' Instead of on the floor, he had spread it like a tablecloth across his desk.

Sebouh thumbed through the pile, reading out loud the names

written in French, while Adrine identified a few orphans—one residing in tent number 2 and two others in number 7.

"This mail has been traveling all over the world," Mardiros said, reading the addresses, also in French. "This one says, 'To Miriam Salibian, Daughter of Garabed of Konya.' The initial address on this envelope says, The Armenian Orphanage in Switzerland," Mardiros continued. "Switzerland has been crossed off and forwarded to, The Armenian Orphanage in Syria. Syria is crossed off, and here in this corner it says, The Armenian Orphanage in Mesopotamia. Is Miriam Salibian in our orphanage?"

Sebouh looked at Adrine, who shrugged her shoulders, "I don't recognize the name."

"We must inquire at every tent," Sebouh insisted. "If no one knows a Miriam Salibian, where should we forward it?"

"Maybe back to Syria," Mardiros moaned, pulling up a hassock for Sebouh and another for Adrine. "I understand there is a new orphanage in Aleppo. She may be there, if she survived the massacre at all."

They left the crumbled, discolored and marred envelopes alone for a moment. The three had stopped identifying and sorting and paused to reflect. The ensuing silence overwhelmed Mardiros. More spiritual than religious, he closed his eyes in memory of the perished Armenians.

Before they started to read and sort again, Adrine touched the undeliverable pile and said. "Perhaps I can ask the students in my class this morning. They may recognize some of these names ..." She stopped short and shook her head. "No! I cannot do that. I do not know how to read in French."

"See, Barone Mardiros?" Sebouh said, addressing Mardiros. "If Adrine learned a foreign language, she could volunteer for such assignments."

"I hear you," Mardiros said. "Maybe I will teach ... or you will learn, in due time." He scrutinized the next envelope. "This is addressed to Adrine Dobajian ..." He focused on Dobajian. Isn't that Mannig's surname? He hid his curiosity, lest it betray his interest in news of her family. "Are you Adrine Dobajian?"

"Yes!" Adrine exclaimed.

"Yes!" Sebouh exclaimed, grabbing the envelope. "It does say, Adrine Dobajian of Adapazar."

"Is your surname really Dobajian?" Mardiros asked, coyly.

"Yes," she whispered, extending a shaky hand. She cuddled the envelope close to her heart and, with tears in her eyes, asked to be excused to return to her tent.

Both men nodded. Sebouh opened the tent flap for her.

She took short, light steps and thanked him for helping her. As soon as she exited she dashed away, yelling at the top of her lungs, "Mannig! Mannig!" Mardiros noticed Sebouh swallowing with difficulty, but dismissed the significance of his reaction, being somewhat emotional himself. Only a few months earlier, Mannig had refused to go to America, saying, "Not without my sister."

Is Adrine Mannig's sister?

33—Surprise, Surprise, and Surprise

Madiros' love was no juvenile crush, but the real thing. At the age of 32, he compared falling in love to going to a bathhouse for the first time—one felt cleansed, senses unusually acute. He heard her cheerful voice a hundred tents away, smelled her presence through variety of aromas and would know her touch with his eyes closed. Visualizing her movements put him in a daze. *Mannig, Mannig.* What a melodious name.

Admitting his passion for her invigorated him. The mere thought of her aroused him. The bulge in his trousers while in her presence would not only embarrass him, but distract him to the point where he could not enjoy her company. The bourgeois decorum implanted in his psyche offered a solution. He dashed to his suitcase and flipped open the lid. He discarded trousers and shirts east and west until he found the heavy bandages he had wrapped around his groin during his athletic feats at Robert's College. He bandaged himself like the Olympian track contender he had been in 1912. He pulled up his white linen trousers and double-checked the buttons inside the fly before he responded to Sebouh's voice. "Come in," he said.

"The orphans are planning a surprise tonight," Sebouh said and, sidestepping Mardiros, sat on a hassock, his after-shave cologne preceding him.

Mardiros smiled, suppressing a chuckle. *The man hopes to attract the orphans.*

Mardiros snapped the elastic of his suspenders against his shoulders and looked into the gilt-framed round mirror, dangling from a pole. Sparkling eyes were reflected back at him. "What surprise?" he asked.

"Actually, the surprise will be on them," Sebouh said, puffing rings of smoke.

"I, too, have a surprise for them," Mardiros said. He thrust aside the navy cravat he'd been considering and selected a green bow-tie that deepened the green of his hazel eyes. The bow also made him look younger—almost like a college student. He proceeded to button the white linen vest, but his reflection in the mirror stopped him. College students seldom wore vests. He threw it aside on his cot. While he put on his jacket, he noticed that Sebouh's thoughts seemed to be flying into space. "You are a happy lark this evening."

"Well," Sebouh said, "the content of the letter from Adrine's uncle gave me great relief. He cannot, after all, sponsor the two sisters in Bulgaria. Apparently he is processing his papers for America. He promises to contact them from there. America is a rich country, he has written. And as soon as he and his family are settled, he will call for them."

"That should have been a disappointment," Mardiros said, angling for a confession.

"For her, yes. But not for me," Sebouh finger-combed his moustache. "I dreaded seeing Adrine move away."

Aha! The man is in love, too!

Mardiros pondered a moment about being in love. How unprecedented in real life, or perhaps even in literature, might a love-affair be that was a by-product of philanthropy? He acknowledged the birth of remarkable friendships among like-minded individuals in the field—his bonding with Sebouh being a tangible proof. However, they shared common ground—affluence, education and selflessness. He reflected upon his camaraderie with Diggin Perouz; an expected relationship with a married lady. The dearth of females in the altruistic arena decreased the opportunities for romance. Nevertheless, affection crossed boundaries of societal mores. Love bloomed at the camp.

Mardiros held his breath. He and Sebouh might be breaking new ground.

Mardiros's philosophical ponderings about how fate had arranged for him to fall in love were disrupted by the smell of Sebouh's cigarette. "By the way," he asked, already certain of the answer. "Which one is Adrine's sister?"

"Her name is Mannig. She is an outstanding young lady herself. Those two sisters outshine any lineage in this orphanage."

Aha! So my own assessment of Mannig's poise is not a figment of my making. Even Sebouh is affirming her nobility.

Mardiros's exhilaration urged him to step into the realm of the orphans. "Help me with my surprise for the girls," he said, handing his friend the accordion file of discs. He swung around and lifted the gramophone. "Tonight, we shall dance."

The singing, wafting from the community tent, beckoned the two to the arena where a large circle of girls, pinky-to-pinky, danced and sang in the center. A few yards from them, a circle of half-a-dozen boys, arms interlocked over shoulders, stomped in sync to the same beat.

Mardiros and Sebouh sidestepped a multitude of spectators and set the gramophone on a table by the tent wall. Mardiros greeted the teachers and staff, urging them to remain seated on the benches. He leaned against a pole and enjoyed watching the ensembles of dancers. To conceal his interest in Mannig, he exerted much effort to appear nonchalant. Not finding Mannig anywhere, he gazed at a few crouched girls. She was not among them, either.

Adjusting to her absence, he decided to manage his expectations. Although disappointed, he remained unruffled. With or without Mannig, he decided to implement his strategy—to break free from the customary girls-dancing-with-girls while the boys danced with boys. Such archaic decorum had been created by people who had lived and died hundreds of years ago. He intended to end the traditional separation of the genders. Only by integrating the boy dancers with the girls could he intermingle with Mannig unobtrusively.

He clapped his hands and signaled to the staff to ring the bell for attention.

"I have a surprise for you," he said, addressing the crowd. "See this music box? This is the latest European invention. It is called a gramophone."

Everybody repeated after him—*gramophone.*

He raised the record for all to see. "This is a disc. Now, I shall place it on the turntable. Then I must crank this handle."

What and How soared up in the air, followed by pushing and shoving for a closer look.

"See how the disc is turning?" he continued. "Next, I shall place the fine needle at the tip of the neck at the edge of the disc. This will bring out music created by an orchestra and then we ..."

Oohs and Aahs filled the evening air.

"Ring the bell again," Sebouh instructed the orphanage manager and suggested that they move the gramophone to the center for better viewing. A more orderly listening time followed, when Mardiros played his favorite record, *"Plaisir d'amour."* The children, awe-struck, listened to the chanteuse's voice reverberating from the gramophone.

Mardiros gazed at their expressions—from the vivid to the brilliant, from the stunned to the romantic—they were immersed in a totally vicarious thrill. *Ah, I wish Mannig were here, too.* His evening was headed somewhere, but not where he had hoped. He replaced the song with a foxtrot, and noticed a smile on everyone's face as some tapped their feet to the beat.

The rhythm stirred the girls. Their youthful bodies swayed and swung; others jounced and writhed. A few girls in head scarves and uniforms flaunted themselves as the 'orphanage elite' locked in, pinky-to-pinky, and devised steps in time with the tempo.

"No, no!" Mardiros said and stopped the music. "This is not a circle dance. It's a couples' dance. It is called the foxtrot. Two people face each other and hold hands—one male and one female ..."

"Oooooooooooooooo!" A big giggle reverberated across the desert atmosphere.

"Come, come, ladies and gentlemen," Mardiros said, walking to the center. "All over the civilized world, modern dances involve one man and one woman. Let me show you how. I need one of you to demonstrate."

He scanned their faces and waited.

No one volunteered.

A complete silence ensued. The girls raised their shoulders bashfully, hid their hands behind their backs and cast their eyes to the ground.

"There is nothing to it," he said, fixing his eyes on one face then the next. "It is only a dance and it is very easy. All I need is one girl. Who will be my partner?"

Sebouh, from the sideline, gestured to stop persisting. But Mardiros ignored him and took a step forward to tap the shoulder of one of the girls, when a voice held him captive.

"I will," the sweet voice uttered. "I will be your partner."

My Mannig! Mardiros thought in jubilation. My dream is becoming a reality.

Mannig made her way through the crowd but suddenly hesitated to meet him in the open.

Sensing her shyness, Mardiros sidestepped the cluster of bewildered girls and extended his hand to her. "Come, Mannig," his voice wavered. His heart beat in his chest like timpani, the booms echoing in his head. A dab of perspiration dotted his eyebrows. "Come, hold my hand."

What am I getting into?

The whole scenario seemed an untidy tactic and he had trapped himself into experiencing it. His plan had become a dilemma. Doing the foxtrot might have been a big mistake, after all. *I should have confided in Sebouh.* His friend probably would have discouraged him from flouting the codes of etiquette at a place such as this. How dare he break the rules about mixing genders? Regrets were too late and, in the morning, he would be looked at as the clown of the orphanage. *What if my passion for Mannig is obvious?* He had planned to express it to her in private.

He wanted to close his eyes to pray for an escape, but his gaze latched onto Mannig's face. His soul clapped its hands at her nervous smile as she approached him. With her almost in his arms, he fantasized about holding her on the Kouyoumdjian veranda in Baghdad.

The two stood in the circle.

The eyes of the crowd were riveted upon them.

His heart's desire was becoming a reality. He faced her. The two gazed at each other, barely avoiding eye-to-eye contact. He put her left hand on his right elbow and slid the tip of his fingers around her waist, not daring to touch her back with his palm. He brushed his sweaty left hand on his trousers before he supported her slender soft hand. He waited a second to catch the beat of the fox trot.

"Follow my momentum," he whispered. "Two steps to the right, like this. And two steps …."

Before he could say, 'two steps to the left,' Mannig was already doing it, her eyes glued to his feet. He wanted to say, 'you already know how to foxtrot,' but was afraid of stuttering. He just smiled and repeated the pattern, while his grip on her back tightened. *Am I in heaven already?*

He hoped time would stop forever—he and Mannig forming one statue.

"Mannig? Mannig?" a boy's voice penetrated through the music. "Is that you? Mannig of Adapazar?"

Mannig withdrew from Mardiros.

Eyes sparkling, she veered toward the voice. "Dikran?" she called, smiling not only with her lips, but with her eyes, eyebrows and obviously, with memories. She dropped her hand from Mardiros' and dashed toward him.

As the two hugged like lost souls, everyone's attention switched to them.

Alas! The kiss Mardiros had been about to place at the peak of his joy soured to envy.

A handsome young fellow was hugging his secret love. The man flaunted a gorgeous broom moustache and eyes that gleamed blissfully beneath healthy eyebrows. Mardiros resented him from the pit of his soul. He turned his back, one eye on the duo's encounter, the other on his powerlessness. Needless to say, he lost interest in dancing.

He replaced the taunting *"Plaisir d'amour"* with Caruso's melodramatic *"Celeste Aida."*

His heart throbbed in his throat; his pain rose higher than the sky, deeper than space. Would this Dikran taint his beautiful Mannig? His garb—that of a cameleer or even a muleteer—was enough to repel anyone. The man had probably not bathed for months.

Mardiros gulped down his self-respect and stooped low to ask Sebouh, "Who is this fellow?"

"He looks familiar," Sebouh said, "but I cannot place him. He must be one of the older orphans who trickled into the orphanage last night." He faced Adrine and, gazing into her face, asked. "Your intelligent eyes are alive with memories. Do you know him?"

"Don't you remember?" she said. "The supervisor expelled him from the Mosul orphanage."

"Why?" Mardiros exclaimed unabashedly. "Maybe he shouldn't be here at all."

"A pretty girl got him in trouble," Adrine said.

"I remember vaguely," Sebouh mumbled, furrowing his brow. "I am amazed that you recognized him, my dear Adrine. Didn't that happen two years ago?" He leaned toward Mardiros and whispered, "As I recollect, a girl—a much older girl—tempted this poor naïve boy into illicit acts. They were caught by the supervisor. Even though he was an outstanding helper, I agreed to expel the two. We needed to protect the morale of the orphans—as well as their morals."

Mardiros kept silent. He ought to forbid the fellow, this Dikran—

or whatever his name was—to inflict any harm on his Mannig. He felt obligated to stop it. Well, first, he himself must certainly purge any of his modern ideas. If he himself danced with Mannig, then this Dikran could do so, too. The ancestors, after all, had been wise to perpetuate segregation rather than adopt current trends. Boys must stay with the boys, and girls with the girls—first matrimony, then unity. Seeing anyone bonding with his beloved angered him. "Why ... is he ... embracing M-M-Mannig?" he stuttered.

"They were inseparable," Adrine said, "until Garina enticed Dikran with adult pleasures."

Inseparable? Mardiros dared not question its meaning. Ignorance was preferable. He must keep an eye on this Dikran, night and day. "Sebouh Effendi," he said, urgency in his voice. "You, yourself, ought to go to Basra tomorrow instead of me. The AGBU officials will be glad to see you. I need to stay here ... for some ... p-p-paper-work ... that I must c-c-complete." He took a long breath to stunt the stuttering that engulfed him when he lied or was angered. "You d-d-don't mind, do you?" He breathed again. "AGBU is expecting news from Jerusalem. The sooner we learn about the future plans for the orphans the better." He took another quick breath. "I'll c-c-cover for you ... do you mind going to Basra?"

"No problem," Sebouh said. "While there, I could go to the bathhouse for a good washing. And ..." he leaned toward Mardiros and whispered, "I wanted to buy something special for Adrine. She has put more life into this orphanage than anyone else. She can certainly teach my classes. She is very capable. She deserves something special."

Another brilliant idea came to Mardiros. "Did you say that Dikran was a good helper? Take him to Basra with you. He can haul the gunnysacks of rice onto the cart."

Sebouh nodded.

I wish Dikran would stay in Basra permanently. His irresistible desire for Mannig blinded his honor or pride. Mardiros wanted Sebouh to do his work in Basra and then return to the orphanage—solo—without Dikran. He never wanted to see that boy's face again. "See to it that the Basrawis give this fellow permanent work in Basra. He should stay there."

Sebouh gave him a quizzical look.

Without shame or blame, Mardiros invented a policy. "We are expected to encourage independence. He looks grown up enough to be on his own. Don't you think so?"

The last tenor note blaring from Caruso came to an end. Mardiros gazed at the sky. The moon reminded him of Mannig—one lit the sky, the other his heart. Her light shone on Dikran tonight, but he knew how to end the glow tomorrow. There was enough silence for reflection, enough moon to douse the stars. He lowered the gramophone lid and latched it. He picked it up to leave but was confronted by a contingency of orphans urging him to sit.

The sea of heads, faces and scarves cascaded beyond the row of the shortest orphans lined up in the front. Overwhelmed, he looked at Sebouh and Adrine. Their eyes were twinkling with mischief.

"The orphans have a surprise for you, Barone Mardiros," Adrine said, sitting beside him while Sebouh signaled to the staff to be seated as well.

A voice from the sidelines said, "Everybody together at the count of three ...." and at the count of three, in unison, the orphans recited the English alphabet to the melody of an ancient Armenian song. They repeated their ABCs up and down the scales several times—some forte, others pianissimo—enunciating each letter succinctly and sequentially. The alto voices harmonized with the prominent sopranos, and the boys' *a cappella* sprinkled an interesting staccato on and off, resulting in a marvelous rendition.

Mardiros scanned the orphans' expressions—jubilant, impish and eager. Their voices came as whispers of love. Sebouh must be the culprit. Who else would teach the English alphabet? Familiar with the melody, he wished Sebouh had confided in him beforehand so he could have accompanied them with his flute. That might have made for an exquisite entertainment. Accompanying the chorus would have won the orphans' hearts, especially Mannig's. That possibility has been the only reason he had packed his instrument and brought it with him.

Listening to the sweet voices, he let his unfulfilled feelings dissipate into the night. He became immersed in the splendor of their affection, gratitude and pride.

"Encore, Encore ..." he yelled, jumping up to applaud at the conclusion. His voice dried up when he realized the children's ignorance of European expressions. "Repeat! Repeat! Sing again. It is lovely," he yelled in Armenian.

The children only giggled and squirmed, then parted in the center, clearing a path for Mannig to come forth. She carried a bunch of wildflowers in riotous colors.

Startled at her sudden appearance, he choked and his heart burned in his chest. He stumbled to his feet, his eyes glued on her.

She knelt before him, head low, and held the bouquet out to him.

"For you, Dear Father of the Orphanage."

34—To Jerusalem

Reclining on a chaise lounge behind his tent, Mardiros doused himself in the farewell rays of the late winter sun soaking Iraqi's southern plains.

After touring the tent classrooms, he rested. Infusing a bit of his knowledge into the Arithmetic Tent of the advanced students and demonstrating classic penmanship at another to the younger ones inflated his ego. Even though his engineering degree existed mainly in the form of a diploma, it enhanced the quality of his teaching.

After a quick soup and bread lunch, relaxing on his cot reminded him of his own school days. Alas, the affluence of his youth! His wealthy classmates had all been dressed in crisp linen uniforms and his surroundings had consisted of ornate, mahogany-walled classrooms. His teachers had been trained specialists. Had he ever valued those amenities at the time? Unlike the thrill he noticed on the faces of the orphans—in spite of their circumstances—he never even once thought of the privileges bestowed upon him during his education. These orphans relished everything —as dowdy as they were, seated on a pillow on straw mats, devouring every word uttered by the volunteer instructors, none of whom were trained in the subjects they taught. It was obvious to Mardiros that, prior to imparting their knowledge to the orphans, the teachers themselves spent hours the evening before mastering the subjects. The orphans then spent comparable numbers of hours memorizing everything.

"Barone Mardiros! Barone Mardiros!" Sebouh's voice interrupted his thoughts. Sebouh dismounted his horse and tethered it to the tent line. "I have news."

Sebouh's return from Basra so soon surprised Mardiros. He jumped up. "I expected your return late this evening," he said. Hoping the news concerned Dikran's employment outside the orphanage, he asked, "What is the news?"

Sebouh handed him the square sheet of a telegram.

Mardiros skimmed it. Seeing how apprehensive Sebouh looked, he re-read it:

> British ship Shuja will transport orphans STOP
> Gharibian team will escort them STOP
> Depart on January 25, 1922 STOP
> Signed Holy See of Jerusalem STOP
> Armenian Church END

"I did expect this message," Mardiros said, "but not the short notice of only three days."

"I'm upset about the Gharibian team," Sebouh blurted out and handed him a second paper listing the names of the escorts. "You and I are excluded. I think they don't need us any longer."

Mardiros grabbed the list and read it several times. His blood rushed to his temples, first in disbelief, then with anger. "But these men have no experience with orphans." He swallowed a lump of resentment. "They are cronies. I wager you—their assignment is the fruit of bribery!" His heart sank with disappointment. "What did WE do wrong?"

"They have other plans for us," Sebouh said and handed him a third paper. "They compliment us for our unprecedented success. But they want us to stay in Baghdad and continue to raise funds for the orphans."

"That's g-g-good and well," Mardiros shouted, needing to lash out at someone. "B-b-but my work is best with the orphans ..." He visualized being separated from Mannig and surely losing her to some dimwit in Jerusalem. "No, I don't like this arrangement at all."

"I had the time to vent my hurt feelings all the way riding back from Basra," Sebouh sighed. "Eventually, I reconciled myself to this predicament." His eyes lowered, he seemed to wonder about his statement. "I must plan for a new future—perhaps get back to managing my businesses in Baghdad." He wiped his forehead and offered to inform the orphans himself, immediately. "The orphans must embark within the next three short days."

Mardiros became lost in thought. Life for the orphans in Jerusalem promised a good future. But separated from them, his life amounted to nothing. It hurt to think his adventures of the last few years were headed to a conclusion. How will I bear a stuffy life all over again?

His eyeballs throbbed with self pity and heart drowned in despair. Resigned, he put on his Topy and sunglasses—wanting to thank whoever invented the tinted eyewear that hid a multitude of emotions. Shame overwhelmed the pity he felt for himself.

Baghdad promised to be a wasteland for his talents. Mingling with the rich, trifling with the ladies and dancing with their unmarried daughters had lost their appeal—not even for the sake of raising funds. Furthermore, he foresaw his mother and sisters-in-law heckling him to settle down and get married. He preferred growing old while visualizing a dance with Mannig on the veranda of his home overlooking the Tigris. Gloom-ridden pain trickled down his spine. He hoped to close the floodgates to his tears before he accompanied Sebouh to announce the voyage to Jerusalem.

Sebouh headed toward the community tent, ringing the hand bell nonstop.

Mardiros followed him.

The kitchen crew stopped their clean-up and followed Sebouh, who now climbed on a bench, still ringing the bell. The endless ringing deafened Mardiros but he was sustained by the sight of the orphans huddling nearby. When the flow of children slowed down and the horde surrounded them, Sebouh silenced the last reverberation with his hand. He waited until all had quieted down before unfolding the telegram and waving it.

"This piece of paper contains big news for all of you."

The hush amid the orphans stifled Mardiros.

"You will be transferred to Jerusalem," Sebouh began.

A thunderous cry of joy arose so instantaneously that a wave of excitement floated above their heads.

Mardiros suffered even more.

The kitchen crew dropped their brooms and screamed in delight. Clusters of girls hugged and hopped and hollered.

Mardiros sighed heavily. Nothing could be sadder than losing Mannig. He could not bear the thought of her absence from the camp, her departure from his life, her voyage on a ship and eventual life apart from him. With folded arms, he sat on a bench—his heart as dry as dust.

All the while, laughter and squealing rose to high heaven.

෯෧

Impatient as the wind, Mannig turned to Adrine and they both—incredulous looks on their faces—wrapped their arms around each other. Not wanting to part, their tears stained each other's cheeks. They jumped up and down, hugging neighbors once and each other over and over.

Jerusalem, Jerusalem, Jerusalem!

Like a carved cross dominating a fireplace mantle in a parlor or dangling around the neck of a priest, Jerusalem represented an image. To Mannig, the name revived the echo of her memory. Her grandmother had earned the Haji-doo title for her pilgrimage to Jerusalem. Now the image was becoming Mannig's destination. *Will I walk where she walked? And will I feel as if I am touching my grandmother again?* It would not be like going back to Adapazar and to her wonderful musical childhood. She understood the irrevocability of life. Her memories sufficed—her yellow organdy dress, jigging to Mama's music while Baba, in his green velvet chair, proudly caressed Sirarpi in his lap and Setrak poked the coals in the brazier.

Mannig dwelt on the memory of her grandmother—Haji-doo, clicking her prayer beads with one hand, hugging the black Bible with the other. Mannig choked up.

She embraced Adrine again. "I am so happy," she said, kissing her sister. At least the two had survived to remember their heritage.

Adrine wiped her own tears. "I am, too. I wish we were leaving today. We don't need three days to pack."

That evening the sisters from Van incessantly jabbered about the wonders awaiting them in Jerusalem: life within real brick walls, incense in the church, meeting young men, getting married. They spoke of weddings, marriage and children.

"Thou wilt invite us to thy wedding, Adrine. Won't thee?" Vanouhi asked.

"When I get married, I will," Adrine said.

"Thou wilt too, Mannig. Won't thee?" Takouhi asked.

Mannig gaped. Getting married activated a unique niche in her thoughts, and Barone Mardiros immediately occupied it. *Hah!* A sarcastic echo rang in her head. She and the Barone? An impossible dream.

"I intend to stay as I am," she said and spread her *boghcha*, square kerchief, on the ground. She placed the new notebook, her treasure, at the bottom, carefully guarding against creasing the pages that had recorded everything of value—words, phrases and sentences about arithmetic, geography and history. Unlike the packing her mother experienced prior the deportation, Mannig's decisions to discard this or pack that were non-existent. One *boghcha* sufficed for all her pitiful belongings. She double-knotted the corners and—*voilà*—she held all her worldly possessions on her arm.

"Remain unmarried?" Vanouhi chuckled.

"Thou wilt marry, when a nice fellow proposeth to thee," Takouhi said.

"I want to finish school," Mannig said. Visions of becoming a teacher like Miss Romella, her kindergarten teacher in Adapazar, danced in her head. Romella had reappeared in her life again in Mosul and, like a soft touch in a hard world, filled a hole left by her mother's death. Although her memories of Romella had gradually faded after she had married a war veteran in Mosul and Mannig had entered the orphanage, the memory of kindergarten resounded loudly in her head. "I will become a teacher," she murmured.

"Thou art a dreamer," Vanouhi said, serving tea in small glass cups before bedtime.

"Let her steep herself in dreams while she can," Takouhi said. "She can't dreameth throughout a whole lifetime—her eyes groweth dim, hair turneth white and joints creaketh like tin. Then she will wake up, and it will be too late."

"And I thought you were my friends," Mannig said, losing appetite for the tea and the conversation.

"Hey, lo!" Vanouhi stroked Mannig's shoulder. "We art thy friends. We art actually schooling thee about realities. The most important thing in life is to have thy own family, real blood family. Thou and I and everyone in this orphanage are cut off from relatives. So we have to start our own new bloodlines. It is our solemn duty to perpetuate our Armenian heritage."

"Schooling will also perpetuate our heritage," Mannig said.

"Maybe it will and maybe it will not. But to get married with thy own kind and procreate is the only sure way." With a sly expression, she whispered in Takouhi's ear, and the two fell into giggles. "It is the enjoyable way, too."

Puzzled, Mannig looked at Adrine, who raised her shoulders impassively.

"Much pleasure cometh in marriage," Takouhi said, giggling some more.

"That is also God's way," Vanouhi said seriously. "God creates children so they get married and beget children. I am sure thy mother wanteth the same for thee, too."

Noises outside the tent silenced them.

"Mannig? Mannig Dobajian?"

"That's Sebouh Effendi's voice," Adrine said. "He is calling you."

Mannig dashed out and said, "I am Mannig Dobajian."

"I know who you are," he said. "I just didn't know in which tent I'd find you. May I come in?"

Eyes sparkling by the lantern light, he scanned the neatly tucked bedding on the cots while he caught a whiff of the allspice aroma from the steeping tea pot. He glanced at the Van sisters and focused on Adrine. "Nicely kept tent. But don't be alarmed. This is not an inspection. I came to fetch Mannig." Turning to her, said, "Barone Mardiros wants to see you, Mannig. Will you come with me?"

Why? Why did the Barone want to see her? As curious as she felt, the calm way she received his request surprised her. Might he be planning a final performance at the farewell gathering for the staff? The thought gave wings to her heart. If the summons were for an audition, she felt comfortable wearing the more formal of the two uniforms. She tightened the belt of the navy blue tunic and squared the pockets. Carefully she smoothed the stiff collar. She stepped directly behind Sebouh Effendi and, making sure he could not see her, she licked her palms several times and smoothed her hair. The sisters from Van often told her she looked pretty when her hair shone and her braid dangled to the side, framing her face. She wet and twirled the end tip of her braid. *I must be pretty tonight.*

Sebouh Effendi stopped at a large tent and tapped at the entryway. "Mannig is here," he said, glancing first at her then at the light beams crisscrossing through the windows veiled with mosquito netting.

"Oh, oh!" Mardiros' voice came in a rush. "Come in, come in, my dear." He reached for her elbow, a jovial smile radiating on his face. He led her in, and thanking Sebouh, he quickly bid him a good evening.

Mannig hesitated in awe. The few square yards of the desert under her feet gave way to a palatial room. Persian rugs covered the floor and tinted kerosene lamps hung from four corners, lighting the tent radiantly. A cluster of small purplish flowers tied in a bouquet scented the spacious area and a soft "*Plaisir d'amour*" reverberated from the gramophone.

Alone with Barone Mardiros? She stepped backward.

As if noticing her apprehension, he held her hand and, with his most generous smile, said, "Please." He encouraged her to sit down on the divan.

She relished the plush sensation of the velvet upholstery against her bare legs. The urge to slide from side to side faded when he sat on a hassock facing her. She pulled her skirt below her stiffening knees. Mesmerized, she gazed at his square jaw, then at his wide forehead, focusing on the changing expression in his eyes—from carefree hazel to serious green.

"Mannig," he whispered. "What I want to say will surprise you," he pulled the hassock closer to her. "I know you don't expect any of it. But I know you are an intelligent girl, and I know you understand the essence of nature."

Mannig liked being called intelligent; but what did he mean by the essence of nature?

"For quite some time now," he continued, "I have been very interested in you ... thinking about you ... all the time. You have been in my mind since the first time I noticed you ... in Mosul ... you were pretending to be a poor starveling wanting to enter the orphanage. Do you remember?"

Mannig blinked in embarrassment. She felt herself blushing from head to toe and prayed it would fade unnoticed.

"Your extraordinary behavior then, and ever since, has inspired me to step out of the ordinary myself," he continued. "I have tried so hard to hide my attraction to you; I have prayed to go unnoticed by you and by others. I have wanted to forget you completely, but it has been impossible. Your presence casts a spell on me every time. Just as I am sure the sun will rise every morning, I am sure I cannot get you out of my mind."

Mannig felt relieved to be seated, since the sensation in her weakened knees could trigger a fall, betraying the affect of his words. Her pulse raced, heart pounded.

"So I continued to volunteer at the orphanage," he said, "hoping to see you again—and God granted my wish. Wherever AGBU assigned me to go, there I found you. Whenever I attended a special program, you glittered like a star. Whatever the message, it sufficed when I heard it from your warm lips. You have won my heart."

And now, Mannig thought, your poetry is touching my heart.

"Seeing you off to Jerusalem tears me apart. Truthfully, my dear, I cannot live without you," he said and apologized for going on his knees. "Traditionally, a mother relays the message I'm about to declare. But we live in unusual circumstances." He took both her hands in his. "I dream of uniting with you. I love you. I want to marry you."

Although he uttered his words very softly, they hit Mannig like a bolt of thunder. She stood up without pulling away.

He arose too. "Will you marry me?" he repeated.

As though the answer had sparked in her head, she knew what he meant by the 'essence of nature.' The words took form and relayed their intent. She opened her mouth, gasped and closed her eyes. *What should I say?*

Immediately, he filled the silence. "You don't have to answer me instantly. I can wait a minute. I know what you're thinking … that I am too old for you and you are very young. I have wished it otherwise but during these past three years, I have seen you act more mature than most adults I know. I trust my heart and my heart knows best. My love for you is the force behind my proposal."

Mannig's timidity had departed outside the walls of the tent. Emboldened, she spoke quietly, confidently and earnestly. "I don't consider your age to be an obstacle. I will be very happy and proud to marry you."

"You will?" Mardiros spread his arms, wanting to fling himself against her, but held back.

Mannig liked his impulsiveness but more so his self control— decorum worthy of an honorable man. "But it's impossible," she said.

"Why? B-b-but why?" he stuttered. "It is the young fellow, right? What is his name? He just arrived … you embraced him …. Do you really like him?"

"Dikran?" Mannig was startled. "Oh, no! I like him very much. He and I became friends. He protected me from the bigger and stronger scavengers when we foraged the streets of Mosul for food. He is my hero."

"Then, why? Why do you think marrying me is impossible?"

"Because I have a special dream for my life," Mannig whispered.

"Tell me, tell me. What is your dream? I have special dreams myself."

Mannig hesitated.

"I urge you to tell me everything … open up your heart … tell me everything … think of me as your …" he stopped for a big laugh. "Not as your Dear Father, please; but let us say, for just a temporary moment … as your Dear Uncle."

Dear Father? Dear Uncle? He seemed as confused as she; the similarity comforted her. "My dream is to continue my studies," she said. "I want to go to school and learn everything. I want to learn everything about the world, everything about life."

"That is not a problem. I will enroll you in a real school in Baghdad. I will find the best teachers for you."

The needle slid beyond the grooves of the disc, repeating a scratchy pattern. Glancing at the gramophone, she said, "I also want to learn music."

"Music? Like what is on this disc?" he asked, rescuing it from further damage.

"No. I want to be like my mother—a musician."

"What do you like to learn to play?"

"Piano. Yes, the piano. My mother played the violin, but she used to say, 'one must learn to play the piano first in order to be a good violinist. She was a very good musician."

"Piano! Oh, wonderful," he interrupted her again. "You could accompany me when I play the flute. Piano it shall be. Baghdad claims some of the best piano teachers. I will hire the best for you."

His promises captivated Mannig. The more they talked the closer to him she felt. Should she take a calculated risk with another request? After all, he did want her to speak openly. "That would be one dream come true," she agreed. "But I cannot go to Baghdad."

He looked stunned, eyes wide and mouth open.

"Because I have a sister," she broke the silence. "She is the only family I have. She and I can never be separated. We make decisions together. We are going to Jerusalem together."

"I know about Adrine," he said, "and I remember your devotion to her since … since that time you refused to go to America without her. The tragic killing of your family, obviously, make you two sisters want to stick together."

Mannig's tears welled in her eyes.

"D-d-do you really m-m-mean th-th-that's your only objection?" he stammered, excitement flashing in his eyes. "That—you d-d-don't want to be separated from your sister?"

"Yes!" she replied definitively.

"That is easier done than you can imagine," he said with a sigh of relief and, leaving considerable space between them, sat on the divan beside her. Took a deep breath.

Mannig's insides stirred with joy. She lowered her gaze and controlled her own delight. She liked him so much that even if he had not said 'easier than imagined' she might have abandoned her sister. She loved him. She had probably loved him for as long as he had been infatuated with her. And just as with him, only now her true feelings took wings.

He told her of his family and asked about hers, but refrained from references to the war. Not once did he attempt to kiss her or even take her hands in his. She was comfortable in his presence. She hoped he, too, felt they would be marrying "their own kind," as the sisters from Van had insisted.

"I will escort you to your tent," he said after they had talked intimately for an hour. "I will speak with Sebouh. He also wishes to get married."

They walked side-by-side, passing the orphan tents without words.

Mannig felt herself a different person—no more the carefree girl. Her head weighed heavily on her shoulders as she cross-referenced her words with his, her reactions to his facial exuberances and finally her heart's desires with his promises. Most of all, she pondered her wonderment about marriage with his determination to please her.

Throughout the night, she turned and tossed, vaguely aware of the summons Adrine received during the night.

⟡

At sunrise, everyone prepared for the departure from the orphanage at Nahr-el-Omar. The breakfast area was cleaned and the tents were evacuated, collapsed, rolled and stored in sheds. The orphans lined up with their bundles in view of Shuja, the British ship anchored off shore. The white ship and its black and red smoke stacks was an awesome sight above the watermark. It beckoned some 900 orphans.

The attendant of the tender singled out Mannig and Adrine, as the first of ten passengers to board, surprising Mannig. She wondered about Mardiros's plans to travel by train to Baghdad. Had he changed his mind? She glanced at her sister repeatedly, hoping for a clue about any changes in plans that might have transpired during the night. Were Mardiros' promises but a figment of air this morning? How embarrassing it would have been if she had shouted her luck to the world, as she had wanted to do?

The puttering of the tender toward the big ship filled her with wonder. Ferrying on the tender electrified her; it was an exhilaratingly fast vessel—diesel fumes wafting, waves chopping against the cruising motor boat. Thoughts about the essence of nature dissipated into nothingness.

Upon boarding the ship the two sisters were whisked to the captain's quarters. When Mannig saw Mardiros standing beside the captain, she lit up from inside, letting out a long dormant breath of anxiety she had held throughout the ride in the tender.

Sebouh Effendi flanked the captain's left, and all three were smiling—the captain most radiantly. In glittering golden insignia and total white regalia, his eyes gleamed and his teeth sparkled. Standing straight and tall, he exclaimed. "The brides-to-be, I assume?"

35—January 22, 1922

The atmosphere of the captain's beautiful cabin intimidated Mannig.

She felt like a mouse. Even her braid dangled like the tail of one. Adrine's tightened grip increased her anxiety until Mardiros rushed to her side.

Knowing she was wanted calmed her. Blithely, she shook the captain's hand when Mardiros introduced her as his bride-to-be. She kept her other eye on Sebouh and Adrine, who followed their lead.

"To perform a double wedding ceremony," the Captain said, "is a unique responsibility for any captain. It is also my first. I shall never forget it."

Mannig glanced at Adrine. "What is he saying?"

"He is an Englishman," Mardiros responded with a smile and proceeded to translate. Then he turned to the Captain. "The brides-to-be don't speak English."

A knock on the door drew everyone's attention. Three gentlemen wearing expensive black suits and ties entered the cabin.

"The witnesses, I presume?" The captain asked Mardiros.

Mardiros took Mannig's hand and approached the entourage, introducing her again as his bride-to-be to Barone Simon Gharibian, Barone Antellias, and Barone Mugurdichian, three leaders of the Armenian community from Basra.

Barone Gharibian held onto Mannig's hand and said, "Mardiros is my best friend. I must tell you he is the shining diamond of Baghdad. He will treat you like a queen. You are a very lucky girl."

"I shall wire about this real-life Cinderella story," Barone Antellias said, retrieving a pen and a small, lined notepad from his jacket pocket. He spoke fast and jotted down even faster. "Just the headline with my monthly byline ought to dizzy the heads in the cosmopolitan cities of the world … Istanbul, Beirut, Cairo and Athens, and Ha! And in the *Baghdad Gazette*, too, of course."

"No one will believe your story," Barone Mugerdichian said. "They will confuse it with a book of fiction I read recently … about a benefactor of an orphanage in America who falls in love with an orphan. I think the book is called, *Daddy Long Legs*."

"They will believe," the Captain said. "They will believe. The presence of the three of you proves it. You are the witnesses to this double wedding, on this 22nd day of January 1922."

A knock on the door heralded the sisters from Van. Seeing how confused they appeared in their rumpled khaki uniforms, Mannig rushed toward them, as Mardiros had done earlier for her, to relieve their distress. She smacked kisses on them both. "We are getting married!" she exclaimed. "Adrine to Sebouh Effendi and I to Barone Mardiros!" She waited for their joyful response, but the sisters remained frozen at the threshold. "Believe me! We invited you, our dear tent mates, to our wedding. We couldn't do it without your presence."

"We wanted you to be part of this ceremony," Mardiros said, putting his hands on Mannig's shoulders.

"I am speechless," Vanouhi whispered to Adrine. "Art thou really getting married?"

Both Mannig and Adrine beamed and nodded.

"But, but, what about a white wedding gown?" Takouhi mumbled.

"Such formalities will come later," Adrine said. "When we go to Baghdad, we will get our white dresses from Sebouh Effendi's big European store."

"Thou art so lucky," Vanouhi said.

"You will find your own lucky mates in Jerusalem," Adrine whispered.

"Maybe we will be as lucky as thee," Vanouhi chirped.

Mannig reached for Vanouhi's left hand, took Takouhi's right, and introduced them to Mardiros, who in turn did the honors with the rest of the wedding patrons.

The wedding ceremony lasted a long time. First the captain read the rites for Mardiros and Mannig in English, and then Barone Mugurdichian translated them into Armenian. Then the whole ceremony was repeated for Sebouh and Adrine. Lengthy indeed, but it flashed in and out of Mannig's head faster than lightening. Mardiros' kiss on her cheek also whooshed by, but she clung to its tender message of warmth, promise, and hope. In embracing the sisters from Van, she poured forth all her love, tears, and joy.

"Congratulations, Diggin Kouyoumdjian," Barone Simon Gharibian said, shaking Mannig's hand and slipping onto her wrist a brilliant golden watch set as a bracelet.

Mannig's gaze flashed at the stark contrast of the glittering jewel against the coarse blue sleeve of her uniform. His words remained whirling in her thoughts.

Diggin? He had addressed her as a Mrs. *Diggin*, which befits grown women, married for many years, mother of children and burdened with chores. She became a Mrs. even before anyone called her Miss. All her life, she wanted to be called Miss, especially as a little girl in Adapazar. When in kindergarten, if someone asked what she wanted to be, she had said, a Miss, meaning to become a teacher like Miss Romella. Visions of becoming a teacher like Miss Romella and being called Miss Mannig evaporated in her foggy head, and dammed-up tears began to roll down her face. Disenchanted, she hugged Vanouhi while she wiped her tears. Then she hugged Takouhi and cried with her some more. She didn't question why the sisters from Van were crying, but they found solace in sniffling together.

Not having time to brood depressed Mannig. She needed to act like a mature Mrs. Kouyoumdjian and not disappoint her groom. "I am so happy you are here," she said to Takouhi. "I shall miss you very much. You and Vanouhi were a big part of my orphanage life and shared a tent with me for so long. So you deserved to participate in my wedding. I will never forget you."

The captain poured cognac into snifters for the gentlemen and passed around a crystal bowl of sugar-coated almonds in a heap of pastel colors. He served Mannig first. "I was told that Jordan-Almonds are a tradition at Armenian engagement parties," he said. "As unconventional as we are at this wedding, we shall celebrate your engagement at the same time as your wedding. One for all, and all for one."

The aromatic vanilla candy nearly intoxicated Mannig. She raised her palm to her nose, sniffing noisily with great relish, when Mardiros caught her eye. He shook his head. Discreetly, she dropped the candy into her tunic pocket. *I'll enjoy it when I'm alone.*

A third knock on the door heralded two waiters in white formal jackets, aproned and carrying silver trays heaped with roasted chicken and pilaf sprinkled with a confetti of raisins and pine nuts. Trays of fruit and vegetables and breads and cakes lined the shelf across from the dining table, elegantly set with purple flowers and candles, all under a shimmering chandelier.

"The chefs of Shuja have prepared a feast in honor of the newly wedded couples," the Captain announced. "Let us sit down."

As Manning was led by Mardiros and helped her into a red velvet chair, she knew he planned to monitor her manners at the lavish dinner. For the next hour, the sterling jingled, the china chimed, and the crystal goblets glittered over and above the dinner conversation. When the butler bent down beside her, holding a platter full of tawny-roasted chicken, she froze in her seat, unable to decide what to do.

"Pardon me, please, ladies and gentlemen," Mardiros said, standing up. "I am seated next to my beautiful bride for a reason." All eyes riveted on him. "Traditionally, I, the groom, am supposed to serve my bride our first meal together."

"Come, come, Mardiros," Sebouh jeered. "When are you going to stop coming up with creative ideas?"

"It sounds very fitting," the Captain said. "Go ahead, Mardiros."

Mardiros served Mannig a few slices of rosemary herbed chicken, several scoops of rice, and spoonfuls of vegetables. Then he leaned toward her and whispered, "Keep the fork in your left hand, always."

The last time Mannig had seen a fork, let alone use it, had been in Adapazar. *My left hand?*

Throughout the meal, he whispered to her to do this or do that, and she emulated all his moves, never needing correction. She concentrated on how to avoid embarrassing him. The rice grains posed a big problem. She decided to avoid the rice after fumbling with the fork for a few grains. Being cautious, thereafter, she hardly tasted any of the wedding feast—the aromatic chicken, the cardamom eggplant stew, or the allspice-flavored rice. When the waiters cleared the table, she felt as hungry as when she had foraged the streets of Mosul for edibles. She had come a long way, but a much longer route still stretched ahead.

The captain jingled his water glass with a knife and stood up. "Ladies and Gentlemen," he began. "I pray you have enjoyed this meal."

"Hey! Hey!" the men responded.

"I asked the chefs of Shuja," the captain continued, "to prepare a special meal for all the passengers this evening. We are not fortunate to experience such an occasion as today often on our voyages. Allow me to make a toast." He raised his wine glass, addressing the two young brides.

"You are the luckiest girls in the world today. You have just married two of the noblest men from Baghdad. Someday you will realize that luck such as yours happens rarely in a lifetime."

Simon Gharibian raised his wine glass and added, "To my friends. Mardiros and Sebouh. You have chosen wisely. I predict that your young partners in life will be the jewels of your future. May God bless these unions."

Barone Antellias raised his glass. "I am honored to witness this double wedding. To you, young ladies! Even though you are married into Baghdad's highest class families, if there is anything you need, I shall be at your service."

"And to the two gentlemen from Baghdad," the Captain resumed his toast. "Your spirit has revived my faith in humanity. I thank you for making me part of your adventure. So my toast to you is: may you live as long as you love, and love as long as you live."

"Hip, hip hurray!" a composite of masculine voices echoed in the dining room. "We will all drink to that."

"In memento of this historic occasion," the Captain continued, "I have a special gift for each bride." He walked to Mannig and pinned a medal-like gold brooch to the lapel of her navy blue uniform. Before pinning an identical brooch on Adrine's lapel, he looked at its back. "The inscription is in English," he chuckled, "but you, young ladies, will learn the language soon enough. It reads 'Shuja—January 22, 1922.'"

Mardiros stood up, gesturing to Sebouh to stand beside him, and then said, "It is with the help of all of you—the Captain, our friends from Basra, the sisters from Van, the shipmates and the kitchen staff .... I hope I am not forgetting anyone ... it is because of you, we can celebrate today. Yes, there will be other celebrations, and yes, even as I speak, Sebouh's family and mine are organizing receptions in Baghdad. They will be fabulous parties, but as you say, Captain, this is an historic day. We thank you, Sebouh and I, for shuffling your schedules to grant our hearts' desire, and we're delighted that our lovely brides agreed to our arrangements. Thank you from the bottom of our heart."

At sundown, the sounds of the historic day faded with the waves of the Shat-el-Arab licking the rim of the sun. The newlywed brides hugged the sisters from Van adieu and, holding their grooms' hands, boarded the tender to return to the mainland.

Once it was a hundred yards away, the tender honked.

Shuja responded with sirens, blasts, and horns.

The Captain, the crew, and 900 orphans waved scarves and shawls and banners. Mannig waved her handkerchief, weighted down with the pain of separation.

The happiest man alive, Mardiros brushed his cheek against Mannig's, rested his chin on her shoulder, and faced the huge white Shuja with her. Soon they would face his Kouyoumdjian clan in Baghdad. His mother would support his life-partner wholeheartedly, and all but one of his sisters-in-law would snub the little orphan-bride. He knew Mannig would naturally win the hearts of his nieces and nephews, whose ages ranged from twelve to mid-twenty. He suspected his role to change from the youngest bearer of the family name to a born-again teacher in the Qasr. He knew the challenges Mannig would face before becoming a bona fide Kouyoumdjian.

"The captain is still waving," Mannig whispered to him, and once again waved her handkerchief.

Mardiros, too, waved. "I liked the Captain's toast," he said. "I shall always remember his words, May we love as long as we live …."

"And," Mannig added, "live as long as we love."

EPILOGUE

1982—Mannig Gets Her Own Banner, At Last

The annihilation of one and a half million Armenians during World War I of 1914 -1918 was one of history's most terrible episodes.

A family, taking a gentle journey to avenge the Genocide, commemorated the memory of those victims with a celebration in Mercer Island, Washington, recently.

The occasion? Mannig becoming a United States citizen, completing the family's Americanization. To celebrate this triumph, Mannig's two daughters and son shared the story of the trek of their 76 year-old mother with 107 friends.

Mannig's three grandsons, suited in white tuxedo shirts, navy slacks, and red cummerbunds, ushered the guests into a venue glowing with jubilation. Poster-sized photographs of Mannig decked the walls of the reception hall. Red, white, and blue balloons embroidered the air, while tri-colored bouquets embellished the lace-covered round tables. The gourmet dinner consisted of an A-A-A feast, that is, Armenian-Arabic-American, and the entertainment featured homespun talents of song, dance, and recitations.

After listening to a brief biography of her life and testimonials, including a personal letter to Mannig from President Ronald Reagan, she approached the microphone.

A petite senior lady, scarcely five feet tall, Mannig flitted onto the stage. She wore an ankle-length navy skirt and a red rose pinned close to her high-collared, white silk blouse. Her olive skin and short graying hair dramatized her patriotic stance beside the towering U.S. flag. She looked radiant.

She tiptoed to an internal rhythm and moved her head to a subtle, inner beat. She whirled her pleated skirt and knelt in a deep bow.

Applause!

She curtsied to her right, then to her left, smiling at the faces with recognition, one after another. She swayed, twirled, and fox-trotted for a full minute with coquettish grace as she approached the microphone.

"When people ask about my childlike movements," she began, "I say I don't want to ever forget my childhood. I want to keep it fresh in my mind. By doing the same movements now as I used to do in Adapazar, my childhood is immortalized in my mind. My mother would be very happy if she knew I survived and can remember."

She scanned the audience.

"I was born in Turkey," she said, "so people think I'm a Turk. I've lived in Iraq most of my life, so people think I'm an Arab. I say, 'No! I am Armenian!' So they say, 'Ah! Then you have lived in Russia.' I have never been to Russia, and I have not even been to Armenia. You see," Mannig lowered her voice, increasing its volume a bit with each following sentence. "I have lived under many banners. M-a-n-y banners. Many banners. Those banners were all temporary." She took a long breath and continued softly. "None of them belonged to me, and I didn't belong to them either." She shrugged her shoulders indignantly. Then she displayed the small flag that had been given to her at the official naturalization ceremonies at the Immigration office. "But when I took my oath and held the American flag in my hand, I was as happy and proud as the astronaut who put the flag of the United States on the moon. Thank God I can say I am an American, and I live under the banner spangled with stars."

GLOSSARY OF FOREIGN WORDS

abaya: head-to-ankle robe, usually black (Arabic)
a-cappella: without instrument accompaniment (Italian)
AGBU: Armenian General Benevolent Union
aggaal: cord part of a male headgear (Arabic)
agoomp: club (Armenian)
Allah kareem: God is merciful (Arabic)
Allah oo akbar: God is great (Arabic)
Allah wiyaak: God is with you (Arabic)
Allah: God (Arabic)
Amahn: Good Gracious (Armenian)
amsagahn: monthly; menstrual period (colloquial Armenian)
Armeny: Armenian (Arabic)
attoba: mud brick
Ayp-pen-kim-ta: A,B,C,D (the first letters of the Armenian alphabet)
Baba: father (Armenian)
bakhsheesh: alms/handout (universal)
Barone: Mister/Mr./Sir (Armenian)
bastinado: lashing of the soles (Latin)
bellem: boat (Arabic)
boghcha: square kerchief used to bundle belongings (Turkish)
Boleess: Constantinople
chaBOOK: scat, quick! (Turkish)
chemise: Slip (French)
cherie: dear (French adopted as an Armenian expression)
chojoukh: child (Turkish)
chors-ankam-ootu: 4 X 8 (Armenian)

Diggin: Mrs./Madam (Armenian)

Effendi: Mister/Mr./Sir (Turkish)

ehh-len wu sehh-len: greetings and salutations (Arabic)

Englaizees: Englishmen (Arabic)

Fils: smallest unit, Iraqi money. 280 *fils* = $1.00 in 1952 (Arabic)

Fransawees: Frenchmen (Arabic)

gabgob: wooden slippers worn in a bathhouse

gatta: pastry (Armenian)

guffa: circular fishing boat (Arabic)

haleeb: milk (Arabic)

hosse yegoor: Come here! (Armenian)

huqqah: water-pipe; hubble-bubble; narguilla (Arabic)

hyereneek: Fatherland (Armenian)

ibriq: water jug (Arabic)

imshee: scat! Go away! (Arabic)

inshaa-Allah: God willing (Arabic)

inteh hadhur: Are you ready? (Arabic)

jahn: dear/endearing terminology (Armenian)

jarbeeg: street-smart (Armenian)

jinni: magician (Arabic/Turkish)

joo'aan: I'm hungry (Arabic)

kaffieh: headgear for men (Arabic)

kaka: shit/dung (slang)

kalak: raft/boat (Arabic/Turkish)

kebab: barbeque (Arabic)

khan: caravansary; inn for caravans (Turkish/Arabic/Armenian)

khatoon: lady (Turkish/Arabic)

khatoon hanum: Grand Lady (Turkish)

khattir Allah: For God's sake (Arabic)

khoobooz: bread (Arabic)

kilo: kilogram (Arabic)

kleecha: date-stuffed cookie (Arabic)

laa: No! (Arabic)

laa w'allah: No! Honestly! (Arabic)

laban: yoghurt (Arabic)

mahhal: place (Arabic)

MangaBardez: kindergarten (Armenian)

manghal : brazier (Turkish)

manqqala: brazier (Arabic)

manyook: fucker (Arabic)

Mare Hyereneek: Our Fatherland (Armenian national anthem)

masgouf: barbequed fish (Arabic)

mateo: Matthew (Armenian)

meg-yergoo-yerek: one, two, three (Armenian)

melisma: music: a passage sung to one syllable of text, as in Gregorian chants (Greek)

Middle East Relief: Organization established by the world community to save the Armenians

millet: ethnic/political enclave (Turkish)

mindare: floor cushion (Turkish)

minging: diminutive (Armenian)

mu'adthin: Muslim prayer chanter (Arabic/Turkish)

murga: stew (Arabic)

mye: water (Arabic)

narguilla : hukka; water pipe; hubble-bubble (Arabic)

oor ess aghcheeg?: Where are you, girl? (Armenian)

Orozdi-Bakk: name of a department store in Baghdad (Swiss)

Pasha: title as Sir/Knighthood (Turkish)

pees kaki hodair: putrid feces smells (Armenian)

Plaisir d'amour: The Pleasure of love (French song)

qabqob: wooden-soled slippers used in bathing (Arabic/Turkish)

qasr: castle (Arabic)

saayyid: Mister (Arabic)

sahib : master (Turkish/Arabic)

sans: without (French)

selamet: Thank God/Peace (Turkish/Arabic)

shakku-makku?: What news? (Arabic)

shalvar: baggy pants (Turkish)

Shat el Arab: The Arab River (Arabic)

sheytahn: Satan (Arabic)

Shuja: name of a British ship

shukran: Thanks (Arabic)

sook: bazaar (Arabic)

subba: prayer beads (Arabic)

tass: cup (Armenian/Arabic/Turkish)

tikkeh kebab: ground-meat barbeque (Arabic)

tutoum kulukh: pumpkin head; naïve; stupid (Armenian)

varjabedanotz: teacher training college (Armenian)

vohr: buttocks (Armenian)

vorpanotz: orphanage (Armenian)

WRO: World Relief Organization (English)

wu salaam aleykum : And greetings to you, too (Arabic)

y'abnayya: Hey, girl! (Arabic)

y'allah: Dear God (Arabic)

yazma: head scarf (Turkish/Kurdish)

yukh: repulsive (Armenian)

zakhnaboot: darn it (Turkish)

Historical Highlights of Armenia

For more information, visit **www.Armeniapedia.org**.

1. Armenia has a historical record of nearly three millennia—mentioned in the Old Testament as the "Land of Aram"; in the King James Version, in II Kings 19:37; and in Isaiah 37:38.

2. In 301 AD, Armenia became the first nation to adopt Christianity as its state religion.

3. In 400-414 AD, a unique alphabet of 36 letters was invented to translate the Bible into the national vernacular. Armenian belongs to the Indo-European family of languages. Two other letters were added to the original alphabet to reflect existing inflections.

4. The cathedral of Etchmiadzin was built in the 6th century in Yerevan, capital of Armenia. It has been the see of the Armenian Apostolic Church since.

5. Armenian kingdoms played significant roles in aiding the European Crusaders in their attempts to recover the Holy Lands.

6. Armenian kingdoms ceased to function since 1375, but its symbolic seat, Mt. Ararat, currently situated in Modern Turkey, remains alive and ticking on the lips of many a poet.

7. Historians estimate 1.5 to 2 million Armenians perished in what is present-day Turkey, during the Genocide perpetrated by the Ottoman Empire in 1914-1918.

8. In 1921, Armenia became one of the Republics of the Soviet Union.

9. In 1991, Armenia ceded from the Soviet Union and established the Republic of Armenia as a sovereign nation and was admitted to the United Nations.

10. Present day Armenia is landlocked in the Trans-Caucasus region. It sustains three million people in a territory of 11,600 square

miles (slightly larger than the State of Vermont). Its boundaries are: Georgia in the north, Iran in the south, Azerbaijan in the east, and Turkey in the west.

11. Yerevan is the capital of Armenia and is situated on old historic Erevan.

12. Outside Armenia, it is estimated that six million Armenians live in the Diaspora. More than a million live in North America.

WHAT MAKES AN ARMENIAN?

Armenians have endured the wars between the Greco-Roman and the Persian East since the first century B.C. Warring empires looted, burned, and devastated Armenian territory, leading its people into captivity, rape, and murder. Each time, the surviving population toiled stubbornly to reconstruct what had been destroyed, as would a swallow rebuild a ruined nest. If asked, what makes an Armenian? The answer would be, "A trek."

Armenians proclaimed Christianity as the national religion of Armenia in A.D. 301, establishing precedence in the annals of the Christian Church. Surrounded by the empires of Rome and Persia, which denounced and persecuted them, Armenians prescribed their own suicide as would a scorpion sting itself when trapped in blazing fires. If asked, what makes an Armenian? The answer would be, "Faith."

Armenians invented an alphabet late in the Fourth Century. It was conceived by St. Mesrop to create a Christian literature in the mother tongue during the most critical epoch of Armenia's political existence and provided the very weapon which, by awakening nationalism, inspired and enabled the Armenian people to survive to this very day. If asked, what makes an Armenian? The answer would be, "Zeal."

Armenians saw yet another foe, the Islamic Caliphate in A.D. 644. Like fragile violets, they were plucked by gnarled hands and mangled by the merciless claws of Arab mercenaries. Never stripped of spirit, all that remained was praying to God. If asked, what makes an Armenian? The answer would be "Hope."

Armenians regained statehood during the Tenth Century, the wages of which spelled compromise. Soon compromise meant change. No Armenian would rather live than see the death of his identity. If asked, what makes an Armenian? The answer would be, "Pride."

Armenians lost their kingdom in 1375. Since then, they have persisted to be Armenian in their own right. They have clung to their culture, traditions, and language like an iceberg (one that doesn't melt) in the North Pole. If asked, what makes an Armenian? The answer would be, "Preservation."

Armenians begot Armenians, perpetuating a conquered people. United, they failed to liberate themselves; independently, they menaced the conqueror. A people without a leader, they safeguarded themselves from falling like wheat at the edge of a scythe, by having recourse to weapons. If asked, what makes an Armenian? The answer would be, "Individuality."

Armenians became dispersed throughout their lands. Robbed of an unalienable land by the invading forces of the Mongols, Persians, Kurds, and the Ottoman Turks, they were determined to survive as a nation. Obsessed with education, they developed a talent for commerce, evolving into an elite Christian minority that catered to a needy Muslim majority. If asked, what makes an Armenian? The answer would be, "Capacity."

One and a half to 2 million Armenians perished in the first Genocide of the Twentieth Century, perpetrated by the Ottoman Turks during WWI in 1914-1918. The survivors were consumed into the Soviet Republic and endured Communism for seven decades. Unlike sheep being goaded into the slaughterhouse, they proclaimed independence and sovereignty in 1991. If asked, what makes an Armenian? The answer would be, "Fidelity."

Armenians established a Christian kingdom at the foot of Mt. Ararat. They have defended their ethnicity from mountains; they have sought refuge in the mountains; and having stood rugged like mountains, they have survived religious, political, and economic persecutions. If asked, what makes an Armenian? The answer would be, "Mt. Ararat."

REFERENCES

1. *The Bastard of Istanbul*, by Elif Shafak, Viking 2007

2. *The Burning Tigris*, by Peter Balakian, Harper Collins Publishers, 2003

3. *Black Dog of Fate*, by Peter Balakian, Broadway Books, 1998

4. *Rise the Euphrates*, by Carol Edgarian, Random House Publishers, 1994

5. *Armenian-Americans*, by Anny Bakalian, Transaction Publishers, 1994

6. *The Armenians*, by John M. Douglas, J.J. Winthrop Corp. Publisher, 1992

7. *Hitler and the Armenian Genocide*, by K. B. Bardakjian, Zoryan Institute, 1985

8. *Armenian Review*, Essays and Douments on Genocide, published by the *Armenian Review, Inc.*, Boston 1984

9. *Brother of the Bride*, by Donita Dyer, Tyndale House, 1982

10. *The Armenians—A People in Exile*, by David Marshall Lang, George Allen & Unwin Ltd., 1981

11. *The Road from Home*, by David Kherdian, Greenwillow Books, 1979

12. *Some of us Survived*, by Kerop Bedoukian, Farrar, Straus Giroux 1978

13. *Passage to Ararat*, by Michael J. Arlen, Hungry Mind Press, 1975

14. *The Forty Days of Musa Dagh*, by Franz Werfel, The Modern Library, New York, 1933

Aida Kouyoumjian was born in Felloujah, Iraq. When she and her sister were old enough to attend school, her family moved sixty miles east to Baghdad.

In 1952 Aida won a year-long Fulbright Scholarship to the University of Washington in Seattle. As the eldest daughter, she was the first in her family to leave Baghdad. The Iraqi government, a monarchy at the time, gave her its blessing. After the year was up, Aida reapplied and stayed another four years. At the end of that period, her father warned her of unrest in Iraq and advised her to extend her stay. Aida married an American—a fellow student—but she still received deportation notices. Her politically savvy in-laws appealed her case to Senator Warren G. Magnuson, who introduced a special bill in congress allowing her to stay in the U.S.

Aida's path to citizenship was further delayed by her engineer husband's frequent moves. Finally his work allowed them to stay in Warrensburg, Missouri, for the requisite two years, thus allowing her to study and pass the citizenship exam in 1962. Her family, which now included three sons, eventually settled in Mercer Island.

After Aida's father died in 1965, she was finally able to bring her mother Mannig to this country. A year later, Aida's brother joined them. Her sister had left Baghdad in 1953, a year after Aida, and settled in South Carolina.

At the age of 69, Mannig was hired by the UW to tutor graduate students in Turkish, Armenian, and Arabic. She remained on the UW staff for seven years before retiring. Not long before her death in 1985 at the age of 79, Mannig was one of ninety survivors who attended the 70th commemoration of the Armenian Genocide in Washington, D.C.

After thirty years of teaching in public schools, Aida currently offers a course on Iraq at Bellevue College and is a popular speaker at schools and public service organizations. She is a former winner of the Pacific Northwest Writers' Association Prize for Non-fiction. She was also awarded first place by the Washington Association of Press Women for an editorial that appeared in the Seattle P-I.

Aida has been active in Seattle's Armenian community since her University days. After Armenia's great earthquake of 1988, she helped organize Seattle's relief effort. In 1989 she spearheaded the formation of the Armenian Cultural Association of Washington (ACA) and was elected first president of its board of directors.

Aida has three sons, eight grandchildren and two great-grandchildren.

You can find Aida online at armenianstory.coffeetownpress.com.